Sex, Men, and Babies

Stories of Awareness and Responsibility

William Marsiglio and Sally Hutchinson

NEW YORK UNIVERSITY PRESS

New York and London

NEW YORK UNIVERSITY PRESS
New York and London
www.nyupress.org

First published in paperback in 2004.

Library of Congress Cataloging-in-Publication Data
Marsiglio, William.
Sex, men, and babies : stories of awareness and responsibility /
William Marsiglio, Sally Hutchinson.
p. cm.
Includes bibliographical references and index.
ISBN 0-8147-5681-6 (cloth : alk. paper) ISBN 0-8147-5696-4 (pbk. : alk. paper)
1. Youth—Psychology.   2. Youth—Sexual behavior.
3. Fatherhood.   4. Single men.
I. Hutchinson, Sally.   II. Title.
HQ797 .M34 2002
305.31—dc21   2002007062

New York University Press books are printed on acid-free paper,
and their binding materials are chosen for strength and durability.

Manufactured in the United States of America
c 10 9 8 7 6 5 4 3 2 1
p 10 9 8 7 6 5 4 3 2 1

Contents

Preface

Several years ago when the first author was writing *Procreative Man*, the idea for *Sex, Men, and Babies* was born. Prior to publication of the former, little had been done to conceptualize men's experiences with procreative issues. That book made clear for us that although scholarly and public interest in young men's sexual, procreative, and paternal roles had recently grown considerably, we knew next to nothing about the social psychology of young men as persons capable of creating and fathering human life. Much of what we did know was based on survey data, most notably the National Surveys of Adolescent Males. These survey data, based on three waves of face-to-face interviews beginning in 1988 and ending in 1995, have provided useful insights into the social demography of men's sexual, contraceptive, and fertility-related attitudes and behaviors. However, survey data do not capture the complexity of the social psychological processes associated with young men's perceptions of self and others; their subjective realities related to specific procreative and relationship experiences; and their decision making about the range of issues involving sex, contraception, pregnancy resolution, and paternity.

What was needed was an in-depth study of the processes having to do with young men's procreative identities and related experiences. A few of the compelling questions that begged for attention: How do men's procreative identities evolve over time? How do men, as persons capable of procreating define their varied experiences? How do men's romantic relationships influence the way they perceive themselves and their involvement in various aspects of the procreative realm? Answering these and similar questions called for a method that would give men the chance to describe in detail, how they thought, felt, and behaved. A project that sought to advance a conceptual map of this terrain was appealing on several fronts because the meanings men assign to their experiences have personal, practical, and political significance.

Although the project emerged from Marsiglio's earlier scholarship and firsthand experience with many of the issues described in this book, it became a reality when he secured Hutchinson's involvement because of her extensive experience doing in-depth qualitative interviews and grounded theory research, an approach described in the first two chapters. Our respective sociological and nursing backgrounds, coupled with our own personal and gendered experiences with reproductive issues, informed the way we framed and interpreted our study.

All studies have their limitations, and ours is no exception. We fully recognize that our choice to conduct in-depth interviews with a relatively small, racially diverse sample of young men at one point in time (for all but two participants) limits our ability to answer a number of relevant questions. Men's present experiences as well as their retrospective accounts of events and transitions in the past, some as long as ten to fifteen years ago, provide the basis of our analysis. Our approach gave the men the opportunity to place their experiences in perspective, to consider the connection between different past events and relationships, and to discuss the influence of these events and relationships on their present sense of self. Even though we do not speak directly to the issues of race, culture, and class, we recruited a purposive sample of men from diverse walks of life who have had various procreative experiences (see Appendix). We adopted a sampling strategy consistent with the grounded theory method, which emphasizes the importance of diversity to the researchers' ability to generate relevant concepts. Our initial challenge—to identify some of the key features of the social psychological processes associated with these young men as sexual and procreative beings—was formidable. Clearly, future studies should look more closely at our conceptual terrain by considering whether and how race, culture, and class issues affect the way young men subjectively experience and express their procreative identities. That work may best be achieved through selective sampling and analytic strategies, including an ethnographic approach.

Because race was not a focus of our interviewing strategy, and did not appear to be a critical factor that shaped the processes of interest to us after reading the transcripts, participants' race is absent from our analysis of the interviews. One practical consequence is that we do not use race as a descriptor when we introduce participants into the text. We initially thought it might bring participants to life for the reader; later we concluded that to do so would be inconsistent with our analytic strategy and would imply that race holds more meaning at this time than mere description. We recognize that at times the vernacular evident in the vignettes or a name may be suggestive of race; even so, our study does not yet let us make substantiated comments about race. Interested readers can determine participants' self-identified race by reviewing the sociodemographic profiles in the Appendix.

We do consistently describe participants by noting age because our discussion implicates the significance of life experience as part of our interpretation of young men's perspectives and behaviors. Age is sometimes a marker for men's opportunities to experience various life situations.

The book, then, sheds light on young men's subjective worlds that have, to our knowledge, not been revealed in the way we represent them here. As the primary architects of this work, we received excellent assistance throughout the project. A great number of students took a keen interest in our study, which for many seemed to hit close to home. We extend most heartfelt thanks to Mark Cohan, who served as a graduate research assistant for a year on the project, and then continued to collaborate with us as a coauthor on several journal articles. His mastery of qualitative methods and his cautionary reminders about our style of interviewing were invaluable. Mark completed twenty of the interviews and was a wizard at managing the computerized, qualitative database. If it were not for his zany personality, the project would have been much more tedious during its labor-intensive data collection and coding phases. Another graduate student, Dan Duarte, completed seven interviews. He enhanced the project team's esprit de corps when, shortly after we launched the project, he coined the contingent of students who worked with us "Pigmy Sperm Whales." In addition to the sixteen undergraduates who adopted the moniker and assisted us in recruiting participants, transcribing data, collecting literature, and editing the book, the twelve undergraduates in Marsiglio's honors course, *Sex, Men, and Fatherhood*, conducted supplemental interviews in the spring of 2000 that enabled us to deepen our analysis of several issues. We would like to thank the following students for conscientious and good-natured research assistance: Mark Alderman, Suleman Ali, Julio Aponte, Kelly Billingsley, Chris Carlin, Sheila Chacko, Nikki Cline, Laurie Dennison, Tricia Duthiers, Jessica Hardy, Tara Hatch, Jim Faubel, Brian Lapinski, Kate McGill, Jenny Miles, Karen Persis, Khalifa Salmon, Elly Sharaf-Eldeen, Angela Sheffler, Jillian Sundin, Paree Taslimi, Brad Tripp, Gustavo Vargas, Eric Walters, Amanda Welton, and Belen Zalenskie.

We owe a special thanks to Dana Bagwell, a former undergraduate, for his data management contributions and assistance with the supplemental student interviews. Similiar thanks go to MacGregor Meyer for his diligent work on creating the index, and Leslie Condrey for her meticulous proofreading. We are grateful, too, for Mr. Marvin Dukes's willingness to assist us in recruiting participants at the Department of Motor Vehicles, Alachua County, Florida.

Betty Seaver (copy editor) and Despina Papazoglou Gimbel (managing editor) deserve praise for their clever, conscientious, and timely editing. They masterfully guided us in our efforts to give life and immediacy to the intimate stories of our young men.

Finally, we appreciate the financial support for this research, which was sponsored by a University of Florida Opportunity Fund Grant (UPN #98041676).

Ultimately, this book was made possible by our participants, who were willing to relate their experiences, some of which were troubling to them. For instance, we heard men speak about their embarrassing moments having sex, buying condoms, and having conversations with parents about reproductive issues; their emotional struggles with their partners' abortions and miscarriages; concerns about their presumed infertility in earlier marriages; heartaches over breakups with previous girlfriends as well as current relationship difficulties; and "deviant" behaviors like encouraging a pregnant partner to take illegal drugs to "promote" their unborn child's intelligence or punching an expectant mother in the stomach with intent to end a pregnancy. Men were also forthcoming when they talked about their joys. They spoke of their love for their partners and children (their own as well as others), future plans to father children, sexual escapades, and deeply felt bonds with parents.

With our anonymous participants' enthusiasm in the forefront of our minds, we are delighted to dedicate this book to these young men. They taught us so much about themselves and presumably others like them. And in the process, they convinced us that properly designed interventions can help many young men become more aware of their identities and responsibilities as persons capable of creating human life.

1

Setting the Stage

Making babies is serious business. At its core, it is a biological process, but a process also steeped in diverse, complex, and controversial psychological, social, cultural, and legal issues. The issues intimately involve both women and men because, as the saying goes, "It takes two to tango." Despite the reality that women and men must both play their respective roles in making babies, men's thoughts and feelings about sex, pregnancy, abortion, babies, and fatherhood have often been ignored or overshadowed by women's voices. One useful response to this disparity is to study the inner worlds of single teenage and young adult men as they come face-to-face with sexual and procreative experiences.

With few exceptions, young men are at least vaguely aware of their potential to create human life. Many actually realize the potential during their teen and young adult years by being involved first with a conception and pregnancy, and then either an abortion, miscarriage, or the birth of a child. In fact, these types of experiences are fairly common. Recent national data show that about 14 percent of men aged 15-19 made a partner pregnant, and about 6 percent of sexually experienced males in the cohort have become biological fathers.[1] Because some teenage females never tell their partners about their pregnancies, these figures are lower-bound estimates. During the 1992 to 1994 period, 21 percent of men had become a father before turning 25, and 50 percent before 30.[2] The men who have children in their teens or twenties are more likely to be high school dropouts, have low or moderate incomes, and be African American or Hispanic. Men in their twenties, fathers or not, are probably more likely, though, to be aware of their ability to procreate than their teenage counterparts. They have more extensive experience with sexual relationships and exposure to friends and siblings who have become fathers.

For some men, experiencing an event or situation involving their potential to procreate represents a turning point in the way they perceive themselves. The joy, pride, disappointment, or fear they associate with creating human life offers them a unique mirror for self-reflection. This inward turn sometimes produces a personal transformation marked by a new perspective on self, sexual partners, children, and perhaps other aspects of life. Those who embrace the news of a pregnancy, even if it is unplanned, may intensify their feelings for their partner and cultivate an idealized image of being a loving, involved father.

Others, living vicariously through a friend's or family member's reproductive experience, can also develop a keener sense of what they might expect under similar circumstances. Procreative novices, those with no prior knowledge of impregnating a sex partner, may at times dwell on their unrealized potential. They may allow it to shape their current identities as well as those they project for themselves. A pregnancy scare, for example, may prompt the inexperienced to ponder the risks of becoming a father before they are ready. As they do, they may entertain a heightened awareness of their identity as fertile men. This identity may come alive in banter with male friends, during a sweaty-palm excursion to a local drugstore to purchase condoms, while having an awkward talk with a parent, or when sharing an intimate moment with a romantic partner. Likewise, some young men's ideas about what it will take to become a "good" father may lead them to grasp the nature of their youthful status more clearly. They may quickly discover that they are not yet ready to be family men; they are, instead, single young men in search of sex uncluttered by paternity, and often unencumbered by a relationship commitment.

And then there are men who remain largely oblivious to their procreative powers. Their indifference is reflected in their thoughts and feelings as well as their practical involvements with girlfriends, "fuck buddies," and one-night stands. Such indifference can be a trademark of men irrespective of their fertility history. It may be of little consequence for some whether they have impregnated a partner or fathered a child. Not only do these experiences fall short of bringing about a significant shift in men's self-perception, they have little bearing on how they feel, think, and act.

Researchers have done well to profile the social demography of men's sexual activities, contraceptive behaviors, and fertility patterns,[3] but much less is known about the social psychology of men's experiences in these areas. Scholars have failed to ask how the presumed or realized ability to impregnate, procreate, and become social fathers affects the way young single men construct and experience their sense of self. How do they become aware of their potential to procreate? How do they subsequently weave that knowledge into the way they construct and present a self, particularly when relating to their romantic partners? Alternatively, how does ignoring this knowledge affect men's sense of self? Little is known also about the complex ways that men's seemingly separate experiences in the procreative realm, often with different partners, affect their lives. How do these different experiences reinforce or negate one another over the course of men's sexual and procreative careers?

Still other compelling questions demand attention as well. How do the everyday contingencies of young men's lives, including those related to their romantic involvements, affect their attitudes, beliefs, and feelings about the critical issues that delimit the procreative realm? Why are some men decidedly more aware of themselves as persons capable of impregnating sex partners? How do men's perceptions of themselves as men and their views on gender relations influence their procreative identity? When and how do young men experience a turning point that transforms their perspective on self and procreative issues? And, for those interested in social policy and programmatic issues, a key question is, How do young men view "responsibility" and orient themselves toward their sexual roles as well as their potential procreative, paternal, and coparental roles?

The search for answers to these and related questions must begin with the social psychological processes implicated when men become aware of their fecundity (ability to procreate) and then negotiate the terrain of sex, contraception, pregnancy, abortion, and fatherhood. Such an approach treats men as evolving procreative beings. As men reflect on the knowledge and experience they acquire over the years, they are able to remake themselves. They can incorporate new insights about matters such as relationships, use of condoms, their fecundity, and the prospects of fatherhood into their inner worlds. As they mature, they can modify their existing beliefs and sentiments to varying degrees. Over time, some men are likely to experience dramatic shifts in how they view their procreative abilities; other men may change very little. But all men are likely to experience some type of change if enough time passes.

Research and Social Policy Context

Research that focuses on the issues just mentioned is timely for two main reasons. First, it is critical to the study of unintended pregnancy as well as childbearing among young persons who may be ill-prepared to face the demands of full-time parenting. Although rates of adolescent pregnancy and abortion have declined in recent years, they remain high relative to rates in other Western countries.[4] Young men, too, are still responsible for large numbers of unintended pregnancies.[5] The vast majority of the 466,000 annual cases where women become pregnant to teenage men involve unintended pregnancies with unmarried men. Among men 25-29 whose partners gave birth in either 1988 or 1994, the pattern is less troublesome but still cause for concern. Fourteen percent said they did not want to have a child and an additional 33 percent indicated the child was born prior to when they had intended to become a father. When unintended pregnancies are brought to term, especially those occurring to teenagers, they are typically associated with poor economic and health outcomes for the women and children. This is a significant pattern even though scholars continue to debate the relationship between poverty status and early childbearing. The key question in this regard: Does poverty status lead to early childbearing or does early childbearing promote poverty?[6]

Second, our research focus is timely because most men spend a great deal of time expressing themselves in their gendered and often meaningful roles as romantic partners and fathers. Hence, to study the social psychology of men's sexual and procreative experiences makes good sense. In short, exploring the dynamic ways men experience themselves as persons capable of creating human life provides a crucial lens for interpreting an important aspect of men's lives as men.

Public and scholarly interest in these issues has grown tremendously since the late 1980s.[7] One indicator is that federal and state policymakers, as well as private foundations, have provided extensive funding for a wide range of research and program initiatives that target young men. The initiatives have dealt primarily with issues associated with sexual activity, contraceptive behavior, paternity establishment, and father involvement. Several of the early programs were the National Urban League's Adolescent Male Responsibility Program introduced in 1986, the National Academy of Sciences Panel on Adolescent Pregnancy and Childbearing (1987), and the Children's Defense Fund report, *What about the Boys?* (1988). Each of these initiatives helped to focus the public's and researchers' attention on male roles in unplanned pregnancy and childbearing.

The early initiatives provided the impetus for an array of local, state, and national research, social policy, and programmatic efforts to promote a better understanding of men's lives in terms of sex, pregnancy prevention, and fatherhood. In many cases, the intent has been to change men's attitudes and behavior. Stakeholders most interested in promoting responsible fatherhood have begun to emphasize that men's roles as fathers begin long before their children are born, or even conceived for that matter. The National Campaign to Prevent Teen Pregnancy, for example, has stressed the need to reach out to teenage and young adult men before they impregnate, or before they impregnate again.[8] By encouraging these men to recognize more fully the potential consequences and responsibilities associated with fathering children, the organization is attempting to ensure that those who do become fathers are prepared to care for their children.

Similarly, the Fatherhood Initiative in the mid-1990s directed by the Domestic Policy Council and former vice president Al Gore's National Performance Review emphasized the importance of understanding men's thoughts, feelings, and motivations prior to their becoming fathers. The Fatherhood Data Team that spearheaded the initiative was comprised of more than a hundred scholars, policy analysts, and public officials. It coordinated a series of national multidisciplinary meetings in response to former president Clinton's 1995 executive order directing federal agencies to support fathers' positive involvement in their families and to ensure that federally funded research on children and families incorporates fathers. The national meetings culminated in 1998 with the publication of *Nurturing Fatherhood: Improving Data and Research on Male Fertility, Family Formation, and Fatherhood*, which reviewed and analyzed the state of theory, research, and data collection on a range of issues related to fatherhood.

Nurturing Fatherhood's recommendations to broaden definitions of father involvement and responsibility were particularly relevant to our study. In the 1980s, father involvement with minor children had been categorized into three basic types: "engagement" (one-on-one interaction); "accessibility" (being physically present to attend to children's needs if necessary); and "responsibility" (active planning of children's lives).[9] *Nurturing Fatherhood* underscored the more recent theorists' proposal to refine and in some ways to reach beyond these forms of involvement by accounting more fully for fathers' cognitive expressions (e.g., prayer) and contributions to children's social capital. This latter notion refers to fathers' contributions to family-based (e.g., sharing parenting styles with a coparent) and community-based (e.g., interactions with children's teachers, coaches, neighbors) relations that typically benefit children's cognitive and emotional development.[10] In addition, *Nurturing Fatherhood* highlighted how recent conceptualizations of father involvement and responsibility are more likely to include men's activities prior to birth and conception. The Fatherhood Initiative has provided an intellectual foundation and incentive for launching a new wave of research on fatherhood while sensitizing policymakers and funding agencies to its relevance.

Overall, the 1990s witnessed a surge in the number of edited journals and books devoted to fatherhood topics.[11] A number of organizations emerged across the country to promote research, social policy analyses, community programs, or the dissemination of information and value-based messages about fatherhood.[12] The directors of major national surveys also have recently responded to the surge of interest in fatherhood by adding questions about fathering to recent and forthcoming waves of data collection.[13] The latest example of this trend is the Male Survey for the National Survey of Family Growth (NSFG), which historically has interviewed only women. Research efforts such as these are novel and significant because they ask fathers themselves about their family roles.

These noteworthy activities have occurred against a backdrop of changes in family life, gender relations, men's declining wages, increases in both women's participation in the paid labor force and men's involvement as primary care providers, and cultural images of fathering.[14] At the same time, heated public debates have emerged over numerous issues relevant to fatherhood. These include divorce and single parenthood, "deadbeat" dads and "involved" fathers, welfare reform, teenage pregnancy and nonmarital childbearing, fathers' rights and responsibilities, the definition of "family," and fathers' potentially unique contributions to child development. The debates often refer to serious social problems assumed to arise from the diverse conditions of "fatherlessness" and "father absence.[15] Despite scholarly disagreement over the meaning of these concepts and the extent and consequences of the latter, the debates influence how the public, policymakers, and the research community frame various questions concerning fathers and families.[16]

Fears about the growing numbers of fathers disconnected from their children have inspired stakeholders to develop organized responses to particular features of fatherhood. Male-only social movements and events such as the Promise Keepers, the Million Man March on Washington, the mythopoetic movement, and fathers' rights groups have each wrestled with fathers' voluntary or involuntary lack of involvement with their children.[17] In the process, they have served to heighten public awareness about the meaning and relevance of fathers in children's lives.

Our Study

Our efforts to understand teenage and young adult men's lives as sexual and procreative beings is consistent with the larger research agenda on fatherhood and the expanded definitions of father involvement and responsible fatherhood. Unlike most previous research dealing with young men's sexual and procreative experiences, our study, based on in-depth interviews, explores men's subjective experiences. With an eye toward the past, present, and future, men in our study share in detail their thoughts and feelings about a range of topics relevant to their sexual and procreative identities. Their candid responses and revealing stories provide the foundation for this book.

Throughout, we have been mindful of how men's experiences are socially constructed and constrained by their reproductive physiology. Accordingly, we discuss how the social psychological processes affecting men's procreative experiences are shaped by the larger social landscape. A view of this landscape reveals that gender assumes a prominent role in organizing how men experience their lives in this domain. More specifically, we spotlight how men's interactions with partners, friends, and family members often enable them to coconstruct their experiences within the procreative realm. In addition, we show how men's relational experiences that involve matters such as their fecundity perceptions, birth control, abortion, pregnancy, and childbirth are affected by their direct physical detachment from all but the coital aspect of the reproductive process. Any meaningful attempt to capture men's lived experiences in this area must take into account the interpersonal aspects of their lives as well as the gendered realities of their reproductive physiology.

Another key feature of our project is to consider men's individual life experiences while taking into account the larger socially constructed landscape of sex and procreation. The larger setting has been influenced by the recent policy and programmatic initiatives mentioned earlier that focus on young men and sexuality, contraception, pregnancy, childbirth, and parenting issues. As noted previously, scholars, policymakers, and social service providers have begun to define responsible fatherhood more broadly to include males' conscientious involvement in sexual and contraceptive decision making to prevent unplanned pregnancies.[18] These and other developments have situated males more squarely in the mix of important policy debates about sex, pregnancy, abortion, paternity, and social fatherhood.

The time is right, then, to listen to young men's in-depth stories about the intimate details of their sex lives, relationships, contraception, abortion, and the visions they have of their future children and roles as fathers. Attending to young men's voices should provide professionals in the field with new ideas about how they can get young men to talk about their personal involvement with procreative issues. Ideally, this research will inform ongoing and future interventions designed to encourage larger numbers of young men to develop a keener sense of their procreative abilities and responsibilities as partners and fathers. Given its theoretical focus, our research should also produce valuable insights for stakeholders interested in promoting men's sexual and reproductive health in other countries.[19]

Theorizing Men's Experiences

Men's ability to become biological fathers ultimately rests on their ability to produce viable sperm and, in most cases, to have sexual intercourse. Although "true" fecundity status is determined with the aid of a laboratory test, men's (and others') perception of their capacity to impregnate can also be a powerful motivating force. Decisions related to having sex, using contraception, and establishing or ending relationships are sometimes affected by whether men (and others) believe that they are fertile or sterile— as well as by their desire to have children. When viewed through the lens of social science, perceptions of fecundity, not the viability of men's sperm, is the defining criterion for theorizing men as procreative beings. From this perspective, the procreative experience involves much more than establishing paternity; it also involves how men manage their awareness of their potential to procreate. The domain of the "procreative being" need not be restricted only to those who have actually had a biological child. It can be extended to include all persons who perceive themselves as persons who can or are presumed to be able to procreate. For some purposes, the spectrum of the procreative being could even be extended to include men who know they are unable to procreate but want to father children.

Subjective Experience in Social Context

Given our interest in the social psychology of men, we turned to the symbolic interactionist perspective, a theoretical framework well known to sociologists and other social scientists who study individuals' everyday life experiences. The perspective helped us formulate the questions we asked our participants and guided our interpretation of their responses and images of self.[20] Each of the competing schools of thought that represent this perspective emphasize a common theme relevant to our work.[21] Meanings individuals associate with aspects of the procreative realm are assumed not to be intrinsic, present in nature, or transcendent in some way; rather, the meanings are viewed as emerging out of a social, interpretive process. What are significant, then, are the social processes by which young men assign meaning to situations, events, acts, others, and themselves as they encounter aspects of the procreative realm. Processes related to men's presumed ability to procreate are particularly important. The definitions men construct in the midst of these social processes are also vital to our efforts to understand men's subjectivity. The definitions typically spring from men's interactions with others, which include their exposure and response to social expectations. Put simply, the relationships men have with others affect how they think about themselves and specific situations.

As young men age, experiencing developmental changes and life-course events along the way, they construct and manage their sexual and procreative identities. A fundamental feature of this evolving process is men's awareness of their ability to procreate. This awareness can be viewed as both a dynamic process and a socially constructed product that is related to formulations of identity and self.

Although men's subjective experiences are in some sense personal, the associated symbolic meanings are social constructions that surface within a value-laden social and cultural context. For example, men's inclination to judge personal experiences in specific ways, such as seeing certain events as turning points, is likely to be affected by their willingness to embrace particular types of broader social and cultural messages. What men see as salient or meaningful is not simply a result of an idiosyncratic process in most instances. Instead, men's perceptions and their efforts to assign meaning to their experiences reflect how they have been influenced by larger social patterns, cultural milieus, and value orientations. Pro- or antinatalist values, religious doctrines, and family and gender ideologies can shape men's perspectives.

Cultural forces often stress the "appropriate" timing of childbearing in relation to other major life-course events such as marriage, education, and work. A male student, for instance, may favor aborting an unplanned pregnancy if he believes he should not have children prior to completing his education and finding a job, even though his religious convictions may contradict this position. Another male may be inspired by the same religious convictions to view his prospective child and his impending status as a father as a gift from God—a blessing in disguise. Competing views such as these are likely to weigh heavily on ambitious young men confronted with an unplanned pregnancy prior to completing their education and/or establishing themselves in the workplace. Although their decisions are personal as to what they should and/or can do, they often concern multiple parties and complex issues.

The cultural forces that come to bear on men's subjectivity are often mediated through men's ongoing involvements with others, the relationship dynamics and situations they experience where sex and procreative issues are raised, and their stage of socioemotional development. Some of the interpersonal ties are informal, close dyadic relationships with friends and family; others stem from more institutionalized and oftentimes temporary arrangements. As for the latter, classroom settings and male responsibility programs that address men's sexual and fatherhood roles can provide men with structured, formal opportunities to explore their personal perspective on a wide range of matters related to relationships and fatherhood. Men's involvements with romantic partners, including their perceptions about experiences they have had with current or previous partners, can affect how they allow cultural messages to influence their stance on procreative issues. For example, when faced with an unplanned pregnancy, men who feel as though they have been betrayed by a partner may be less susceptible to Catholicism's pro-life doctrine. If they are worried that a partner is likely to cheat or leave them at some point, they may reason that the advantages of terminating a pregnancy outweigh any possible religious sanctions.

Self and Identity

Because the study of the self and subjectivity go hand in hand, an exploration of young men's inner worlds as they relate to procreative issues should emphasize the relationship between men's procreative identity and their larger sense of self. Such an exploration must also acknowledge how language can shape men's self-knowledge and expression. With the exception of being the father of a child, the English language does not provide men (or women) with ready-made folk terms to think of themselves as individuals capable of procreation. The term "father" is obviously a familiar label. It signals men's relationship to a biological child, in some cases a stepchild, and it defines men's identity as it relates to another person who already exists; it is an identity or category of experience that has been, in effect, realized. Academics tend to use labels such as "father-in-waiting" or "prospective father" to identify men who have impregnated a partner. But men in everyday life do not have access to a folk term that represents their impending identity as a father. Men do not even have legal standing relative to a fetus prior to a child's birth.

Men's inability to gestate a fetus and thereby visibly announce their identity to others (as women can do, especially during the latter months of a pregnancy) also reinforces the ambiguity of this prospective status. Having no visible signs of being a "father-in-waiting," men will be less likely to elicit responses from others that would acknowledge their status. This means that men who have never fathered a child must work at seeing themselves as persons who are capable of procreating. Presumably, they will associate images of their procreative potential with their more accessible identities as men and romantic partners. Thus, while men's awareness of themselves as persons capable of creating human life is qualitatively different from their identities as men or partners, they may anchor their procreative identity in their everyday life experiences as sexual and romantic partners, or as men. By thinking about their future fatherhood responsibilities and opportunities, men can also try to make sense of their more elusive identities as partners of women who are pregnant with their children.

Persons who have written about these prospective identities have used the language of "possible selves" to convey the notion that individuals project themselves into the future. Thus, "possible selves" represent the "cognitive manifestations of enduring goals, aspirations, motives, fears, and perceived threats. Because 'possible selves' provide a relevant way to relate the meaning, organization, and direction of these dynamics to the self, they also provide the essential link between the self-concept and motivation."[22] In addition to providing individuals with a purpose to act, contemplating "possible selves" offers individuals a standard to evaluate their current standing and behavior. In other words, as individuals attempt to create ideal images of what they would like to accomplish and how they would like to see themselves, they implicitly juxtapose these images against their current and past self images. This type of mental imaging is particularly relevant during key transitional periods throughout the life course. A case in point would be men who visualize themselves as first-time fathers.

Even though we did not firmly align ourselves in this study with any specific perspective on the self, our orientation has been consistent with some of the main themes associated with the theoretical tradition we mentioned previously, symbolic interactionism. The self, as conceptualized within symbolic interactionism, is distinctly social, multifaceted, and dynamic.[23] Viewed as a social construction, the self represents a fusion of countless social experiences that individuals have endured, interpreted, and assimilated to varying degrees. Emphasis is on how individuals adapt to their perceptions of how others see them. Thus they come to develop and express a sense of self through interactions with others, or at times, through imagined interactions.

This social self brings to light individuals' reflexive abilities, their inclination to express themselves as both subject and object. As people think about themselves as objects, that is, as potent men, romantic partners, fathers-in-waiting, and fathers, they often mentally traverse their previous and projected life courses to express their subjectivity and assign meaning to their self. Some may wander back through time, lamenting a lost lifestyle as a teenager or young adult when they had far fewer responsibilities, when proving their manhood was about sexual conquests and posturing for peers; thoughts of being a financial provider and responsible father were far removed from their images of manhood. Others may gaze into the past and recall a less desirable self, a lonely person with no educational and career ambitions, addicted to drugs and alcohol. Such a critical self-appraisal of a former self may stem from a newfound perspective on romantic partnerships and on the day-to-day pleasures of being an involved father. Another spin on these imaginary exercises is displayed by men when they think about how they can mold their life to achieve their ideal image of a future self.

These examples illustrate that if we are to understand how men subjectively experience aspects of the procreative realm, we must consider how men work with a past, present, and future self-image as they construct and present a self. Although there may be any number of factors that affect men's ability to realize their fantasies, apprehending how men think and feel about procreative issues is a necessary first step.

One implicit consequence of viewing the self as multifaceted is the notion that the self is a type of miniature social structure comprised of different identities and dimensions. The theoretical debates about how this structure can best be conceptualized,[24] though not directly relevant to our purposes, have prompted us to take into account men's multiple identities as single men (including notions of adult manhood), romantic partners, and prospective or real-life fathers. In some instances, men juggle the identities as they attempt to privilege their commitment to one over another. In other instances, they work to fit them together in a manner that they find appealing or that they suspect is appealing to others. The potential overlap and tension points between the identities can therefore represent an important site for discovering how men subjectively experience themselves in the procreative realm.

As mentioned previously, we are interested in how men change. The dynamic features to the self are therefore of considerable interest to us. By viewing individual men as active agents who play a major role in creating their own experience and self, we focus on the ways men organize their self-perceptions and learn lessons through their personal and vicarious experiences. Thinking about men as evolving procreative beings, as we do, leads us to study men's inner worlds involving their sex lives, procreative experiences, and visions of fathering. We assume that we can gather meaningful insights about men's inner worlds by encouraging them to talk about their thoughts, beliefs, and feelings relevant to various aspects of the procreative realm. Men's inner worlds that relate to their current and previous sexual and romantic partners are of particular interest to us.

Procreative Bodies, Gendered Lives

Theorizing about men's subjectivity calls for us to be sensitive to how men's biological sex affects their self-perception, and how gender, as a cultural construct, helps to structure their lives, especially their relations with women. Although we do not treat consciousness as being completely distinct from the human body, we realize that the connection between men's awareness of themselves as procreative beings and their physical self is rather limited because of their reproductive physiology. For men, it is more the absence of this mind-body intersection than its presence that shapes their awareness of their procreative self.

Despite recent efforts to promote gender equality, there is simply no escaping the fundamental sex differences in reproductive anatomy and physiology. Much has been made of the fact that women conceive, gestate, and give birth to human life and that men's direct role in the procreative process is limited to the contribution of sperm during intercourse (or the donation of sperm in noncoital reproduction).[25] Human reproductive physiology is uncompromising; postconception, it excludes men from the ongoing physical processes associated with making babies. It even fails to alert them to their procreative potential on a regular basis, whereas most females, once they experience menarche and prior to undergoing menopause, are reminded of it monthly. Men have close and frequent encounters with their sperm through masturbation but presumably interpret these pleasurable moments as part of the erotic realm replete with mental fantasies. Some of our participants' stories also brought to mind that teenage males' exposure to sperm first produced in their "wet dreams" can usher in personal thoughts about their emerging manhood and fecundity.

Aside from experiencing ejaculation, men do not have the same types of direct and experiential connections to the reproductive process as do women. Men, therefore, do not have specific physical events that would be included in what Alfred Schutz calls their relevance structures, that is, the set of circumstances or symbols that prompt a person to focus on an aspect of reality in a particular fashion.[26] Yes, modern sonography technology offers some men (and women) the opportunity to see the fetus they have helped to create. And, yes, men can serve as a birthing partner who "assists" with a child's birth. But these experiences cannot fully produce the type of body-mediated consciousness that women can achieve.[27] Whatever consciousness men have of themselves as procreative beings, including a desire to pass on their genetic material to their children, is bound to be a social accomplishment, at least in part. Hence, gendered cultural and social processes fashion the opportunities men have to give meaning to their personal experiences in the procreative realm.

Men in the United States, generally speaking, are seldom involved in social rituals related to fertility and babies. They also are less likely than women to be exposed to commercial or interpersonal messages that emphasize pregnancy and/or babies. And they are less likely to have occasion to be involved in group bonding experiences that focus on reproductive issues, for example, baby showers. Men's homosocial bonding experiences are more likely to occur within the context of the erotic realm (e.g., the viewing of men's magazines, trips to strip clubs),[28] but a number of programs have been introduced around the country that bring teenage and young adult men together to talk about issues related to sex, procreation, and fatherhood.[29] These and other interventions may ultimately revamp how some of the cultural and social features of the procreative realm are gendered, but dramatic changes are unlikely to occur in the immediate future.

Changes may also take place in how men and women approach certain aspects of their romantic relationships, but these too are likely to evolve slowly. If we were to take the field of evolutionary psychology seriously, we would have to conclude that the prospect of altering some of these patterns in any significant way is a long, uphill battle. From this perspective, certain aspects of our mating patterns are ingrained in our unconsciousness because reproductive strategies fundamental to our species are based on critical sex differences, and have been for millennia. The sex differences supposedly have been produced throughout human history because men and women have faced different types of opportunities and risks in the sexual and reproductive arenas. Altering these patterns is possible, but doing so goes against the path of least resistance.

John Townsend, a cultural anthropologist, embraces this controversial perspective and vigorously argues that men's and women's conscious and unconscious approaches to love and commitment in Western societies today stem from their basic and divergent reproductive strategies and sexual psychologies. Simply put, men are thought to be predisposed, as men, to maximize their opportunities to copulate and procreate with multiple partners. On the other side of the sexual/reproductive mating equation, women are inclined to be more selective in choosing a mating partner. They ultimately desire a mate who will invest in a partner and children who may be born to the couple. Although such investment can take many forms, women today are assumed to seek material and emotional investments from a serious male suitor.

We do not base our study on this type of evolutionary perspective; however, researchers in this area have produced intriguing findings that warrant mention, given their possible connection to our study. For example, researchers continue to show that men are more willing than women to have sex outside a committed relationship and to have sex with a stranger.[30] Studies based on experimental designs using law and medical students also indicate that men and women differ in the criteria used to evaluate a potential sex partner and, to a lesser extent, a marriage partner. Men, on average, are more likely than women to emphasize a potential romantic partner's physical attractiveness when considering whether they would be interested in a sexual encounter with a particular person, or be willing to consider a person as a marriage partner. For their part, women are more likely than men to evaluate a potential sex partner's ability and willingness to make material and emotional investments in them and their offspring. When it comes to marriage considerations, women are clearly more likely to assess a potential partner's ability and willingness to be an economic provider. Even professional women tend to acknowledge the importance of socioeconomic criteria, preferring to mate with a man who has a higher or at least a similar social and economic status. Men, meanwhile, appear to be more likely than women to wonder about a partner's willingness to be the hands-on caretaker of the children, and suitability for the role. Still, men's concerns about these matters may not be as salient to them, relatively speaking, as women's concerns about a mate's ability to be an economic provider.

To what extent these differences are due to social, biological, or some combination of factors is unclear and beyond the scope of what we hope to accomplish here. What does seem clear is that the differences have persisted to some degree despite significant efforts to bring about gender equality. Irrespective of their origin and persistence, these patterns may color the subjective worlds of young men and women, influencing how they form and express their sexual and procreative identities.

How do men's sexual psychologies relate to their personal thoughts and feelings concerning procreative issues directly relevant to them? When men are having sex or fantasizing about having sex in a casual arrangement, they are seldom motivated to have vivid fantasies about having a child with that partner. In these situations, men are often capable of separating their physical and emotional selves, experiencing the physical pleasure of the moment without fantasizing about a long-term commitment that might ultimately involve childbearing. Some men, however, may worry at least fleetingly about the prospects of having a child with a woman whom they look upon primarily as a casual sexual partner—or a more serious partner, for that matter. In some instances, this kind of uneasiness raises its head when men experience regret having had unprotected sex with a recent sexual partner. Such regret, does not necessarily entail a clear-headed assessment of what it would be like to father a child under a particular set of circumstances. Rather, men may tend to have an abstract and muddled impression that they are not yet ready to deal with the significant life changes that a baby may bring.

The way men interpret and manage specific relationships can also affect their procreative identities. Men often link their sentiments about paternity and social fatherhood for specific children to their feelings for the children's mother. For these men, feeling committed and attached to specific children is contingent on being involved romantically with the children's mother. Scholars have coined this tendency the "package deal."[31] Not surprisingly, the connection between men's subjectivity involving procreative matters and romantic relationships may tend to be stronger after the children have been born, or at least once men have learned that they have impregnated a partner. Once men's romantic relationships dissolve, however, their identities as fathers to the former partner's children often wane. Another twist to this pattern is that men are less likely than women to yearn to have children outside a romantic involvement. Single women, for example, pursue single parenthood through adoption and assisted means, including modern technologies, at significantly higher rates than is so for men. The evidence is rather clear that compared to women, men's procreative identities and commitment to fathering roles tend to be more closely tied to men's romantic involvements.

"Sensitizing" Concepts

When we theorize about young men in this study, we aim to generate a rich, broad, and practical understanding of their subjective experiences. Most important is how they construct and express their identities as procreative beings. Consequently, our purpose is not to estimate how many men, or what types of men think, feel, or act in a specific way. Our questions do not deal with the social demography of men's lives. Such questions are best left for studies based on large, nationally representative surveys. In qualitative studies like ours that search to uncover social psychological processes, we, in agreement with other qualitative researchers,[32] think it is critically important not to presume that membership in a certain race, cultural group, or social class holds any special significance. Instead, we use our in-depth interviews to deepen our theoretical understanding of the complexity and range of men's subjective experiences in the procreative realm. By taking this path, we hope to uncover some of the possible ways young men frame their procreative experiences in their minds and hearts. True, the nature of our sample limits our ability to generalize our results with confidence to various subgroups of young men. But our study enables us to break new ground by exploring in great detail facets of young men's inner worlds that have gone uncharted. Future qualitative research that builds on our conceptual developments, particularly ethnographic work that examines men's lives within an ecological context, will be better suited to consider how young men's procreative identities may be affected by race, culture, and social class.

We use as our starting point the first author's theoretical scheme for conceptualizing men's multifaceted lives as persons capable of creating human life. This model, discussed at length in *Procreative Man*, emphasizes men's subjective experiences and interrelated identities as sexual partner, father, and masculine male. As a flexible analytic framework, it outlines ways of thinking about men's subjective experiences in the procreative realm that provide scholars a starting point for studying specific aspects of men's lives. We describe below two of the broad concepts that are pivotal to this approach: procreative consciousness and responsibility. In addition, the "turning point"[33] concept provides us with a useful conceptual tool with which to explore some of the changes men experience in their identities and perspectives as they deal with various procreative issues.

We work with the three concepts as if they were what qualitative researchers refer to as "sensitizing concepts."[34] Closely tied to one version of symbolic interactionism,[35] sensitizing concepts are provisional conceptual tools. They also highlight the unique properties that may be associated with a class of data—men's procreative identities in our case. The concepts offer researchers a general sense of reference and orientation without unduly restricting new paths for theoretical discovery. Thus, sensitizing concepts, by definition, are loosely defined and dynamic.[36] In contrast, definitive concepts have more precise, rigid meanings. Sensitizing concepts enable scholars to locate an entry point for developing a line of inquiry while allowing them "to see those meanings that people attach to the world around them."[37] In the words of one theorist, they provide "a starting point in thinking about a class of data of which the social researcher has no definite idea and provides an initial guide to her research. Such concepts usually are provisional and may be dropped as more viable and definite concepts emerge in the course of her research."[38]

Typically, sensitizing concepts emerge from the research process and are closely tied to research participants' thoughts and words, although they remain more abstract "second-order" concepts, one step removed from the data. In our case, the "sensitizing" concepts we used initially to orient our study and then in a more limited sense to interpret men's reflections about their experiences, are a bit more abstract than usual. Nevertheless, they help us generate new theoretical insights about the social psychology of young men's experience with procreative issues. Because these concepts were instrumental in guiding our interviewing and analytic strategies for our current study, we describe them briefly here. We discuss in subsequent chapters other concepts we discovered and developed during our analyses of the data that could serve as sensitizing concepts to guide future research on young men.

Procreative Consciousness and Responsibility

Theorizing about men's subjective experiences in the procreative realm must account for the attitudes, beliefs, feelings, and impressions men have of themselves in relation to various aspects of procreation—including a self-image as prospective father. Relevant experiences include men's conscious thoughts about the possibility of conception and pregnancy, as well as related efforts to figure out how to bring about or impede conception. Men's attempts to nurture or abort a pregnancy are significant, as are men's visions of their own children not yet born, in some instances not yet conceived.

By using the phrase *procreative consciousness* to capture the diverse subjective phenomena just described, we earmark aspects of men's "wideawake" consciousness. When individuals are attentive to aspects of their everyday-life worlds or demonstrate self-awareness by projecting themselves into hypothetical situations, they are conscious in a distinctive sense. This type of awareness is unique in that individuals are attending to aspects of their environment and themselves in a conscious fashion. The awareness can still vary, though, in both sharpness and duration.

Of course, most men also have fertility-related motivations that are not prominently featured in their immediate lived experience because the motivations are neither influencing behavior nor being expressed as part of a "wideawake" consciousness.[39] The motivations, residing in men's latent procreative consciousness, can be viewed as untapped potential. Lying dormant, beyond immediate conscious reach, they can be set in motion by an appropriate stimulus or set of circumstances. Hearing a partner talk regularly about her desires to have a child in the near future or within a specified time frame can prompt men to sit up and take notice of their own unexpressed fertility desires. They may find themselves thinking, "I definitely want to have kids someday, but I don't want to be having kids now, I don't have the time or money," or "Well, I've always wanted kids, maybe I should just go for it, I'm not getting any younger."

Though fascinating, this complex layering and connection between "wideawake" and "latent" consciousness is largely beyond our theoretical interests in this study.

We do, however, focus on both the fleeting and more enduring aspects of men's procreative consciousness. On many occasions during involvement in a specific activity, men actively attend to procreative issues for a relatively short period of time (though sometimes quite superficially). We refer to these experiences by using the phrase situational (or situated) procreative consciousness. Here we find men involved with objects or props (e.g., condoms, pregnancy prevention advertisements, pamphlets discussing fatherhood), and/or people (e.g, a sexual partner, clinic staff, friends, parents) in a specific kind of situation (e.g., sexual encounter, discussion about contraception/pregnancy, a consumer purchase). For example, listen to Sean, a 23-year-old participant in our study as he talks about those times when he's lying naked next to his current partner:

> [when] I am not wearing a condom, I want to put some type of barrier between us. But she feels that's breaking the moment if we're just lying there. And I am trying to explain to her that well, if I get excited I have heard that some sperm can exit . . . and she feels I'm being overly paranoid and so I try not to listen to the voices when they tell me you need to put underwear on or pull the sheet over her or something.

Sean's fears of impregnating his partner under the circumstances he describes may be unfounded, but his concerns are nonetheless real. These fears heighten his momentary self-awareness as someone who has the potential to procreate when he's lying naked next to his partner. Sean implies that his procreative identity becomes salient to both him and his partner in a particular type of situation. Although his ephemeral thoughts apparently fade into his latent consciousness once he and/or his partner alter the situation, that is, one of them gets up and/or gets dressed, they resurface when he finds himself in a similar predicament.

Men are also likely to possess more general thoughts and feelings about themselves as persons capable of creating human life. Though relatively stable, such thoughts and feelings are often muddled and obscure. The term *global procreative consciousness* is useful here. This type of awareness is likely to be affected by men's own experiences with contraception, abortion, pregnancy, and childbirth, or indirectly through their exposure to others' experiences. Thus, it may arise at various times and in numerous ways, although it is probably most distinct during prolonged and identifiable phases of men's lives. An identifiable period might include, say, the time between when a man's partner informs him that her period is late and her announcement that her period has arrived.

Marcus's comments suggest that global awareness is not always framed by a neatly defined, identifiable phase of a man's procreative life; rather it can reflect a man's current mind-set more generally. This 19-year-old with some college experience alludes to his global awareness when asked if he thinks about pregnancy.

> I think about it a lot. That's why I just, I stopped. I just don't do it [have sex] as much. . . . I just don't think about it as much. I jis' don't be like a little dog and trying to holler [hook up with someone to have sex] at everything, just something like that. Just in general that's like being, being responsible, being smart not hollering a lot, trying [to] take on a lot of girls.

Marcus's comments reveal that he is now much more conscious of and concerned about his ability to get a girl pregnant than he was earlier in his life. According to him, his new self-awareness, or global procreative consciousness, has led him to become less preoccupied with the idea that he needs to persuade lots of girls to have sex with him. He also appears to have adopted his present outlook on girls, sex, and pregnancy outside a time frame that is marked by an identifiable set of sexual or reproductive circumstances.

Another useful theoretical distinction can be made by considering the mode or basis of men's procreative consciousness as it is expressed in either the situated or global context. On the one hand, men sometimes develop perceptions and feelings about specific domains of procreation that they associate with a particular romantic and/or sexual relationship. In other instances, men develop views that are largely independent of a specific relationship.

How can men's procreative consciousness and sense of responsibility be influenced by specific features of a romantic relationship and a partner's views about reproductive issues? One answer to this question comes by way of Todd, a 27-year-old, who was homeless and a father of a two-year-old when we interviewed him. Todd spoke at length about how his troubled relationship with his former live-in partner prompted him during her pregnancy to think about the prospects of being a single resident or nonresident father. These thoughts came on the heels of his partner's and his hoping that the pregnancy would end without a live birth. Responding to a question about whether he had thought about being a father during his former partner's pregnancy, Todd says:

> Yeah. I sure did. . . . [W]e wanted this baby to go away. It wasn't right or whatever, it didn't seem right. And, then, when that wouldn't happen, . . . then I started thinking about it, what it would be like to be a father, what it's gonna entail, you know, once she started leaving me and all this crap while she's pregnant, which, you know, that's just the way she is, she's really like, capricious, and if one of her friends or something tells her, . . . that I'm a piece of shit, she's gonna believe them, whether she feels that way or not, or whether its true or not. So, once she started doing that, I kinda like, I talked to everybody about that, and, even like my family members and stuff were like surprising me by going. "[S]o what, she's pregnant with your kid, what's that mean to you?" . . . I'm just like, what do you mean what does it mean to me, Jesus, you people are so insensitive. . . . [S]till, I had to go through thinking about what its gonna be like to have her raising the kid, or me raising the kid that we both have, stuff like that, and then it went back to, oh, okay, now we're gonna do it together, you know, its kinda, fluctual.

Todd's perception of his partner's negative attitude toward him plainly influenced how he thought about his upcoming fathering experiences, apparently contemplating how he might be forced to manage certain responsibilities on his own.

Many men have personal beliefs, attitudes, and preferences about individual procreative issues that are not confined to or necessarily the result of their ongoing involvement in a particular romantic relationship. Their ideas and feelings about procreative issues may be relatively stable for extended periods of time irrespective of whom they may be involved with at any given time. Some men may have strong pro-life views or may be inclined to view contraception as always a shared responsibility among sexual partners regardless of any particular romantic relationship between them. For a specific example of someone who maintains his own ideas separate from any ongoing romantic relationship, and seemingly independent of any specific situation, we can turn to Reynaldo, a 17-year-old participant. Reynaldo shares his feelings about the prospects of getting someone pregnant at this point in his life, and in the process clarifies how his parents, his father in particular, helped him to develop his own independent and global perspective.

> Like, my dad has another son and he had him when my dad was seventeen and so like my dad was telling me, you know you shouldn't do those type of things [having kids at a young age] because they end up hurting the kids more than anything. And that's really when I started understanding that I could do something like that. And not really ruin someone's life but, you know, pretty much mix it up because if a girl gets pregnant she has to take care of that kid and I'd probably have to pay child support. You know, and I don't want to go to jail. It's going to ruin someone's life one way or the other.

Reynaldo's description of his procreative consciousness brings us to the procreative responsibility notion, with its important social policy implications. This sensitizing concept represents a unique form of procreative consciousness. Given its significance, it deserves to be treated separately even though we see it as being a special type of expression of procreative consciousness. It identifies men's beliefs about their obligations and their involvement in various areas including sexual decision making, contraception and conception, pregnancy-resolution discussions, childbearing activities/rituals, and, to some extent, paternal activities (perhaps more precisely labeled as paternal responsibility).

Procreative responsibility covers two closely related yet conceptually distinct areas of activity involving men's perceptions and men's interactions with others. These domains include (1) men's perceived sense of obligation to acknowledge paternity and fulfill particular social fatherhood roles, and (2) the practical aspects of events related to procreation (including its prevention) ranging from sex to contraception to conception to gestation to pregnancy outcome (e.g., choosing a contraceptive method, accompanying a partner for an abortion). Defining male procreative responsibility precisely is no easy task because diverse and sometimes contradictory definitions of responsibility exist on individual, familial, peer group, community, and societal levels. What is perceived to be responsible behavior in the eyes of some stakeholders, in fact, may be irresponsible to others.

Competing concerns about how single men can act responsibly are most immediately apparent when considering men's involvement with an unplanned pregnancy. Should unmarried men propose marriage to "legitimize" unplanned births? Are men supposed to step back and support whatever decision a pregnant partner wants to make, including abortion? When a woman chooses abortion, should her male partner assert his willingness to accompany her through all phases of the abortion process? Or, should a man, when faced with a partner's desire to abort, do everything in his power to prevent the partner's going through with it? These are clearly timely, difficult, and value-laden questions worthy of debate. However, because we are interested in the social psychology of men's experiences, not men's morality, we focus where possible on men's subjective definitions of responsibility when we interpret our data.

We get a glimpse of how one rare, albeit persistent, version of procreative responsibility can be conveyed when Desmond, a 30-year-old with a flare for colorful language, says:

> Well, I don't think you're a man unless you can be responsible for the sex, cause sex does bring on responsibility when you release that load, if you will. Ah, that's responsibility. It doesn't seem that fair, but that load, boy, can take you into a tailspin of thousands and thousands of dollars, just for that little load.

In this instance Desmond views responsibility in narrow, monetary terms. He makes no mention of the social aspects of fathering that entail taking care of a child's daily needs. Desmond's other comments also reveal how his views on procreative responsibility are affected by his conception of the gendered nature of the procreative realm we described previously.

> First of all, it feels good being a man. . . . A man is potent a long, long time. Um, that feels good. . . . There's some machismo about the part . . . all men have to be worried about is paying money when they can pretty much spring clear. They don't carry anything for nine months . . . the kid's not gonna want to nurture off of his breast. You know, men, I think, have a biological advantage, and it feels good to be a man.

Touting the pleasures of being a man, he seems to rejoice in a man's limited responsibility of only "paying money." He gives no evidence of having envisioned himself as a social father or of being in an enduring relationship with his own child.

A final point about these conceptual issues is that much of men's conscious thinking, feeling, and activity in the procreative realm is connected to their ongoing interpersonal relationships. As a result, men's subjective experiences often meld into the evolving "self" they present and manage in connection with the relationships they have with their partner(s). As a result, it is sometimes difficult to isolate these experiences as distinct thoughts, feelings, or actions because they become entangled in men's more elaborate presentation of self.

Turning Points

Given our interest in exploring the dynamic aspects of males' personal careers in the procreative realm, we make use of the "turning point" concept. A situation or event can be thought of as a turning point if it prompts an individual to experience a fundamental shift or transformation that leads the individual to become someone other than he or she was before. This developmental moment occurs "when an individual has to take stock, to reevaluate, revise, resee, and rejudge."[40] As this process unfolds, the individual is compelled to "try out the new self, to explore and validate the new and often exciting or fearful conceptions."[41] From the symbolic interactionist perspective we described above, what ultimately matters is whether the individual is aware on some level that these events and related processes have altered his or her identity and perspective.

It may not always be possible, though, for the individual to identify the unique contribution some turning points have for altering his or her identity and perspective. Although we treat turning points as relatively discrete events that affect some aspect of men's lives in the procreative realm, they may sometimes be embedded in processes associated with more general developmental transitions common to adulthood.[42] Turning points in some instances may also consist of a set of intersecting experiences rather than a discrete event. Men may still view them though, in retrospect, as a specific, identifiable event. Looking back in this way may muddle the way men interpret the dynamic processes that have altered their perspective and identity.

These caveats notwithstanding, we discuss at length in chapter 4 how diverse types of turning points affect men's procreative lives. Included among the many voices we will hear as part of that discussion are those of

Arthur and Andy. Arthur, a 21-year-old working-class participant shares his story about how his partner's secretive abortion devastated him, leading him to take a personal vow never to date a pro-choice woman again. We learn from Andy, a 30-year-old, well-educated participant, how his desire to marry and father his own son was awakened after he cared for his cancer-stricken father during the father's final months. We use these and other examples to show how procreative experiences can serve as turning points, and how nonprocreative events can also come to be defined as turning points that alter men's subjectivity in the procreative realm.

A Grounded Theory Approach

As we discuss more fully in chapter 2, our effort to make sense of men's rich narratives and reflections is guided by our use of the sensitizing concepts mentioned above and the grounded theory approach.[43] This inductive strategy places a premium on remaining "close" to the qualitative data at hand. Transcripts are to be read intensively, with participants' comments being compared repeatedly until concepts and theoretical insights emerge. Thus, beginning a study armed with definitive concepts and a formal theory is inconsistent with this method.

Because the grounded theory approach eschews a priori theorizing, preferring instead to build theory from the data themselves, using it in conjunction with the model outlined in *Procreative Man* required us to be vigilant in treating procreative consciousness and responsibility as sensitizing concepts. This was challenging because, unlike many studies based on the grounded theory approach, we initiated ours with considerable familiarity with the theoretical terrain. Likewise, we were knowledgeable about substantive issues—trends and concepts relating to sex, contraceptive use, abortion, procreation, and fathering—that are likely to function as "social facts"[44] and influence men's procreative identities. We therefore turned to the sensitizing concepts to formulate some of our initial questions and probes; they alerted us to fruitful areas of inquiry. At the same time, however, we fostered a research process that enabled participants to assume the role of teacher with us. We sought to discover new concepts and ways of thinking about men's procreative lives and identities. So, although our research strays a bit from the path grounded theorists typically pursue, our line of inquiry is still illuminated by this inductive approach.

The grounded theory approach allowed us to achieve two basic aims. First, we used it to deepen, expand, integrate, and to ground in empirical data notions about procreative consciousness and men's experiences with fertility issues. Second, we discovered new concepts and their properties that shape how young men construct and express their identities as persons capable of creating human life. Unlike typical grounded theory studies, we did not aim to generate a grounded theory. Rather, we expanded Marsiglio's original conceptual framework in order to account for how men construct and express their procreative identities over time. In doing so, we linked substantive concepts close to men's daily experiences to the more abstract sensitizing concepts, procreative consciousness and responsibility.

Although confident that our study addresses these two aims in considerable detail, we recognize that our research does not answer important questions related to men's developmental processes, race, and culture. Given our relatively small sample, we are handicapped in making credible statements about young men's procreative identities and their stage of socioemotional or cognitive development. Likewise, we are limited in our ability to compare young men who are African American to those who are white or Hispanic, or poor men to those who are more economically well off. Instead, we have generated new concepts that appear to be relevant to all of them while expanding other concepts that reveal the complexity in young men's procreative lives.

In choosing our emphasis in this initial study, we remain true to the grounded theory method. The purpose of grounded theory analysis is to achieve analytic generalization, the generation and expansion of analytic and sensitizing (meaningful) concepts in an area that has not been explored fully. These concepts need to have explanatory power, which requires that they are abstract enough to be useful in understanding "multiconditional, ever-changing daily situations."[45] They should also be meaningful enough for nonacademics to understand them and find them useful in their work. Achieving this explanatory power requires a diverse sample to ensure that the data are rich and complex enough to be conceptualized in a manner that adequately accounts for the phenomenon of interest. Thus, conceptual understanding more than description and representation (distribution of men among categories for statistical purposes) is the goal of our research at this point in time. We have tried to be sensitive to and explore all theoretically meaningful issues with our sampling strategies rather than making the *a priori* assumption that social structural or cultural variables were more important. For this initial study, we interviewed men of many ages, races, and economic circumstances. We did this in order to maximize differences so we could achieve a higher level of conceptualization instead of focusing on only one group (e.g., African American teenage males) to minimize differences. We maximize differences to foster greater breadth of understanding; in subsequent studies we will minimize differences in order to study more closely our newly generated and expanded concepts/categories.

Generally speaking, when the grounded theory method is used, no one variable is presumed important until it surfaces as such from the data. In examining our data, we have not yet heard that race or socioeconomic standing influence how men respond to our questions about their procreative lives. We suspect, however, that there may be situations where race, class, and cultural features of men's lives do bear upon how they experience their procreative identities within their local ecological context. Age (developmental stage), on the other hand, does emerge in our interviews as important in some situations and we discuss this in places where the men felt it was an issue. For example, some men described feeling differently as they got older about the possibility of an unplanned pregnancy. This finding supports the value of conducting additional research that focuses on a more restricted category of older adolescent men who are at a similar stage of development.

With this caveat in mind, we proceed in the chapters that follow by sharing the lessons we have learned from our focused set of analyses. At the outset we discuss how men use different strategies to assign meaning to the discovery of their procreative potential. We then show how a romantic partner helps men coconstruct their procreative consciousness, including efforts to help male partners actively attend to issues of procreative responsibility. Most important, we deepen our understanding of procreative consciousness by identifying four properties: *knowledge (with an emphasis on fecundity perceptions), emotional response, temporal orientation,* and *child visions.* Studying these properties illustrates the breadth and complexity of how some young men think and feel as they personally attend to different aspects of the procreative realm.

This initial analysis of procreative consciousness sheds light on how men evolve in the way they think and feel about procreative issues. Our discussion of men's nascent procreative consciousness gives way to our more extensive treatment of the ways men modify their subjective experiences throughout their teens and twenties as persons capable of creating human life. Although we are interested in all types of experiences that facilitate change, our main interest rests with the "turning point" events relevant to procreation. We therefore rely heavily on Strauss's general typology of critical junctures or transition points in identity to guide our analysis.[46] After identifying five general types of turning points relevant to our study, we refine the turning point concept by elaborating eight properties: *degree of control; duration; presence of subjective and/or behavioral changes; individual or shared experience; vicarious or personal experience; type and degree of institutional context; centrality; and emotional response and evaluation.*

In reviewing men's stories about their turning points and other life issues, we became acutely aware of the relationship between their romantic involvements and their subjective experiences with sex, birth control, and procreation. We therefore highlight the relevance of relationship issues for understanding men's procreative identities. How men categorize types of women and their relationships with them is sometimes relevant to how men think about their ability and desire to procreate.

We then illustrate the complexity of how young men, many of whom are not yet fathers, envision fatherhood while we selectively show how personal and relationship issues affect men's perceptions. Here, our research reveals two interrelated substantive concepts. *Fatherhood readiness* signifies men's sense of being ready to become a father; *fathering visions* references men's views of ideal fathering, their images of the ideal or good father, and their visions of fathering future children. We sharpen our understanding of these concepts by introducing five interrelated theoretical properties: *degree and form of collaboration, focus of attention, temporal orientation, experience*, and *degree of clarity.*

In the concluding chapter we propose how our work can inform various programmatic efforts that target young men. The most relevant ones are designed to prevent unplanned pregnancies and promote responsible sexual, contraceptive, and fathering behavior. We also show how our research relates to a conceptual model of fathering that focuses on three trajectories men experience as fathers (*self-as-father, father-child*, and *coparenting*).

The core of our work is clearly defined by the theoretical and substantive insights we generate from the analyses just described. In addition, we address many of the methodological and programmatic issues relevant to our area of study. Not only do we describe in the next chapter the basic aspects of how we sampled and interviewed young men, we systematically reflect on our research experience in this study. In essence, we offer a backstage account of how our research project evolved. By sharing our insights in this manner, we aim to inspire qualitative researchers and social service providers to think in fresh ways about how they might study and work with young men on a broad set of issues related to sex, relationships, and fathering.

2

Studying Young Single Men

When we began to study young men's thoughts and feelings about their relationships, sex, contraception, pregnancy, abortion, and fatherhood, we were venturing into largely uncharted territory. Survey researchers have attempted to answer various questions concerning these substantive areas in recent years, but their approach is ill-suited to delve deeply into men's inner worlds. Likewise, little has been done to study how men's experiences with different procreative events are related to one another, or how men's procreative consciousness evolves over time. Our journey into men's subjective lives within the procreative realm has therefore produced exciting challenges and lessons for us along the way.

Unfortunately, social scientists have seldom asked young men candid, open-ended questions about the issues of interest to us. Although a few researchers, including the first author, have asked teenage and young adult men relevant questions in focus group settings, and some have completed ethnographic work on related issues,[1] the paucity of research in the area led us to believe that there was much to be gained by eliciting men's stories and reflections about their sexual and procreative lives.

We suspected too that what we would learn would not be limited to substantive and theoretical insights about men's thoughts and feelings in the procreative realm. True to form, and in keeping with the qualitative research tradition, we have benefitted by reflecting on aspects of the in-depth interviewing strategy we used to tap into young men's experiences. We provide an overview of our methodology in this chapter, but our discussion of how we went about studying young men goes far beyond describing the ways we identified our participants and secured their participation. We do more than simply describe our sample's social and demographic characteristics and the types of questions we asked. In addition to clarifying the basic features of our research design and sample, we want to sensitize researchers and social service providers, as well as ourselves, to the challenges of conducting qualitative interviews with young men. Consequently, we make a concerted effort to frame our comments about the research process as a reflexive exercise. In particular, we discuss a variety of methodological issues that come into play when doing in-depth interviews with young men about personal issues dealing with sex and procreation.[2]

We evaluate our project in order to provide others with insights relevant to their own research and clinical work with young men. Because the quality of in-depth interviews directly influences data analysis, qualitative researchers studying young men stand to benefit by considering the methodological issues that have emerged from our self-evaluation. Researchers interested in formulating survey questions may also want to think about how the issues we raise can inform their pilot study work and questionnaire development. Meanwhile, social service providers, given their opportunities to talk extensively with young men about sexual health, pregnancy prevention, and fathering concerns, should benefit from our reflexive approach. Our contribution will be most apparent when we address issues that other professionals find relevant to their own conversations with young men, and if we are able to encourage them to reflect on their own studies and interviews.

Using our research project as a case study, we underscore the tight connections between a study's purpose, data collection strategies (including the interview guide and other aspects of securing and interviewing participants), and data analysis. Some of our concerns are general; others are specific to qualitative research with young men. We organize our reflexive comments around seven specific methodological concerns:

(1) overlap between theoretical and methodological perspectives;
(2) efforts to gain access to young men's personal thoughts about potentially sensitive topics;
(3) questions about how participants' and interviewers' age, gender, and race may affect the interviewing process;
(4) efforts to account for participants' sexual and procreative experience as well as their level of maturity;
(5) temporal issues involving interviewers' attempts to take into account men's inclination to move back and forth in their narratives among previous, current, and future self-conceptions;
(6) collection of data on various types of experiences that are embedded within the interview narratives;

(7) researchers' and participants' use of language related to sex, relationships, and procreative activities.

We then describe six indices that can be used to assess the interview process and the data we obtained.[3]

The bulk of what we offer in this chapter can be viewed as a story within a story. No doubt some readers may skip this material and jump to the more "exciting" substantive story that captures how young men describe their sexual and procreative experiences. The larger story can still be read and understood by those who choose this route. However, the subplot—our self-reflexive, detailed account of how we experienced and guided a qualitative inquiry into young men's lives—is a valuable story in its own right. Our account of the data collection and analytic processes also places in perspective how we represent our participants' voices in subsequent chapters.

How Men Have Been Studied

To date, most research focusing on adolescent and young adult men's views on aspects of contraceptive use, pregnancy, and abortion, and their beliefs about men's sense of responsibility toward children they or others might sire has been based on survey methodologies.[4] Much of the survey research that is at least remotely relevant to our study is based on data from one of the three waves of the National Survey of Adolescent Males first fielded in 1988 when respondents were 15–19 years of age (NSAM-1, NSAM-2, NSAM-3), the new 1995 NSAM cohort, and the sample of men who were 20–39 years of age in the 1991 National Survey of Men (NSM). Research using these and other survey data has done much to document the social demography of young men's beliefs and attitudes. However, the structured-interview format these studies use makes it difficult to uncover the social psychological processes that affect how men perceive and express themselves as sexual and procreative beings. Survey-based studies are therefore ill-equipped to clarify how men construct and assign meaning to their various experiences. They also are poorly suited to study how men's subjective experiences unfold within a dynamic, social context.

Recent focus group studies, ethnographies, and qualitative interviews have begun to supplement survey research and, in the process, enhance our understanding of the social psychology of men's involvement in the sexual, pregnancy, and childbearing domains.[5] These qualitative studies, guided largely by a perspective that accentuates the social problems associated with irresponsible male behavior, have contributed to our understanding of young men's (and women's) beliefs about contraception, pregnancy, and paternity. They have also revealed some of the individual and interpersonal strategies individuals use to make sense of and negotiate their interests in these domains.

The above qualitative studies have their own set of limitations though. Most important, they do not explore fully the complexity of the conceptual terrain associated with men's efforts to develop and alter their self-perceptions as persons capable of procreating. They do not systematically consider, for example, how men may express an awareness about procreative issues that is either situated in a specific context and time or is more global and enduring. Nor do they focus on how men weave their sexual and fertility-related experiences over time into particular types of self-images. Relatedly, little work has considered the consequences of men's ability to orient themselves toward past, present, or future images of themselves and their experiences as procreative beings. Existing research also does not examine closely the separate and interrelated aspects of men's individual and relationship-based ideas about procreative issues. Finally, the research has focused disproportionately on poor, inner-city youth. Hence, much remains to be learned about the social psychological factors associated with young men's experiences (especially those who live outside the inner city) as they begin to define and then express themselves as sexual and procreative beings. Many of the key questions in this area implicate how men assign and interpret meanings to their sexual and procreative experiences, as well as to their romantic relationships.

Notwithstanding these caveats, survey and qualitative research has provided us with insights that have informed our understanding of the conceptual and empirical terrain we explore in this study. For instance, some survey data speak to the idea that young men's initial awareness of their presumed ability to procreate is largely indirect, cursory, or nonexistent. Because we know that a large percentage of men (married men in particular) report using condoms to prevent pregnancies rather than STDs, we can assume that these men have given at least passing thought to their presumed fecundity.[6] Although findings from focus group work are consistent with this inference, both young females and males tend to assert that males think less about pregnancy prior to having sex than do females.[7] We also know from national survey data that a high percentage of men report that they expect to father a child. Findings from the NSAM 1995 cohort (15–19-year-olds) show that almost 95 percent expected to father at least one child.[8] The statistical average for the ideal family size is 2.3 for this cohort, with African American and Hispanic men wanting slightly larger families.[9] Reports from the same data set indicate that 5 percent of these teenagers reported that getting a girl pregnant would make them feel like a man "a lot."[10] Though admittedly small, the percentage is not inconsequential.

One ethnographic study of teenage and young adult men in Brooklyn, New York, touches upon the "consciousness" or "awareness" theme of interest to us.[11] Some of the participants in the study felt that they were too young and not sufficiently mature to impregnate a partner. Some spoke of their ejaculate as "dog water" or mentioned that they were "shooting blanks," yet the majority were aware that sex could lead to pregnancy. The study also highlights the notion that men's perceptions and attempts at negotiating definitions of themselves as well as situations are imbedded within specific community contexts. Many seemed to adopt a fatalist approach to the prospects of paternity that the author of the study posits as probably being due to their exposure to either a lower- or working-class cultural ethos. Research with the initial wave of NSAM finds some support for the idea that young men living in poor neighborhoods (not controlling for city size) would be less upset and would anticipate greater rewards from becoming a father than youth living in more affluent places.[12] Young men from disadvantaged environments may view paternity as a source of prestige, especially if they do not have long-term educational and employment goals.[13]

Recent focus group research,[14] and earlier interviews with abortion veterans,[15] highlight issues related to the interpersonal context that shapes young men's views and behavior in terms of fertility-related matters. Individuals' perceptions of what sex means in different types of relationships are important to consider. So, too, are issues associated with trust. Some African American young men, for instance, speak of their concerns about not being able to trust all of their sexual partners to use effective contraception. At the other end of the spectrum, some young men report that they know of male peers who want to get their partners pregnant to secure their hold over them. The popular-culture stereotype tends to portray women as using their fertility as a form of "entrapment," but men apparently entertain this strategy occasionally as well.[16]

Some research focuses on issues related to young males' contraceptive use, views about responsibility, and pregnancy-resolution choices. Data from the NSAM show that after young men learn that they have impregnated a partner, they are more likely to report higher levels of sexual intercourse and lower levels of condom use.[17] Researchers working with these data speculate that young men may be more likely to engage in risky sexual behavior because they perceive that few negative consequences are associated with a previous pregnancy experience, and this experience may make them feel more masculine while generating support from their male peer group. Unfortunately, researchers' understanding of the underlying social psychological forces that contribute to these types of patterns is rooted primarily in speculation because the young men have not presented their own detailed accounts of their behavior. In a related vein, the literature does not address the situations in which the young men learn that a partner is late with her period. When do men consider these experiences pregnancy scares? How do they think and feel about these situations? When and how does the experience affect the way they pursue relationships and deal with birth control issues?

Analyses using the NSAM do indicate that a relatively large percentage of young men report that they have what many would define as a responsible orientation toward sex and contraceptive issues.[18] Small-scale studies have also shown that some young fathers are interested in and committed to being actively and positively involved with their children.[19] At the same time, recent analyses using a national cross-section of adults indicate that both men and women report that women tend to anticipate greater personal responsibility for children they bear than do men who are the fathers.[20]

Many young men clearly feel that prospective fathers should have a stake in making decisions about how a pregnancy is resolved. In one study using the NSAM, 61 percent of adolescent males reported that they did not feel that it would be all right for a woman to have an abortion if her partner objects, indicating a possible gender conflict of interest over the abortion issue.[21] Other research supports the idea that men tend to want to have more control over the decision to abort a pregnancy than women want to relinquish.[22] Although the NSAM data are silent on this issue, we suspect that men are likely to associate their sense of paternal obligations, and their rights, with their level of involvement with and feelings for a sexual partner. Another study that compared NSAM trend data from similarly aged cohorts in 1988 and 1995 found that the general approval for abortion declined among white teenage men.[23]

Getting Our Men Involved

A number of theoretical and practical considerations helped us decide what types of men we ultimately invited to talk to us about their thoughts, feelings, and experiences. We wanted to include a subset of teenagers, for example, to ensure that we had the opportunity to talk to young men who were aware of their fecundity but were not too far removed from the time when they first began to understand that they could probably father a child. This strategy ensured that the youngest men in our sample had reasonably recent memories about their experience and were articulate and comfortable enough to share their personal stories with us. For these reasons, we decided that the youngest participants would be 16-year-olds. At the other end of the age continuum, we chose to limit our study to men no older than thirty. We reasoned that participants in their mid to late twenties would have a number of life experiences relevant to our study. We assumed that men in this age range would provide us with insights based on their numerous and diverse types of relationships, that is, casual, close friends, serious dating, cohabiting, and previously married. Including such men meant that we could learn a great deal about the transitional experiences and early turning points in men's lives that involved their procreative identities. It also increased our opportunities to discover how some men reinvent or modify their procreative identity as they encounter various fertility- and nonfertility-related experiences with different partners over time. Thus, listening to these "older" young men allowed us to learn how men managed and related their subjective experiences with different relationships, sexual experiences, and procreative events.

To maximize participants diversity, we used a combination of purposive and theoretical sampling strategies (selecting participants by using conceptual criteria) and recruited participants in a number of ways. Most of what we discuss is based on our main or core sample of fifty-two men, though we also gathered more limited data using a supplemental sample of thirty-six men. Because our primary objective was to develop theoretical insights into men's subjective experiences, we did not attempt to secure a random sample in either case. Rather, we stopped collecting data when interviews no longer provided new conceptual information. This strategy "permit[ted] the deep, case-oriented analysis that is the raison d'être of qualitative inquiry."[24]

We constructed our sample to include men with different fertility events because we wanted to study a broad range of men's subjective experiences and behaviors in order to develop fresh theoretical insights, ones that could be generalized on analytic grounds. Thus, the intent of this sampling strategy was not to establish the basis for examining differences and commonalities among participants with different procreative profiles but to ensure that our sample was as diverse as possible.

As for the particulars, our screening interviewers (undergraduate and graduate students) arranged sixteen interviews with men who were visiting a local department of motor vehicles office, and we identified the remaining thirty-six participants through abortion clinics, a prenatal clinic, a prepared-childbirth class, a local employment agency, a homeless shelter, personal contacts, and word of mouth. After reviewing data for our first forty-two participants, we used theoretical sampling to identify the final ten. Interviews with the final ten men dealt more explicitly and extensively with the turning point theme discussed in chapters 1 and 4. With the exception of two early pilot interviews, all interviews with the main sample were conducted between April 1998 and December 1999.

In our main sample, we used our selective site sampling and screening interviews to ensure diversity in procreative life experiences, age, race/ethnicity, education, financial status, and relationship status. Among our participants, twenty-eight (ages 16–30) had no pregnancy or fertility experiences; twelve (ages 18–28) had partners who had aborted a pregnancy (typically within the previous twelve months); seven (ages 20–28) were involved with a partner currently pregnant with their child; four (ages 22–29) had experienced a miscarriage; and nine (ages 20–29) had biological children prior to the interview. The numbers suggest that some participants had more than one fertility experience. Three men with biological children reported having had a partner who aborted a pregnancy (one of these men was also with a pregnant partner), two other fathers had a partner who had had a miscarriage. We also conducted follow-up interviews one to two months postpartum with two of the men who earlier had a pregnant partner; accordingly, we conducted a total of fifty-four interviews with our main sample.

The racial/ethnic composition of our main sample is 29 white; 15 African American (one biracial); 4 Hispanic; 2 Native American Indian; and 2 Native African. The mean age of the sample is 22; eight men younger than 19, and fifteen 26 or older. Three participants were still in high school; three were high school dropouts; twelve had no college experience; twenty-eight had some college experience (one had not completed high school); and four were college graduates. Two were graduate students. Twelve participants labeled themselves as "poor" and one "nearly poor" when we requested, "Please describe your own money situation." Five participants were divorced, and one was separated ("nearly divorced"). All of the participants lived in Florida, including both urban and rural areas. Thirty-nine lived in the north central region of the state and thirteen in the northeast region.

In addition to our main sample, we secured brief and more focused taped interviews with thirty-six men aged 18–29 in spring 2000. Their mean age was roughly 21, with 9 percent identifying themselves as African American; 66 percent, white; and 20 percent, Hispanic. Thirty-one of these men had never to their knowledge impregnated a woman, three had personal experience with an abortion, and one man whose partner was currently pregnant also had previous experience with a miscarriage. All but four had spent at least some time in college; most were currently enrolled. After being trained to conduct in-depth interviews, twelve undergraduate students conducted these supplemental interviews as part of a class project in the first author's honors course, *Sex, Men, and Fatherhood*. The interviews dealt primarily with the young men's experiences with becoming aware of their procreative ability and the turning points they experienced relative to relationships, sex, and procreation. Students prepared memos for all thirty-six of the interviews and fully transcribed eighteen. We selectively draw from the subset of fully transcribed interviews to augment our analyses of men's stories and reflections in particular areas. We have constructed two detailed tables that profile the participants for both the main and supplemental samples in the Appendix.

Interviewing Strategies

As researchers using a grounded theory approach, we treated our study as a loosely structured, evolving project in which the theoretical ideas were often generated inductively from the data. We placed a premium on our ability to modify various aspects of the interviewing format on a continuing basis as we and our interviewers gleaned methodological and substantive insights from the interviews. In short, we examined our data throughout the data-collection process, using our emerging insights to adapt our questions and interviewing style to enhance subsequent interviews. Before we conducted the main interviews, we wrote detailed interview guides suited to interviews with men with various procreative experiences, focusing on men who had never impregnated a woman; men who had experience with an abortion and/or miscarriage; fathers-in-waiting, fathers of newborns; and fathers of young children. We structured the interview schedule such that participants would answer not only specific questions relevant to their profile(s) category but also a series of more general questions about their views on and experiences with relationships, fecundity, birth control, pregnancy scares, discussions with peers and family, and fatherhood.

To secure our participants' trust, we used strategies common to qualitative researchers. For instance, we arranged for a private, comfortable setting; provided up-front time to discuss the project and the informed consent (assent for the participants ages 16–17); emphasized participant anonymity and the confidentiality of answers; provided each participant the chance to ask questions before and after the interview; told each he could choose not to answer any questions; and, after the interview, inquired of each as to his psychological comfort with the questions and the interviewer.[25]

A recent overview of strategies for interviewing men provided the theory and language that explains and supports why we did what we did.[26] The authors caution that good interviewing technique is not enough, especially if the research emphasizes gender. Interviewers need to be alert to men's need to "signify, in culturally prescribed ways, a creditable masculine self," a self that is portrayed by control, autonomy, rationality, risk-taking, and sexual desirability. Our strategies aimed to make the men feel at ease and safe enough to share intimate feelings and experiences. Although all of our questions were personal, we began with more general, less sensitive questions and moved to more specific and intimate questions. We attempted to tune into their needs and anxieties, to present a nonjudgmental attitude, and to convey our belief that we saw their responses as worthy and valuable. In our repeat interviews with new fathers, we reviewed their earlier interviews when their partners were pregnant so that we could look for correspondence between the two interviews.

Our interviewing team consisted of two white males, an African American male, and a white female, aged 30, 40, 45, and 55 respectively. They conducted semistructured, audiotaped, face-to-face interviews that lasted between sixty and ninety minutes in on-campus offices, public libraries, and other locations convenient to the participants. We sought to understand participants' experiences while treating the interviews as an opportunity to access subjective information relevant to our sensitizing concepts (procreative consciousness, procreative responsibility, and turning points).

Theory and Method Overlap

As alluded to earlier, classic grounded theory research emphasizes an iterative method whereby researchers simultaneously code participants' answers using different levels of codes (concepts attached to participants' textual excerpts), write memos to capture the main concepts of the narratives, and undertake theoretical sampling to further explore the concepts. These procedures help researchers discover concepts and their properties in order to generate a theory based firmly in empirical data.[27] Typically, upon completing the research, the proposed theory with its phases, dimensions, and properties is compared and contrasted with existing theories.

We restricted our use of the grounded theory approach to help generate substantive and theoretical codes. Unlike typical grounded theory researchers, we began our research well versed in some of the substantive and theoretical issues relevant to our study. Consequently, we used the grounded theory method for two main reasons: (1) to deepen, expand, integrate, and ground in empirical data previously proposed theoretical notions about men's procreative experiences, and (2) to generate new concepts and their properties. Unlike most grounded theorists, we are not at this time attempting to produce a full-fledged grounded theory. Our more modest goal is to develop a conceptual framework that accounts for how men construct and express their procreative identities over time and in different situations.

Given our approach, with time and experience we came to appreciate the necessity for interviewers to learn about the conceptual underpinnings of our interview guide. Interviewers needed to become clear on the meaning of terms like *procreative consciousness* and *procreative responsibility*. Although we did not use this highly specific language in our interview guides, our basic understanding of the procreative consciousness and responsibility concepts permitted us to focus the detailed, semistructured guides. This language is directly related to our primary study aims of expanding existing concepts and developing new ones. However, until we fully understood how critical it was to educate our interviewers in detail about the substantive foci of the research, the initial interviews were sometimes off the mark. They concentrated instead, for example, on the evolution and dissolution of relationships or sexual behaviors rather than procreative experiences. We quickly came to appreciate how we could use team meetings and informal debriefings throughout the data collection phase to encourage reflexivity and keep us on track.

We also discovered that knowledge about the grounded theory method was helpful to interviewers. And it is here that we again broke from the traditional use of the method.[28] Because we were attempting to ground existing concepts in our data, we were interested in how participants attribute causes, contexts, contingencies, consequences, conditions, dimensions, phases, and properties to procreative events. For example, if a man discussed condom use, the interviewer was expected to ask questions about who initiated it, under what conditions, the consequences of condom use for each partner, for the relationship, and so on.[29] We used this approach to obtain rich description to help us develop, expand, and integrate concepts. When interviewers were cognizant of the approach, it directly affected the interview process, making it more goal directed. Thus, our early experience taught us the importance of training interviewers in both our theoretical and methodological perspectives.

Eventually, however, we found ourselves questioning the use of very specific interview questions designed to have men talk about issues related to our sensitizing concepts. We wanted to strike a balance between wanting men to provide very specific details in order to make the concepts more dense and simultaneously wanting participants to have enough freedom during the interview to take us to places in their minds and hearts that we would otherwise not find. We expected that these places could enable us to generate new concepts. Although the detailed interview guide was helpful in some ways, at times it appeared to limit spontaneity. It altered the rhythm of the interview and left us wondering what serendipitous findings may have emerged had we not been constrained by the guide. Listen to an interviewer's postinterview notes:

> I felt like the interview guide sort of worked against me when the flow of the interview allowed me to cover a lot of things without direct questioning. The guide is good because it's so specific, but that can be bad because when the interview has good flow, it becomes difficult to avoid asking redundant questions from the guide. I tried to handle this by taking extra time during interview lulls to try to figure out where I had already gone

and where I needed to go. It worked okay, but I think people who use this guide in the future need to be aware of this dynamic.

The issue at hand concerns our desire to acquire extensive, rich details that accurately reflected how the men felt about their procreative experiences when they occurred, details essential for generating concepts and their properties. At the same time we wanted details that addressed predetermined topics comprehensively. The complexities associated with this dual purpose highlight the interplay between theory and method. After identifying what we believed were almost competing goals, we then began to see the similarities between our sensitizing concepts and the theoretical codes/concepts that we generated with the constant comparative method. This data analysis technique emphasizes an iterative process of comparing incident with incident, category with incident, and category with category. The sensitizing concepts we identified prior to our study, procreative consciousness and responsibility, and our empirically generated concepts guided our data collection and analysis as it unfolded.

Our awareness of these issues caused us some concern about whether our sensitizing concepts and those we generated might restrict our thinking during subsequent data collection and analysis. It seems that the grounded theory method provided some safeguards that are inherent in the data analysis methods. By using the constant comparative method, we were able to tease out similarities and differences in codes, yielding dense codes that have analytic power. One significant finding involved our learning that some men had experiences that drastically altered their procreative consciousness. Some of the experiences included having a partner who aborted the man's child, betrayal by a partner, and death of a father. When we interpreted the comparison between these incidents and categories (abortion guilt, loss), we arrived at the theoretical code of "turning points" that has been a valuable concept in our data analysis. We found that close examination of the data coupled with more abstract questioning of the data ("What is this interview about?" "What is going on in the data?") helped us to avoid force fitting the data to the codes/concepts. Throughout, we sought flexibility in our thinking because this enabled us to discover fresh theoretical insights.

Other issues relevant to our approach concern coding and the structured interview questions. We coded each interview separately and then jointly to enhance dependability.[30] Over time it became clear that the questions that reflected our sensitizing concepts appeared to lead directly to specific codes, affecting interpretation of data. For example, we asked, "What kind of a father do you want to be?" and then coded many answers as "father visions." Even though our structured questions have enabled us to deepen, expand, integrate, and ground in empirical data our original concepts, we wonder what information is precluded by this approach.

Because men's thoughts are critical to our study of the evolution of procreative identity, we decided early in our research to modify our interviewing style to explore men's spontaneous productions rather than relying solely on our own interview structure. In this same vein, and in contrast to the standard survey approach that forces respondents to provide information on one sexual partner at a time while not asking them to make explicit connections between partners, we decided to delve more deeply into the men's experiences and the connections between them. To honor men's impromptu productions, we became more reluctant to shift a participant's attention to thinking about similar or dissimilar experiences with the same partner or previous partners until the participant seemed ready to move to another topic.

A related issue involves our sequencing of questions that tended to elicit information about sexual relationships in a chronological fashion. Upon reflection, we realized that our interviewing strategies essentially led the men to construct their sexual histories and accompanying procreative experiences in ways that were remarkably sequential and monogamous. It was only in one of our later interviews, when an interviewer happened to ask about a participant's experiences with maintaining multiple sexual partners, that we considered the need to explore how these contemporaneous circumstances might influence men's consciousness about their procreative identity. Similarly, men who learn that a sex partner has multiple partners of her own may have unique ways of thinking about their procreative identity.

Armed with a clearer sense of our theoretical and methodological perspectives, a significant amount of data, and our initial analyses of men's interviews, we improved our ability to explore men's evolving procreative identities with an eye for critical junctures, stages, phases, dimensions, consequences, and contexts. As we altered our roles, we modified our use of the semi-structured interview questions. We relied more on the rhythm and direction that emerged from the interaction between interviewer and participant, while being more attentive to the full range of men's experiences at a given point in time.

Getting Young Men to Talk

Although conventional folk wisdom paints young men as reluctant to talk honestly and sensitively about romantic relationships, sex, and procreative issues, we took it upon ourselves to offer the men a safe environment to share their intimate perceptions and stories. Given the nature of the topics we covered and some of the men's limited experience talking about them, we needed to ease our participants into particular discussions carefully.

We were aware that female interviewers may have difficulty establishing rapport with adolescent males if sensitive topics are discussed in a narrative form.[31] This is a concern for this general area of research because female interviewers are the norm when conducting national surveys with closed-ended questions about related topics. Answering such questions, however, is likely to be less threatening than sharing intimate details about one's specific sexual and procreative experiences. We also knew, however, that even though some research has found that male interviewees preferred talking about pregnancy with women interviewers,[32] other research with women interviewers has found that gender was not sufficient for ensuring a successful interview.[33] These disparate findings kept us alert to interviewing issues throughout our study.

As in any interview situation, our interviewers needed to avoid judgmental statements or responses, to work to gain the men's trust, and to provide them with the freedom and psychological comfort to "expose" themselves and whatever uncommon beliefs they might possess. When we interviewed the men about sexual topics in particular, we wondered about their need for bravado.[34] From our collective interviewing experience, we found little evidence of any kind that they were prone to embellish their experiences to convey a stereotypical male response. For many, their interview was the first time they had ever talked about some of the issues; it was clearly the most formal context. We wondered about the types of contexts and under what conditions men typically discuss sexual topics and procreation.

Throughout the interviews, we recognized the need to be reflexive about our behavior or presence that might limit the men's sense of personal confidence and willingness to speak of their fears, anxieties, and experiences. We established a few strategies for engaging them initially and sustaining their active involvement in the interview process. Of the procreative novices—men who had never to their knowledge impregnated anyone—we typically asked about their current dating habits, taking our cue from the way the first author had conducted focus group interviews with young men in Denver.[35] Of the others, we asked several questions about their fertility history to orient them and ourselves. We then began the interview by asking each of the men to talk about the relationship that involved the most recent fertility experience.

In retrospect, we wonder if we should have made more extensive use of prefatory warnings about particular questions, such as "This is a very personal question and you don't have to answer it if you don't want to," or, "This is a rather unusual question yet some men have . . . " Reminding the participants of the option not to answer any question is in keeping with the idea of process consenting,[36] in which informed consent is viewed as dynamic rather than static and with the belief that men want control and autonomy.[37] The warnings can facilitate participants' comfort and, therefore, positively affect data quality.

At times we tried to meet moments of discomfort by acknowledging a participant's feelings and reiterating the reason for the question:

> I: Was this you giving her oral sex or?
> P: Uhm, pretty much anything new that we did, like.
> I: Okay.
> P: I don't know what I am trying to say.
> I: (laughs) I know this is tough. I don't know how to make this more comfortable for you, if there is any way that I could do that. I'm just trying to get a sense of what her experiences were like.

Sometimes the interviewer moved to a less threatening aspect of the topic. In the previous example the interviewer left the details about oral sex, to ask: I: "Did you guys talk about—either before, during, or after—what you did or how things went?" In this case, this segue appeared to decrease the man's discomfort yet still focused his attention on relevant issues.

Interviewer Characteristics

Who can best conduct in-depth interviews with young men about sensitive, highly personal issues concerning sex, birth control, abortion, procreative consciousness, identity, and fatherhood? An older woman? A younger woman? A young male? An older male? Should an African Amer-

ican male interview an African American male, or can a white female gar-
ner detailed, richly textured information about what is meaningful to an
African American man? Or are these variables, generally considered significant, irrelevant to obtaining quality data when experienced interviewers
conduct in-depth interviews? What preconceptions and stereotypes do the
interviewer and participant hold that may affect the interview process?
What facilitates rapport, builds trust, and encourages spontaneity? We
raised these questions knowing that the interviewer could serve as "surplus threat,"[38] an extra threat above and beyond a baseline threat inherent
in all interviews that place male participants at risk of giving up control
and losing their public persona. When the interview deals with gender-re-
lated issues, interviewer gender and the intersection of gender with class,
race, and age concerns may also increase or decrease surplus threat.

Some have suggested that people are more inclined to share information with others like themselves.[39] One researcher suggested that "the sex
of the interviewer becomes crucial as the subject matter becomes more
sensitive."[40] Yet, in most cases, our participants reported that age, gender,
and race were irrelevant to interview success. We were acutely aware of the
need to obtain rich data from our participants, yet we remain a bit uncertain whether any personal variables associated with the research team affected the quality of the information the men provided.

To better evaluate each interview, we kept reflexive personal notes that
documented our assessment of it, and methodological notes in which we
suggested directions for future interviews based on it.[41] We also ended
most of our interviews by asking the following questions about our
methodology: Can you make suggestions about questions my research
team should be asking men that I didn't ask you? How comfortable are
you talking about these kinds of issues with an interviewer? What kind of
interviewer would help you to feel most comfortable talking about these
issues? (Man? Woman? Age? Race?)[42] Can you explain why? Because we
did not require closed-ended answers, some participants did not indicate a
firm preference, and a few revised their initial statement as they worked
through their comments. Generally speaking, slightly over a third indicated they preferred a man, and about the same proportion indicated that
it did not matter. Only four said they would prefer a woman. As for interviewer age, about a third of the participants said that it did not matter;
most of the rest said that it would be best if the interviewer were about the
same age or slightly older. More than two-thirds mentioned that interviewer race did not matter at all, and only two participants (both African

American) clearly said that they would prefer an interviewer of the same race; one white man indicated he would prefer a white interviewer.

Though few of the men indicated a clear preference for their interviewer to be of a particular gender, Desmond connected his preference for a man to his use of sexually laden slang. When asked his preference, he replied, "I, would probably say male because, ah because . . . I mean I could not have said the things that I said [if the interviewer had been a woman]. You know, if I'm talking about a load [sperm], and, ah, you know, because, I've heard guys say that some women only serve as, you know I guess, sperm buckets, sperm dumpsters, and stuff like that, and no woman's gonna take that very kindly."

We are aware that the quantitative data we gathered on preferences do not illuminate sufficiently the relevance of age, gender, and race issues. We recognize, too, that the interviews provided the men with opportunities for identity work and that participants could have understated and/or omitted their perceptions, experiences, and concerns, providing instead, socially and gender appropriate answers. These data, however, clarified our original belief that the interviewer and participant socially construct the interview.[43] Of course, each interview is different, depending on participant and context. And age, gender, and race are only a few of the variables that may be influential. Still, according to what our participants say, the interviewer's personality and style, and perhaps experience, appear to be most critical to the interviewing process. In the words of one participant who reported that he had no preferences for an interviewer based on demographic characteristics: "I try not to differentiate or conceptualize relationships based on gender, I look at my relationship with anyone, it all depends on that person, it doesn't necessarily depend on the person's gender, it depends on who that person is. What characteristics that person might have, what that person likes to do, how that person treats people, how am I able to relate to that person."

Participants' Experiences

At various times in this study, we were reminded that men of different ages and emotional maturity present interviewers with different challenges. In particular, we attempted to understand the difficulties and strategies associated with doing quality interviews with younger men who have limited sexual/procreative experience. On two occasions, with participants aged 16 and 21, we acquired limited information and had a sense of discomfort about the interviews, feeling as though we were "pulling teeth." One of the interviewers wrote, "During the interview, [Jody] was limited in his ability to capture the essence of what he felt and thought during that time." We wondered if participants' lack of experience and prior thought about the issues contributed to limited disclosures. In postinterview notes, the same interviewer wrote, "Does the complete absence of information and experience that many young men have with regard to kids make the concept 'baby' as ambiguous, abstract, and potentially mind-numbing as 'God' or 'Death'?"

In one of the two interviews the participant repeatedly used words like "weird." In the other, the man said, when asked what happens on a date, "Nothing." In the former, we may be dealing with a limited vocabulary; in the latter, we do not understand his use of the word "nothing." In situations such as these, we learned that it is critical to employ multiple interviewing strategies in order to represent young men's experiences more clearly. We also learned to focus on whether our youngest participants were inexpressive as a result of age and/or limited experience, or if they felt threatened and therefore inhibited.

The interviewer's being nonjudgmental is critical, particularly with younger men who may be experimenting with new behaviors and/or feel uncertain about the behaviors' "appropriateness." One helpful tactic that underscores this nonjudgmental perspective involved the use of general data from previous interviews to reveal the acceptability of a range of behaviors. For example, we sometimes said, "Some of the other guys we interviewed told me *x* while others told me *y*. What are your thoughts/feelings?" Or, if the young man said *x* we sometimes said, "Others have told me *y*." This corroborated our earlier message to the participants that there are no right or wrong answers. Countersuggestion is a technique that interviewers use to convey that beliefs and behaviors alternative to what the participant described are common. The technique may be especially important when interviewing young men who may think that they need to know all the "right" answers about sex and related issues.[44]

Temporal Orientation in Men's Narratives

An important feature of our interviewing style was that we sometimes asked the men to move back and forth in their narratives among their past, present, and future selves in order to capture developmental changes in their perspectives. We tried to do this with care because we wanted them to describe and reflect on their experiences, thoughts, and behaviors, rather than imaginatively construct answers to questions they may never have considered. Our goal was to avoid leading the participants to "come up" with answers to questions that were really beyond their experience or their own prior thinking. The latter could be a particular danger with young and/or inexperienced men. By differentiating perceptions that the men had processed prior to the interview from those that were constructed in the interview itself, we attempted to avoid misinterpretation. For example, we could have been led to believe that our participants had a much more active procreative consciousness (including thoughts and feelings about their fertility, contraception, pregnancy resolution, and abortion) than they really did if we did not clarify the timing of their thinking. Our evolving awareness of this issue caused us to begin to ask the participants if they had thought about a topic under discussion prior to the interview. We did not discard thoughts constructed in the interview itself, but carefully designated them as originating at that time and interpreted them accordingly.

We sensitized our interviewers to the issue, training them to ask specific questions at different points about whether participants had ever thought about something prior to the question/interview. For instance, questions that dealt with men's thoughts and feelings about becoming fathers, being fathers, and having biological children were preceded by a question about when the men first had these thoughts and feelings and how they evolved over time. Likewise, when we asked for information about their child visions—imagining their child prior to conception or birth—we needed to understand which images occurred prior to the interview and which were constructed during the interview itself. If future efforts to encourage young men to become more aware of their procreative ability are to succeed, determining men's preexisting level and type of consciousness about these issues is critical, not only for researchers but for those who work with young men in pregnancy prevention and fatherhood programs.

Interview Narrative Foci

We took notice of the different types of foci embedded in the participants' narratives. Some foci represented instances of the men's active procreative consciousness during episodes tied to specific situations (e.g., buying or using condoms); others occurred throughout more enduring periods of men's lives (e.g., experiencing the gestation process with a partner). Moreover, we recognized that expressions of a situational or enduring procreative consciousness can also be experienced in the context of a sexual relationship or individually. These complexities in the conceptual terrain present unique challenges to qualitative interviewers as they try to capture and make sense of participants' subjective experiences.

Our response to the above challenges was to adopt an interviewing strategy that enabled us to consider how men sometimes develop relationship-based perceptions and feelings about specific domains of procreation because of their association with a particular partner—some of whom may have played an active role in helping them coconstruct their experience. We asked: "Did your partner ever ask you to have intercourse without a condom?" "What reasons did she give you?" "How did you feel about her asking you to do that?" "Have you ever thought about having children with [partner's name]?" "How often have you discussed kids with her?" We also asked questions that explored men's personal beliefs, attitudes, and preferences about specific procreative issues that were independent of any particular romantic relationship. With these ideas in mind, we asked questions such as "Can you remember what types of thoughts and feelings you had when you figured out that you could get a girl pregnant?" "How often, if ever, do you think about this possibility?" "Were there specific situations that brought it to mind?" As our research unfolded, we came to see that this expansive interviewing strategy enabled us to capture more fully the complex ways men think and feel about procreative issues.

Language Use

Language was especially meaningful to our type of study, both in terms of how we as researchers used it to guide and code the interviews, and as it was used by the participants during interviews and then interpreted by us. We struggled with the dilemma of what words to use in our interview questions for the men, many of whom had not necessarily thought a great deal about procreative issues. For example, in our analysis we discovered that many of the men emphasized the importance of what we call "turning points"[45] in their lives. As we moved to theoretical sampling and a new round of interviews, we wondered about different strategies for accessing information about turning points. Under what interview conditions, if ever, would it be useful to use the term *turning point* if participants had not yet introduced it themselves? What words could we use that would get to the notion of turning points for the participants? After listening to their narratives about a particular experience (e.g., abortion, pregnancy scare, miscarriage), when is it okay to ask selected participants whether they thought of the event/experience as a "turning point?" We resolved the matter by listening for the men to talk about "change," how some event or experience changed the way they think and/or feel about an issue, or, in some cases, how they act. We learned that some, for instance, have become adamant about using condoms because of a previous pregnancy scare or a partner's pregnancy and abortion.

Yet people can change their behavior without considering the causal experience(s) to be a turning point, of course, so we asked the participants to describe the intensity and meaningfulness of their experience(s), to reveal if they actually have had turning point experiences or more minor changes in thoughts, feelings, and actions. Following up on this discovery, we did theoretical sampling and interviewed the men specifically about turning points, or "major changes in feelings and/or actions." We remain reflexive, however, struggling to learn what types of strategies would be most effective to help us understand men's perspectives without unduly influencing their feelings about a particular procreative experience. Researchers must be attuned to participants' diverse opinions on these types of issues. Varied opinions, informed by different situational contexts and different kinds of participants, should help tease out the complexities of the interview situation.

Toward the same end, we cautioned ourselves to be mindful of what we called the product of a pregnancy. If we called it a "fetus," a different image was conveyed than if we called it a "child," "baby," "daughter," or "son." Accordingly, it was necessary to wait and listen for the language that the men used, so that our language did not create their experiences or diminish the rapport between the interviewer and participant.

Our choice of language highlights another methodological issue. During coding, we realized that we were unclear about some men's rationale for engaging in certain behaviors. For example, we coded some interview excerpts "alternative sex" and others "non-coital sex." Over time, we came to realize that these are not particularly useful codes if we do not understand the meaning men assign to these activities. Did the men engage in alternative sex to avoid pregnancy, an STD, or an HIV infection? Perhaps they were seeking pleasure, or they were not ready to have sexual intercourse with a particular person, or perhaps there was some other un-known reason. By reviewing our theoretical coding, we grew cognizant of the necessity to alter our interviewing strategies to obtain a more complete understanding of behavior in context. Because our aim was not simply to document or describe patterns of behavior, we needed the additional information to interpret the men's experiences.

The participants' use of certain words and the meaning they attached to them required us to become more vigilant in assessing communication clarity. In one instance, a participant indicated he was having "unsafe sex." The interviewer assumed that the term meant he was ejaculating inside his partner. As the interview progressed, the man declared he would never ejaculate in a woman; he was thinking of withdrawal as unsafe sex. We also learned the varied ways participants used the word *protection*: most used it to refer to condom use; some used it to mean a partner was on birth control pills.

Several of our participants used a vernacular that seemed easy to un-derstand in the context of specific questions, but some usage was less clear, more open to conjecture. For example, we were privy to words and expres-sions such as "bring her up," "nuttin," "pre-cum," "raw dog," "covering up," "a load," "talkin to her," "runnin to her," and "holleren." In some instances, we were tempted to assume that we understood participants because we interpreted their comments in context, in accordance with the content and flow of the interviews. We sometimes found it easy to encourage the men to continue talking because we did not want to interrupt the rhythm of their response. However, after we realized our assumptions could lead to misinterpretation, we agreed that it was important to interject quick ques-tions in order to seek clarity from participants.[46]

In several other interviews, we became aware of the marked distinction between the meanings of the words *female* and *girlfriend*. It appears that some of the men categorize women; "females" are women who can be used for recreational sex without emotional commitment. These men rarely talked to "females" about protection or about much of anything; however, girlfriends become conversational partners. How the men think about women, which is reflected in the language they use to describe them, appears to affect their sense of procreative consciousness and re-sponsibility. For example, those with a girlfriend openly discussed protec-tion, birth control, and, in some cases, fatherhood; the men who involved themselves with "females" assumed responsibility for protection (con-doms) or did not, without comment.[47]

Because misunderstandings during the interview can affect the ambience of the interview, the quality of the data, and data analysis, attention to language should inform future research in this area. Our experience has highlighted the importance of avoiding assumptions and of understanding the social psychological contexts of individuals' experiences when doing interpretative research.

Indices for Interviewing Success

Because the quality of a study based on in-depth interviews is intimately connected to the quality of the interviewing process, we thought about ways that we could assess an interview's quality during and after the interview. By scrutinizing the interviewing process, we were able to propose the following six qualitative indices for assessing our interviews: (a) emotional accessibility, (b) view of interviewer as counselor, (c) collaborative behaviors, (d) declarations of comfort, (e) detailed, dense, personal information, and (f) narrative revisions.

Emotional Accessibility

The interviewer's ability to build and sustain rapport with the participant is a vital feature of conducting a successful in-depth interview, particularly on sensitive topics. In our study, rapport seemed evident when the young men exhibited emotion during the interview, such as positive affect by joking, laughing, smiling, or providing information with a very serious demeanor in almost confessional tones; hanging around to talk after the interview; and spontaneously commenting on positive feelings about the interview or the interviewer. One interviewer's personal memo highlights this point nicely:

> I was able to develop good rapport with AP, which really was no small feat considering that we come from different planets. He is ex-military and has very traditional family "values": "A person [read 'woman'] who wants to work rather than be with her child shouldn't be a parent." Apparently, he was very comfortable, because he hung around and talked with me for about a half-hour after the interview was over.

Although the participants who showed a great deal of emotion during their interviews did not always provide more information than those who were less emotional, their overall enthusiasm for the interview process appeared to be associated with the quality of information they provided. Relatedly, some qualitative researchers have referred to "key informants" as persons capable of teaching the researcher.[48] Such persons generally enjoy sharing their knowledge with the researcher and have good communication skills; they are emotionally accessible. Even though we did not identify key informants per se, some participants provided us with opportunities to probe for specifics, to ask hypothetical questions, and to test developing hunches. Awareness of the degree of emotional accessibility was useful in guiding us as we navigated an interview. An emphasis on emotional accessibility seems to suggest that we can get really good information from only a certain kind of participant, but key insights can be offered by participants who use a variety of interaction styles.

View of Interviewer as Counselor

For some of the young men, telling their stories to an unfamiliar interviewer was probably similar to what they might have experienced if they had talked to a counselor. As they spoke about the intimate details of their lives, they were revealing things about themselves that in some cases no one else or very few people knew. Although the interviewers did not offer advice or encourage participants to modify their thinking or behavior, some may have seen the interviewer as a counselor.

In one interview, a 17-year-old briefly discussed his 24-year-old friend who has a 37-year-old partner with a 16-year-old daughter. The participant recognized his friend was having problems with the relationship and said, "I think if Pete came to you guys, you could help him sort things out . . . or, figure things out for himself . . . by thinking about it." In another situation, a 27-year-old stepfather and a father-in-waiting noted some difficulty in "not being fully developed in a relationship where we are having a child together." At the end of the interview, he requested the name of a couples-therapy counselor. A participant's view of the interview process as useful or even therapeutic indicates positive feelings toward the interviewer and a belief in his/her goodwill and potential helpfulness.

Collaborative Behaviors

Some of our participants appeared to take the role of collaborator. A feeling of mutuality, of having joined the team, seemed to prevail. This was especially notable when a few of the young men spontaneously suggested friends or coworkers they thought might be willing to be interviewed. One of the interviewers later ran into a previous participant who said that he had some friends who had expressed an interest in participating in the study when he had discussed his interview experience with them. Although money may have been a motive for the friends, the man told the interviewer how much he himself had liked talking about the issues, and he seemed to think his friends might also.

Tim provides a different example of how the participants showed their interest in working with the interviewers. At one point, while Tim was attempting to explain how it is that he has a son with a woman yet is not serious with her, he asked that he not be rushed: "I don't know if that clarifies anything. But it's difficult to put these things into words. You've got to be patient." In this case, Tim appears to be motivated sufficiently to work to get the interviewer to understand his complex feelings and comfortable enough to request patience.

Some of the men collaborated by offering ideas for additional questions and areas of focus. One thought we should ask for more details about his sexual activity; another encouraged us to ask men about "nesting" behaviors, that is, how men prepare themselves to settle down and have a family of their own. Our approach was to think of these young men as our teachers; some of the interviewers made this explicit. Trying to learn from our participants, we sometimes asked, "Is there something that we should have asked but did not?" Perhaps these strategies facilitated collaborative behaviors. Pleased at being given an opportunity for self-expression, the participants demonstrated interest in the question, considered it, and then offered their ideas. Only a minority offered concrete suggestions, but a spirit of collaboration was present when they did. Their involvement in this way provided yet another indicator that our interview style was successful, even if we did not ask all of the questions they thought might be relevant.

Declarations of Comfort

During our interviewing, we not only attended to content and narrative flow but also listened for cues to the level of emotional comfort between interviewer and participant. In one interview, the white female interviewer, aged 55, listened to a 24-year-old father-in-waiting discuss the evolution of his trust for his partner.

> P: I can just feel people. I, mean, if you're goin' to do some harm to me or anything of that nature. Like, you know, try to be devious with me, I can kind of tell off the bat.
> I: Mm-hmm. And when you say people, do you mean girls or guys or.
> P: It don't matter.
> I: Anybody.
> P: It don't matter. You could be old, young or whatever. It doesn't matter.
> I: You've got a good intuition.
> P: Right. Cause I got a good intuition about you, that's why I'm doin' this interview.
> I: Un-huh. Is that right?
> P: Yeah.

In this case, the participant spontaneously provided positive feedback to the interviewer and, in so doing, denied the importance of age, gender, and race.

In another instance, a participant seemed to find comfort in the fact that the interviewer was a stranger. When asked how comfortable he was answering our questions, Arthur said, "Okay. Now, you being a complete stranger, no problem talkin' witcha. Pretty much anything you wanted to know." However, this same man, who used extremely graphic language and a lot of slang to describe sexual activities, acknowledged that if he had been interviewed by a woman, "some of my answers would have been toned down."

Declarations of comfort let us know we were on the right track, that we were able to put the participant at ease, facilitating the possibility that he would be willing to share personal beliefs and perceptions about his procreative experiences. Social psychological comfort is the sine qua non for successful research interviews.

Detailed, Dense, Personal Information

Because we were concerned throughout the interview process about our need to obtain rich, detailed information, we measure our success, in part, by the quality of the information. When this type of information was elicited, especially on topics that are sensitive, socially unacceptable, or that do not reflect positively on the participants, we were confident that we had obtained quality data. For example, a 20-year-old related feeling "afraid" when confronted with his partner's pregnancy. He described his regrets about two pregnancies with different partners and an abortion attempt. He discussed his "slip-ups" when he did not use a condom and related that to his fear that interrupting the rhythm of the experience to get a condom may cause the girl to change her mind about having sex. Similarly, Tim felt comfortable enough to be self-critical and share the following personal information with the interviewer: "I haven't been on many dates in a long time and I went on this date and I kinda made some mistakes." Continuing, he described how he later met with the young woman and asked her, "Did I do something wrong, maybe you were uncomfortable, maybe I shouldn't have done this." Later in the interview he again shared his evaluation of his behavior with the interviewer: "At the time she became pregnant I freaked out and didn't know quite how to react to the situation. I didn't handle it very well."

Todd, a 27-year-old, talked of how his partner and he first tried to abort their fetus, using a variety of "herbal stuff." When that did not work, Todd embraced the idea of fatherhood. He shared an unusual perspective: During the later stage of the pregnancy he pressured his partner to use drugs in order to "improve" the baby in some way,

> I did insist that she [partner] do LSD and psychedelic mushrooms [I: Uh-huh.] while she was pregnant. I didn't insist, but I strongly suggested it and suggested that that might be a good thing you know. As it turns out I think it probably was. It's because I don't buy the chromosome, uh, thing, you know where as they say it screws up your chromosomes or whatever, some kind of crap that the government dumps on us. . . . I think it totally can make children smarter.

Some of our participants were more attuned to details than others and were able and willing to recreate scenarios, including conversations, feelings, and events, with or without insightful analysis. Interviewers attempted to recognize and appreciate participants with this ability so as to acquire the rich details that are needed to enhance data analysis and interpretation.

Narrative Revisions

Occasionally, participants quickly revised their statements during the interview, behavior that we believe is reflective of a desire to be accurate. For example, when asked if he told his partner how he felt about having children, one of the men began by saying he had and then corrected himself saying he really had not but that she knew that he didn't want kids now because of his age. He caught himself being less than accurate, corrected himself, and provided more detail. Another participant first said he had paid for his partner's birth control pills but then offered that it was really her mother who had paid for them; he had driven her to the store. In these examples, the men seemed to value exactness, causing us to believe the data are credible.

Because many of our questions were value laden, we recognize that some of the men may have supplied information that made them "look good." A revision that concerns a highly sensitive topic(s) is especially noteworthy. So, too, some men, as they worked to reconstruct events that had occurred some time ago, would revise their account as their recollection of specific features of a situation became incrementally more complete as they filled in the details. Generally, being attuned to narrative revisions helped us assess accuracy and how the men viewed the interview situation. Men who demonstrated that they want to be exact showed an understanding of our needs: obtaining true-to-life recollections. By revising their accounts as they went along, or retrospectively, they demonstrated that they value what we value and, in so doing, enhanced their credibility.

Implementing Our Lessons from the Field

The absence of clear instructions on how to interview men about their developing procreative identities inspired our use of "critical self scrutiny."[49] This hallmark strategy of qualitative research encourages researchers to evaluate their role in the research process in an ongoing fashion at the same time that they are collecting and analyzing data. The cautionary tales that we present suggest lessons that can inform future qualitative research and programmatic interventions that focus on young men and procreative issues.

Although we do not believe that what we learned reflects the experiences of all males, we believe that much of what we say should be meaningful and relevant to many. The details may vary in different contexts, yet we expect that the concepts should be useful in providing a way to think about young men's procreative identities. Our detailed analysis of our in-depth interviews with a diverse group of men aged 16 to 30 taught and reinforced for us the following important lessons:

(1) We should be aware of our own theoretical and methodological perspectives and how these affect the interview situation.

(2) Access to participants' thoughts, feelings, and experiences requires constant attention and strategic moves to remain connected throughout the interview.

(3) Age, gender, and/or race of interviewer and participant may directly affect the interview experience in a small percentage of cases, but most participants are receptive to either experienced or attentive interviewers.

(4) The experience and maturity level of participants may present particular difficulties in interviews dealing with procreative experiences.

(5) The directions of the interview in terms of temporal issues and focus require our attention during the interview process.

(6) Interviewers need to be aware of how they and participants use language and of how language affects the interview process.

These lessons should assist other researchers and social service providers by sensitizing them to the value of reflexivity and, in particular, about the individuals with whom they work.[49] In academia and in practice, how we ask questions, when we ask them, the content of the questions, what we expect when we ask the questions, and who we are all influence to greater or lesser degrees the interview occasion.

3

Becoming Aware, Being Aware

For most boys, the journey through puberty and adolescence is marked by an accelerated interest in how their bodies work, change, and provide opportunities for physical pleasure. One way boys learn about their bodies is by comparing them to those of other boys and girls. The comparisons focus on overall size, weight, and musculature, as well as signs of pubertal development and emblems of masculinity, such as body hair and voice pitch. One distinctive feature of this body-oriented focus, of course, is boys' fascination with their penis.[1]

Some boys find their penis intriguing, beyond seeing it merely as a pleasure-producing organ. They eventually discover that it provides them the opportunity to procreate. For some, their awareness of and response to their procreative potential furnishes a meaningful subtext to how they experience their adolescent and young adult lives. Not surprisingly, the experiences are sometimes tied to young males' feelings about their emerging manhood. Unfortunately, most boys in the Western world do not have an explicit road map to guide them through this transitional period; they travel along without any well-defined puberty rituals. As a result, some feel confused and even anxious about the nature and meaning of the changes.

At an early age, prior to becoming aware of their procreative potential, most prepubescent boys are captivated by the pleasurable sensations they experience when their penis is rubbed or touched in a particular fashion. Much to their delight, they quickly learn that they can produce these sensations by their own playful efforts. No doubt parental and/or religious pressures cause some to feel unease, shame, and/or fear when they touch their penis, or even think about this form of self-pleasure, but most find the temptation irresistible. When boys do indulge these urges, they often develop a unique experiential bond with their penis. The distinctive physical attributes of a penis, most notably its highly visible and sometimes unpredictable tendency to change size and shape, bolsters males' orientation toward—sometimes preoccupation with their penis. Boys immediately see and feel the results of their playful behavior. They experiment with self-pleasuring techniques, noting all the while how their penis responds, eager to get it right. At the same time that boys often come to see their penis as a vital part of who they are as persons, as something they should master to enhance their sexual competence, they also sense that it has a "mind of it's own." The spontaneous erections they "achieve" while having a sexual daydream or casually looking at real or media images of others—typically females—reaffirm that their initial physical reactions are often beyond their control. Add to this mix of experiences the erections that boys experience for no apparent reason, sometimes awakening them in the middle of the night. Despite their apparent randomness, the spontaneous erections direct males' attention to their penis. These intimate, typically private moments often prompt young men to bestow a special status on their penis, treating it as an object in its own right, separate from yet connected to their larger self.

The folk language of male "culture" reinforces the pervasive penis-centered, male psychology. It even offers males opportunities to personify their penis, to nickname it, and to assign it personality traits. Some males may become so "addicted" to the process of fondling their penis that it becomes one of their daily routines of personal maintenance, sometimes being blended into sleeping and showering rituals. In the absence of reliable national data to document the particulars of males' private affairs in this area, we rely on anecdotal evidence to suggest that the previous description is consistent with many young males' lives.

Young men's same-gender peer culture also accentuates this penis-centered mentality. It does so by emphasizing phallic connections to sexuality rather than procreation; and the connections become personalized by young men. Granted, young men's increased use of condoms since the late 1980s[2] may mean that more males are encouraging their friends to wear condoms, but many of our participants were as likely or more likely to mention condom use to friends to heighten their awareness of STD/HIV issues than for pregnancy prevention.

When most boys first begin to experiment with masturbation, they seldom associate what they are doing with their own sexuality. They are likely to have little if any understanding of the socially constructed erotic realm. Their experience is largely a sensual activity aimed at achieving physical pleasure and comfort. Eventually, though, boys will begin to introduce sexual fantasies into their personal rituals, a mental shift that changes the symbolic nature of their masturbation activities. Although the exact timing of the shift varies, it seems safe to assume that boys on average experience it at a younger age than previous generations of teenagers, because of the growing pervasiveness of sexual imagery in contemporary media. We also know that on average boys venture into this sexual, private arena at an earlier age and more regularly than do girls.[3]

Not all boys, however, have a clear understanding of how their penis and its ejaculate play a role in making babies. Inadequate formal and informal sex education is largely to blame. Boys are probably even more uninformed about the role their testes play in sperm production. Eventually, these same boys experience some type of "awakening" as they move through adolescence on their journey to manhood. They become more cognizant of their ability to procreate and, in the process, begin to see how their sexual and procreative abilities are linked. Once males make this connection, they adopt conscious and unconscious ways of managing their newfound awareness as they pursue romantic and sexual involvements. This awareness and practical knowledge will sometimes be a part of young men's wideawake consciousness; at other times it will fade, becoming part of latent memory. Either way, it will be incorporated into young men's stock of knowledge that ultimately can shape their procreative identities if the right set of circumstances arises.

When viewed in this way, how boys orient themselves to their bodies affects how they will express their procreative identities over time. Some of these experiences will be connected to key transitional periods in young men's lives, inducing them to occur on occasion. In other instances, they will be of little consequence for their evolving identities.

Acquiring this basic knowledge about paternity is typically not a profound experience for boys, but awareness is necessary for males to experience a subjectivity that includes self-awareness of their involvement with aspects of the procreative realm. This initial awareness represents a logical starting point, then, for our analysis of young men's life stories about sex and procreative issues. We begin with our participants' first recollection of becoming aware of their procreative ability, but the main segment of the story line we explore has to do with young men's accounts of how they subsequently experienced romantic relationships and dealt with issues associated with sex, contraception, abortion, pregnancy, and fatherhood. It is here that we have sought to identify key properties and their dimensions that can be used to highlight the complexity of men's procreative consciousness. We consider the meaning their procreative knowledge initially had for them, as well as their accounts focusing on responsibility issues related to this life domain. In other words, we have tried to unpack the varied and interrelated aspects of young men's subjective experiences as persons capable of creating human life.

Because young men are likely to change the way they express their subjectivity in the procreative realm over time, it is essential to consider how transitional experiences emerge and then evolve. Young men will experience all sorts of changes in the way they think of themselves as procreative beings, some small, others more pronounced. Sometimes the changes will be folded into key transitional periods in young men's lives. In the next chapter we consider at length the more significant types of turning points men experience relevant to the procreative realm. But first we turn our attention to the process by which men become aware of their procreative abilities and remain aware. This is our initial step in revealing the conceptual complexities associated with our sensitizing concept, procreative consciousness.

The process of becoming and being aware assumes, too, that individuals have various cognitive resources at their disposal that enable them to focus on and make sense of their reality. Thus the "relevance structures" mentioned in chapter 1 come into play here because the process by which men become and remain aware of their procreative ability is connected to men's preexisting and evolving frames of reference, or bases of knowledge. What types of previous experiences and stimuli prompt males to process insights relevant to how they develop and express their procreative identities? To talk about the evolution of procreative identity—to treat it as a process—requires us to be attentive to the varied resources young men use to orient themselves to the procreative realm.

Becoming Aware

How do young males initially become aware that they can presumably impregnate a sex partner? The question has significant implications from a social psychological and social policy perspective, but little is known about the process. To understand young men's lives more fully as persons capable of procreating, we clearly need to address researchers' ignorance in this area. With this in mind, we explore the "becoming aware" experience for young men by considering three main issues. First, the context or source of this awareness. What types of interpersonal situations and information sources provide young men with the means to recognize their procreative potential? Second, we explore the nature of "knowing" and males' affective response to this experience or state of mind. Third, we study how males work with this awareness and how it evolves over time. Thus, we not only focus on how our participants came to recognize their procreative potential (becoming aware) but also consider what the potential means in terms of participants' thoughts and feelings (being aware) and of their behavior (being responsible). Our discussion emphasizes how becoming and being aware of one's procreative potential are features of a dynamic process that unfolds in numerous ways because of personal and contextual circumstances.

During our interviews, we asked participants to look back over their lives and talk about the thoughts and feelings they had when they first realized that they were probably capable of getting a girl or woman pregnant if they had sex. We also asked them to comment on how they currently thought about their potential to create human life. Given our participants' range of ages, our request meant that some had to think back as far as fifteen to twenty years; others only needed to recall experiences of several years ago. Generally speaking, these young men, regardless of age, seemed comfortable and capable of remembering relevant events and their perceptions of them. In a few cases, though, the men's recollection of this period in their lives was rather fuzzy; their foggy memories often reflected the uneventful nature of the process by which they learned about their procreative ability and the fact that they had not encountered a specific event or experience that marked the transition in their lives. Marcus's narrative exemplifies the vague responses, although he eventually ties his awareness to becoming sexually active. Asked if he recalled what he first thought when he realized that he was probably capable of getting a girl pregnant, Marcus replies:

> I don't really, I can't really say I mean [pause] I really, I still don't know if I can get a girl pregnant if I just. I mean I ain't gonna say I am not shootin. I'm not having, like, any problems with my cum or anything, but I don't really, I ain't gonna sit there and try it. But I'm sure I'm capable of doing it. But I don't know when I was really conscious, I mean when I could,— probably, I mean, probably when I started to have sex a lot. I mean I knew I could get somebody pregnant.

The passage illustrates how Marcus, a 19-year-old procreative novice, struggled during the interview to clarify his thoughts about his procreative abilities when he made the transition from being ignorant of procreative issues to becoming aware of men's (and his own) potential contribution to procreation.

Typically, when our participants talked about their initial awareness and understanding of their ability to procreate, they provided us with a window into their intrapsychic lives as adolescents and young adults. Some of them reported becoming aware of their fecundity as early as 8 years of age; a few, as late as 19 or 20; and most, between their early to middle teen years (12 to 15). They often referenced this event by first identifying the grade they were in when they took a particular course and then calculated their age. Some participants developed a general sense of their procreative potential in their early teens and then went on to talk about having experienced additional changes during their late teens and twenties. The changes included developing a greater sense of clarity about their procreative potential and responsibilities.

As we highlight below, some of our young men had an immediate and clear recognition of their ability to procreate. For others, the certitude came over time, often in conjunction with a procreative event such as a pregnancy scare or an actual conception. In situations where the men's awareness of their ability to procreate has this developmental quality, we find that some experienced a steady, burgeoning evolution of awareness, whereas others had more sporadic flashes of insight sprinkled over time. For those in the latter group, moments of awareness tended to be intermittent and undulating. Whatever the path, the men displayed a range of responses to this knowledge.

Source of "Knowing"

Most of our participants mentioned that they learned about men's ability to father children through a sex education course, talks with parents and friends, pregnancies and subsequent childbearing among their peers, books provided to them by their parents, or some combination. Thinking about his initial understanding of his ability to procreate, Tripp, a 23-year-old, engages in the following exchange with the interviewer:

> T: I suppose probably around, I guess it really dawned on me probably 8th grade, 7th grade, I guess. I went to Catholic high school so,

Catholic grade school all my life and high school after that and we had, we started sex ed in like the 5th grade, but you know like everybody sits there and cackles while the nun draws a uterus and a penis up on the board.

I: Do you remember the reason why it dawned on you?

T: No, I remember my parents got me a book. . . . It was probably 6th grade, and it was your basic facts of life book 'cause they didn't want to sit me down so they gave me a book. But yeah, I just remember me and my friends would sit there and laugh at all the pictures.

I: Yeah?

T: But yeah, but that's I mean, I guess that's when you're like "Oh yeah, okay that's where babies come from, fantastic."

I: Is that the point at which you realized that you personally were able to do that?

T: Yeah, I guess so. I knew I was a, I knew I was a guy and I had a penis and that was about, yeah, it took me, yeah, yeah.

As Tripp recollects how he thought about this earlier period in his life, he suggests that both the Catholic sex education class and the book his parents bought him enabled him to piece together an understanding of how he was capable of making a baby because he "had a penis."

Another concerned mother presented her son Gavin with the book *How Are Babies Born?* after learning about her son's wet dream. The son, now an 18-year-old, had gotten up in the middle of the night when he was 12 to wash his clothes after he thought he had "peed [his] bed." His mother, curious about why her son was washing clothes at that hour, questioned him about it. Once she learned that he thought he had peed in his bed, she informed him about wet dreams. Soon thereafter she presented him with the book that Gavin describes in the interview as a "cartoon type book for kids."

Parents provided information directly through talking or indirectly through providing their kids with literature; friends and peers often played a role by providing young men with opportunities to learn from others. Some of the learning was observational. Along these lines, Mitchel comments that he learned about his ability to procreate because "my friends in high school or people that I know that they started having children, they started getting pregnant and I was exactly the same age and it was a splash of water that shuuhh you know if I do this now, then I can have a child. Through other people'[s] experiences that's where usually I've learned everything."

Although many men explicitly spoke about the role that teachers, parents, and friends played in helping them discover their ability to procreate, Austin offers an example of an alternative and more private path. This 21-year-old anchored his new perspective on his fecundity on the first time he masturbated to orgasm when he "was really young." "When the realization came, it was a new feeling. . . . I remember being young and thinking, 'Wow, I could, impregnate a woman.'. . . It wasn't like a sense of power or anything like that. It was just an unusual feeling that I'd never had before." Others may have indirectly set the stage for Austin to make the connection between his orgasm and his procreative ability, but he describes his initial realization as occurring while he was alone exploring his sexuality. He labels this discovery as a "fascination" even though he admits that he "didn't really sit around and think, 'I could get a girl pregnant if I wanted to.'"

In light of the "boy" subculture and traditional adolescent male values,[4] it should not be surprising that relatively few of our participants mentioned that they explicitly learned about their ability to procreate by talking to their friends. Boys spend a great deal of time hanging out with other boys, yet little of this time is spent on in-depth, informative talks about the practical aspects of sexuality and fertility. Discussions of sex tend to be superficial and often involve some form of masculine posturing. Moreover, unlike women, men seldom participate in all-male groups that celebrate aspects of procreation that might lead them to form a clearer understanding of their potential role in creating human life.[5] Despite these patterns, male friends were at times instrumental in helping other young men gain their initial understanding as well as a more heightened appreciation of their procreative abilities. Seeing other young persons involved in unplanned pregnancies, whether male or female, friend or relative, appeared to be an equally common source by which young men developed a keener awareness of their own procreative potential.

Derrick and his best friend, both of whose partners had had abortions, "traded stories of what happened." Derrick told only his best friend and only some months after both abortions. He realized after his first abortion experience why his friend "was like so, really like emotional about it . . . he said like 'Fuck!' and so after I went through the same thing I got like a better understanding of why he was so emotional about it." Derrick admitted he had never thought about the possibility that he could get a girl pregnant before he did.

"Knowing": Meaning and Emotions

In addition to being exposed to different sources that helped them realize they had the ability to procreate, our participants varied considerably in the way they initially experienced their understanding of their fecundity. In other words, "knowing" meant different things for participants. For some, their awareness about their fecundity represented a significant developmental and personal experience. These males saw it as a sobering transformation of consciousness and self, a realization that was, on occasion, intimately tied to their understanding of how their procreative ability—in essence their ability to bring about an unplanned paternity—could profoundly impact their life course. This sentiment is aptly captured by the comments provided by four procreative novices when asked how they initially thought and felt about their newly discovered procreative capacity. Note how, without prompting, Alex, Cecil, and Terence each explicitly link their presumed procreative ability to paternity and the impact they believed it would have (or would have had) on their lives.

> It was scary. It's a change of life, it's a big commitment, big decision. I think it's something very sacred and should only be used if in such certain extents [*sic*] like marriage and to have a child, and it's something very serious. [Mitchel, age 22]

> Kind of scary and overwhelming. Just 'cause it's a really big deal, you know. And, never really thought about it before that. It's just, I don't know, it just kind of opened my eyes a little bit. [I: What did you see when you, when your eyes were opened?] Just real life. 'Bout how it could actually happen. . . . And how much that could change things or mess things up and make it so you're not going to be able to do what you hope to do. [Alex, age 18]

> I mean, I just thought it would be a crushing responsibility, right, to have to take care of a kid when you were 16 and a lot of freedoms would, just you know go away, you know. [Cecil, age 26]

Terence, a 25-year-old, comments that although he probably "always" knew that he was able to create a child, it never "dawned onto" him until he was in the 7th or 8th grade. That's when it became a "worry" for him because that's when he started to "get into girls." He goes on to say that "I definitely didn't want to have one [a child] because I was so young then. I had a lot to look forward to like high school, finishing high school, and going to college. So I definitely wou-, probably wouldn't of finished college if I had a son or daughter."

For those with experiences similar to those of the four men, developing this type of expanded understanding of self can be instrumental in moving young men along a developmental trajectory of sorts, one that helps them transition from an adolescent to an adult identity. As evidenced by the comments above, and as we discuss later in the chapter, this developmental transition for some young men is accompanied by a heightened sense of awareness that one's procreative potential can affect others' lives. For other young men, their primary concern is their own well-being. In either case, by becoming more acutely aware of their fecundity, some begin to recognize how their procreative potential can alter the course of peoples' lives, including their own.

The "knowing" experience was relatively straightforward for some of the men in our sample; others presented a more muddled picture of their procreative identity. Once Alex, Cecil, Mitchel, and Terence understood the basic physiology of reproduction, they simply assumed they could impregnate someone. Their emotional response was grounded in their perception of their fecundity. Technically though, until a man is faced with a situation where he is confident that he has actually impregnated a female, a distinction can be made between his perceived potential to procreate and the experiential knowledge of procreating. Although most of our participants did not highlight this distinction, some did. Take for instance, Butch, a 21-year-old who expresses uncertainty about his own procreative abilities. Asked about when he first realized that he could actually procreate or have a child, Butch replies:

I guess until you really get someone pregnant, you kinda doubt you know. You're like, man, whoever taught these little guys to swim? That's what I always thought. When she [current girlfriend] had the miscarriage, I kinda knew. But, I had always thought, there's a chance, you know, there's always a chance that maybe you don't have enough, high sperm count. Maybe she can't. But when she had the miscarriage, I definitely knew then after that, if I kept doing what I did there's a chance she could get pregnant.

Butch's ambiguity about his earlier procreative identity is underscored further when he responds to the interviewer's request that he specify the age at which he had developed his awareness: "I mean I always thought I could. I'm sure that I could've before [prior to pregnancy resulting in miscarriage]." But, a few minutes later in the interview, when talking about his use of condoms with this partner, Butch appears to revisit his uncertainty:

> [I]f I wasn't using a condom, would she get pregnant? And, I guess, it's not really doubt, or maybe it's not really like your failure, but it's the fact that "can you?" Can you get her pregnant? But that was pretty much, I always had it, pretty much, until she got pregnant. I probably had that feeling when I was like eight. Can I get a girl pregnant, when the time comes?

Butch's rambling narrative points out that the experience of "knowing" as it relates to a man's perceptions of fecundity can involve a complex layering of ideas and fleeting thoughts. Thus, it is a challenge to capture and interpret the essence of some of the men's narratives about different aspects of their procreative consciousness.

In this instance, it appears that Butch at an early age came to "know" that men impregnate women and that, as a male, he could probably impregnate his girlfriend. At the same time, he had a faint but lingering doubt in the back of his mind about his ability to "get her [a partner] pregnant." Not surprisingly, Butch was relieved when he verified this ability to procreate when his partner had her earlier miscarriage. Knowing for sure was important to him because he was a "family oriented person." The experience let him know, without a doubt, that he could have a family in the future. He was "just happy that everything was working in order and everything." Butch's narrative makes evident the value of examining how particular experiences affect the evolution of men's procreative identity over time.

Although we encountered several notable exceptions, the newly found potential to impregnate a woman was typically not interpreted as an experience that induced a monumental shift in the young men's sense of self. The urge to have sex may actually restrict some young men's willingness to think seriously about their procreative ability. Note that Cecil, now 26, associated the possibility of an unplanned pregnancy in his teenage years with "crushing responsibility" and a loss of freedom. He remembers, however, that as an adolescent his desire to have sex kept the possibility of pregnancy remote in his mind—a tendency that he believes is common among young males who crave their first sexual experiences. "[W]hen you're young, you wanna have sex so bad when you're like a 15-year-old and 13-year-old. . . . [Y]ou don't necessarily think that you're gonna get somebody pregnant." Cecil's comment reminds us that the adolescent mind-set often features naive, wishful thinking and a sense of denial or invincibility. Armed with these powerful psychological tools, some young men pursue their sexual interests without seriously considering the consequences of their actions.

Given the adolescent mind-set, we were not surprised to find that for some of the young participants initially learning about their ability to procreate was largely an insignificant moment in how they experienced themselves. A 23-year-old, Sean, recalls his nonchalant reaction during a sex education class: "I was thinking, 'Oh I can get somebody pregnant now,' okay. . . . It didn't really have any, I guess impact, on my life. . . . I was thinking that every other guy in that class would do the same thing, so I really didn't see how it separated me from them." Similarly, 30-year-old Desmond made sense of his newfound knowledge by comparing his circumstances to those of his peers. He elaborates on his perceptions by saying, "I could not feel any power, at the time, because it was something natural. All guys did it; so I was no more special than anyone else." Desmond conveys the idea that knowledge of his fecundity did not have a dramatic impact on his self-perception; he was largely unchanged. This appears to be the case because his interpretive focus is tied to the comparisons he makes with his peers, rather than to his own development. In the language of social science, he aimed his "comparative appraisals" at his peers not himself—a practice that was described or hinted at by others. He apparently did not actively think about his own developmental changes because he was aware that everyone else was experiencing similar changes. He also was aware that some (as he mentions elsewhere during the interview), were actually being confronted with the consequences associated with unplanned pregnancies and births.

Evolutions in Awareness and Identity

Reflections such as Cecil's underscore the importance of understanding the diverse ways in which young men over time acquire, interpret, modify, and incorporate information about sex and procreation into their sense of self and identity. They also highlight the need to consider how young men's perceptions about the consequences associated with fatherhood may evolve over time. By listening to Reynaldo, an insightful 17-year-old participant, we gain a glimpse of how a young man's procreative identity, including his sense of responsibility, may change.

> Well, at first it was like, well it [procreation] can't happen to me I'm just, you know, too good. . . . I started seeing the reality of things on TV. . . . Talk shows and like. Those shows . . . [about] teenagers that are pregnant. . . . I guess it settles in and when I was like 15 and one of my friends got pregnant and she decided to keep the baby. She had to . . . get out of school for awhile . . .'cause she had to get a job and her parents weren't really too happy with it. And that's pretty much when I started seeing the truth. Like first, it's just like oh having a baby is good, but when you think about it, it's too much responsibility. I'm going to wait until I'm older.

Reynaldo's account of his initial perspective about procreative issues is consistent with the unrealistic, though common, adolescent mind-set described above. Here, then, we see a significant developmental feature of adolescence at work. Coupled with the limited understanding that many youths in the United States have about sexuality and fertility issues, the adolescent mind-set fosters a situation wherein Reynaldo, and others like him, have a distorted procreative identity. Fortunately, being exposed to others' fertility dilemmas through the media and his friend's experience prompted Reynaldo to redefine his own reality. Part of his maturation process involved his realization of the consequences of unplanned fatherhood and, implicitly, that he was not immune to impregnating a partner.

Reynaldo developed an appreciation for his fecundity indirectly through observing others, but some young men develop a meaningful appreciation for their fecundity only when they have an experiential connection to it. Take for instance, Jeffrey, a 21-year-old who contrasts his relative lack of procreative consciousness when he was a virgin (spoken in the present tense) with the awareness he developed as a result of the first time he had intercourse:

> [T]hey say you can get a girl pregnant if you do this [have sex]. Well, I've never done it [had sex]. It sounds kind of abstract to me until I'm actually faced with it. So I think when, I think the first time I had sex I was like this, and I guess I learned what it means to ejaculate, that God, this really

could do something. . . . I think when you're there in person and you physically feel it that you have the potential to do that.

Jeffrey points to his first experience with ejaculation during vaginal intercourse as a turning point in his perception of his procreative identity.

The procreative consciousness of some men is not affected in any significant way by their sexual experience(s). For them, a heightened consciousness is accomplished when they encounter their first pregnancy scare or actual fertility experience. Asked about when he came to realize that he was capable of "making" a child, Harper, a 29-year-old, replies "I was just doing my thing, then, you know. I never really thought about fatherhood or having kids." Later on in the interview, Harper adds: "I always knew you could, okay, you know, I could get a girl pregnant but when you are at that point when you are going to have sex I never thought about it, you know." Having revealed his youthful efforts to downplay or dismiss his thoughts about his own fecundity, Harper goes on to say that he had never recognized how serious it was to impregnate someone until he and his partner had a pregnancy scare. Only then, when he was faced with the prospect of becoming a father, did he develop a deeper sense of what it could mean to be a procreative man.

Men's stories about how their procreative consciousness emerged reveal the richness and variability of their experiences. Because few young men have firsthand experience with the concept of paternity, some may have a difficult time identifying with this seemingly irrelevant or remote life experience. As one of our interviewers suggested, the experience may be similar to many young men's understanding of death. This is especially true for those who are neither sexually active nor currently involved in a physical, romantic relationship. From a practical standpoint, being sexually active, particularly when vaginal intercourse comes into play, draws men closer to the procreative realm, literally and figuratively. Having sex, then, enables some to perceive paternity in a more realistic light.

As we saw above, another way that procreative experiences can become more concrete is by spending time with friends who share ideas and stories related to their own experiences. This type of sharing can provide less experienced individuals with new pieces of information or at least a sensitivity to certain issues that can broaden their cognitive relevance structures. In turn, the information can trigger the initial opportunity—and subsequent times—to think about their own procreative potential. Listen to Harper, a 29-year-old, describe his friend's admonition:

Oh yeah, [he] became a father. He was telling me, "Oh you gonna have to start doing this and doing that." I'm like, "Man, I ain't gonna have no kid." He talked a lot about changing diapers, you have to get up, you have to save money, buy diapers, you have to, the baby's crying at night, you gettin up or you have to take it to the babysitter. . . . [I: . . . Did that get you to think about being a father and what that meant?] It, yeah, it did actually. It did make me start thinking about a lot of things. About things I hadn't been thinking about.

Likewise, a younger, 18-year-old participant, Gavin, recalls having been cautioned by relatives against the mistake of having children. "[T]hat's what my dad and my cousins would tell me, 'kids are like another disease. You got really two deadly diseases that you can't get rid of, HIV and kids. And kids, they're not as bad a disease as HIV, but they can kill you. Kids will run you into the ground." These kinds of scenarios underscore the need to explore the dynamic qualities of young men's procreative consciousness, specifically their awareness of themselves as persons capable of impregnating women and producing children.

Being Aware and Being Responsible

Once young men become aware of their presumed ability to procreate, the knowledge can be experienced in a variety of ways. As mentioned earlier, men's experiences and perceptions related to the procreative realm encompass situational as well as more enduring or global features. Moreover, men's self-perceptions and actions in the procreative realm are often shaped by their involvement with romantic partners who can play a pivotal role in helping them coconstruct their experiences in this area.

Types of Procreative Consciousness

Being aware of their own procreative potential may lead some young men to an active self-awareness and sense of responsibility about their fecundity. The awareness can be expressed in a more or less general way and on a regular, continuing basis. It can also manifest itself when it is connected to specific events such as pregnancy scares or seeing a friend who is pregnant. However, some males may have the basic knowledge about their fecundity, but it may not affect them in a practical sense because they do not actively think about their potential to father a child. Raymond, a 19-year-old participant, provides us with an instructive example that captures part of the complexity of a few related issues. He summarizes his latent awareness or procreative consciousness this way: "Well, I mean, I know it can happen to me. I just don't think about it. I mean, if I already know it, then there's no need to really think about it." By itself, Raymond's comment seems to imply that he is largely or completely inattentive to his potential role in preventing a pregnancy. On the contrary: although his partner has been taking the pill for awhile, Raymond indicates that he doesn't "cum inside of her" because it's a "bigger risk." He mentions that when they had sex for the first time together, he practiced withdrawal [a method he learned from the movies] without seeking approval from his partner. Raymond explains his reasoning for practicing two forms of birth control:

> in one drop of sperm you got like millions of you know, even though, she's on the pill, I mean, it's still not a hundred percent. And out of those one million, one could get in there [inside an ovum]. . . . [I: Why don't you want her to get pregnant?] Because . . . I know I can't take care of a baby right now and go to school and work, all that stuff. And, she's still in school too.

Raymond's initial explanation, comments he made earlier in the interview, and his reply to the interviewer's question, all illustrate that he is cognizant of and concerned about preventing a pregnancy. However, we learn even more about Raymond's procreative consciousness and responsibility when he is asked if he thinks about pregnancy when he withdraws. He replies: "It's second nature, I guess, not to [cum inside her], to go ahead and withdraw." This response, taken in light of Raymond's previous comments, demonstrates the multilayered nature of procreative consciousness. It appears that Raymond has a basic or global self-awareness of his ability to procreate, but he no longer actively thinks about it during intercourse with his current partner because withdrawal has become habitual for him, and his partner does not question him about it. He therefore does not have an active situated procreative consciousness.

For some men, like Raymond, knowledge about procreative abilities remains backstage in their consciousness for extended periods. Other men, though, experience this knowledge as a more active feature of their "wideawake" self as they navigate the terrain of their everyday life world. Some appear to link their awareness to specific situations; others have a more global sense of their procreative consciousness. Harper, for example, demonstrates a highly active procreative consciousness when he replies to a question about how often he thinks about his ability to get women pregnant: "Every time I have sex, every time I think about it, like, a lot. . . . [I]f she's not on birth control or I don't have a condom then I'll probably like no [not have sex]." Desmond, on the other hand, assesses his procreative consciousness without referring to a specific situation. He observes that compared to when he was a teenager, the "stakes are higher now" and he will "be held accountable" for his actions. "[N]ow I feel like I do have somewhat of a, I'm not going to call it a lethal weapon, but I have this potency that can really, ah, change the course of anyone's life. Now I clearly understand it." Desmond's metaphoric reference to his "lethal weapon" vividly conveys how he has embraced new imagery to capture his self-image as a man capable of creating human life.

Procreative Consciousness: Active and Inactive

During any given day, young men's minds are likely to visit a range of topics, including sports, parties and drugs, friends, religion, school, work, music, TV, and their social standing among peers, to name but several. For many, thinking of their girlfriends or others with whom they would like to "hook-up" occupies much of their time. To a lesser extent, young men may even find themselves having passing thoughts about or pondering issues related to their presumed ability to procreate. Though these thoughts typically occur less frequently than sexual thoughts, they can be highly significant, given the potential consequences associated with them. They also are usually grounded in men's practical experiences, such as purchasing and using condoms. Some of these everyday life events are more important and unique than others.

Explicit or implicit references to unplanned pregnancies were a common impetus that led numerous men in our study to think more often and sometimes differently about their procreative potential and sense of responsibility. In several ways, these experiences activated the men's procreative consciousness, bringing preexisting and new thoughts and feelings related to procreation into their "wideawake" consciousness.

At times, our participants thought about a hypothetical unplanned pregnancy scenario privately or occasionally discussed it with others. They grew more attentive to their procreative abilities when they tried to imagine how an unplanned pregnancy would alter their lives and the lives of others. We previously introduced several men who recalled how they had first thought about the ways fathering a child would affect their own and others' lives. Gavin, a high school basketball player, adds to these stories by commenting on how an unplanned pregnancy would affect his life right now: "I know too many like student athletes that have babies and it takes so much out of them. Try to do both things or—you can either let it take things out of you or not. And I'm not the kind of person who's just going to like just push it to the side . . . so it would take a lot out of me." Seeing fellow athletes struggling to juggle sports, school, and fathering responsibilities has given Gavin reason to pause and think about his priorities and sense of procreative responsibilities. Later in the interview, Gavin adds how his mother has reinforced his reflective outlook because "she lets me know from the start, that 'if you get a girl pregnant, I'm not going to be the one paying for it, cause, you can't go to college, I'm not going to push you to go to college, if you can, but if not you will pay for that child's expenses, you know what I'm saying?'"

Sean also provides us with a useful example of how discussions about hypothetical pregnancies can accentuate men's procreative consciousness. He recalls the occasional talks he had with his partner, who asked him what he would want her to do if she got pregnant. Sean laments the fact that her "obsessive" worrying about pregnancy led him to have his own fears:

> [E]ven though I know there's pretty much nothing to worry about, she'll obsess about it, but she'll try not to tell me and it's like I know when something's wrong with her, so then that's when I start to think . . . so what if she is pregnant, what are you going to do? . . . [T]his job at the library can barely support you and the dust bunnies under your bed. And that's when I start seriously thinking O.K., I'd have to drop out of school, I'd have to get a full-time job, probably won't be able to come back to school for a while, if ever.

Sean's comments highlight the social malleability of procreative consciousness. His description of his interactions with his partner reveal that his situated procreative consciousness is a collaborative accomplishment. Left to his own devices, Sean might not actively be aware of his procreative potential. But his partner's worries force him to think about it and subsequently articulate how he perceives his procreative responsibility.

Another permutation of the unplanned-pregnancy scenario involves men's immediate concerns when a partner confronts them with news that she might be pregnant. The conversations may or may not be tied to a specific sexual episode or come on the heels of men's worrying about the prospects of an unplanned pregnancy.[6] Most of our participants had not worried much prior to the disclosure; some had already begun to worry because they had had sex without using contraception, or they had begun to question the effectiveness of something they had used, or they had assumed or knew that there had been a contraceptive failure (e.g., a condom's breaking). Francisco, a 20-year-old father and one of two men interviewed prior to and after the birth of his child, captures the flavor of these types of postsex worries when he describes why he did not use a condom and how he felt about that practice when he had sex with a particular partner for the first time.

> I mean, I remember taking the condom out, but I just said, "Aw, screw it." And I just went—then the next day—and I just went for it. The next day I woke up feeling guilty. I'm like "shit. I could—I'm in jeopardy here." I was just—I was living it up. I had this feeling of—that I was invincible.

Most of the participants did not articulate it as succinctly as Francisco; but there were others who felt that they were "invincible" in the sense that they could have sex without worrying about the potential consequences.

The participants differed in how surprised they were to find out that a partner was late with her period, but most seemed relatively surprised when told by a partner. They responded in a variety of ways that included indifference or fear. The news seemed to activate the men's procreative consciousness; in a few instances, it represented the first time they had given serious thought to this aspect of their self. It was usually an opportunity to think more seriously about things they had already considered about their fertility and the pregnancy process, including previous pregnancy scares. A partner's remarks may have encouraged most of the men to bring their thoughts and feelings about procreation to the fore, a type of consciousness not necessarily sustained beyond the immediate time frame. Whereas some worried constantly for days about it, others were largely or completely able to distance themselves from the potential pregnancy and their relationship with the partner. Desmond, now 30 years of age, recalls how he callously responded to pregnancy scares in his early twenties.

It's kind of shocking when she comes to you and tells you, "Well, I think I might be pregnant." I mean, it's amazing how you change because I remember, actually getting a little mad. I said "What do you mean?" And, it's just amazing how, how with some guys, I'm not going to say all guys, but I immediately tried to distance myself from it or, it was just, I wasn't ready to deal with that. And, when I look back at it, that was not fair to her because I probably hurt her feelings at the time. But, when you're young and immature, you just, sometimes you're not in control of your feelings.

The men's responses to a partner's disclosure appear to be related to the type of relationship between the pair, although it is difficult to unravel the processes connecting the men's reactions to the relationship status. In general, they seemed to be more concerned about the prospects of an unplanned pregnancy when they were emotionally involved with a partner. They were less interested when it had been only a fleeting sexual encounter or were no longer dating their sex partner. We hear the importance of this emotional connection in the words of 25-year-old Ricky, who described separate situations he had with two former girlfriends who had confronted him with pregnancy scares. Ricky indicated that he explicitly told the women that he would assume responsibility for his child if one were born. Commenting on the most recent incident, he says:

> . . . I told her that I was really in love with her and I told her yeah I'm sure we can get married, I didn't say I was going to marry her, I said I'm sure we can get married but I didn't want the baby to be a reason for us to get married, so I told her I would support her and if anything got between us, I would still support her—to help her with the kid.

From a practical standpoint, situations such as Ricky's make it easier for men to maintain an active procreative consciousness. Being actively involved in a partner's life generally meant that the men in the study had more opportunities to be reminded of their potential role as a father-in-waiting.

Participants who were less involved with their partners seemed to spend less time thinking about their potential paternal status. One 20-year-old man, Mario, nonchalantly recalled one of his self-defined pregnancy scares with a girl he had sex with for the first time in a dorm room while her roommate was there. "[M]y penis was inserted into her vagina without a condom for a short period of time and I never knew if any precum got into her or not, but this is now six months later and her stomach does not look big at all. So I'm glad to know that I didn't father a child from her." Given Mario's depiction of this scenario and the fact that he mentioned that he had never talked to her about the "pregnancy scare," it appears that his thoughts about his "pre-cum" were not sufficiently strong to sustain an active procreative consciousness in connection with the situation. Although the sexual event happened without Mario's having a clear understanding of his partner's birth control practices, he went on with his life without inquiring about her well-being.

Some of the men commented on how their response to a partner's telling them that her period was late was affected by the nonmonogamous nature of their relationship. For instance, upon being told by one of his casual partners that her period was late, David, a 28-year-old, recalls having said, ". . . [I]t's not really my business. I mean, 'cause you've seen other people. You know, so, why even tell me? Unless you know for a fact that you're pregnant, don't even bring it up. 'Cause, I might not even be the father, so why tell me?" David's comment highlights how the gendered nature of reproductive physiology can foster ambiguous situations when women have multiple sex partners within a specific time frame. Put simply, being uncertain about their paternity can shape men's initial and subsequent responses because they have no way of knowing for sure during gestation that they are responsible for a pregnancy.

Additional factors may affect how men assess a partner's revelation and, in turn, influence the extent to which their awareness and feelings about their procreative ability are brought to the fore. As alluded to above, a partner's comments may or may not lead men to view the situation as a real-life pregnancy scare that should be taken seriously. We suspect that men's sense of a partner's perceived familiarity with her body as well as how predictable the partner's menstrual cycles are may be important in this regard. Men may place greater stock in a partner's assessment, for example, if the partner has experienced a pregnancy and therefore has first-hand knowledge about the associated physical changes.

Despite some women's efforts to reassure a partner, not all the participants were confident that a partner was in a position to assess her pregnancy status. Commenting on how he was "more strung out" than one of his sex partners, Joseph says, "She was like, I just don't feel like I'm pregnant. And I was like, what does that mean? She's like, I think I'd know if I was pregnant. And I was like, all right. So she was much more calm than I was. I was really bothered by it, not like angry or—I was just thinking about [it]." Joseph appears to have been reluctant to accept his partner's blind assessment of her pregnancy status. She may have reassured herself, but she did not completely eliminate his concerns.

Men's more general understanding of women's menstrual cycles can also affect how they see potential pregnancy scare situations. Todd had previous sex partners tell him that they were late with their periods, but he never worried about it because "girls miss their periods all the time, it seems like. I don't [get] worried. . . . [G]irls are irregular with that all the time . . . [it] has to do with all different kinds of stuff besides being pregnant." Given Todd's mind-set, it is not surprising that he acknowledged having sex with partners who were not using birth control and that he did not define situations as pregnancy scares even though partners told him that their periods were late. Derrick offers an assessment of the menstrual cycles of a select group of young women: "I know that a lot of athletic females have, you know what I'm sayin', irregular cycles." By leaning on alternative reasons for late periods, some of the men were able to remain relatively calm in the face of events that others among the men found highly stressful.

Being attentive to the practical issues associated with a pregnancy scare provides men with opportunities to sustain some level of awareness of their procreative abilities. Talking about the pregnancy scares that have occurred in each of his three long-term relationships, Marcel gives a general description of the patterned way in which his conversations with these partners have evolved:

> So usually the first thing that you talk about is the specific mechanics of failure. What happened and how do we assess that risk? And then usually, it's gonna sound militaristic, but the problem solving phase—what do we do about this shit. Where do I drive you? What do we need to seek out? . . . Which is what happened. I never actually with any of those women said hypothetically if you are pregnant what will we do then. It's always how do we run damage control on this error. And make it go away. And I think it goes away. . . .

Scenarios such as these, where men like Marcel grapple with how to manage the process of sharing information about a potential pregnancy and contemplating a course of action, reveal how men's procreative consciousness can be indirectly awakened.

Finally, some of the men learned that they had actually impregnated a partner. Most received this news while a partner was still pregnant; a few discovered it after the fact—after a partner had aborted the pregnancy or a miscarriage had taken place. In both cases, though, the men's procreative consciousness was accentuated, at least briefly, because they were led to think about their role in bringing about a pregnancy. In the former situations, the men were looking ahead to the impending prospect and responsibilities of fatherhood; in the latter, they were contemplating what fathering experiences they might have had.

The significance of an unplanned pregnancy may even go beyond the prenatal period into the postnatal period for some young men. When we interviewed Francisco the second time, after his child had been born, we reminded him of a comment he had made during his first interview while his partner was pregnant, that it was sometimes hard for him to think of himself as a father. Now, several months later as a real-life father, Francisco is surprised to find that he is still not always aware of himself as a father.

> [E]very once and a while, I'll be walking around school, and I still, you know, it will just come to me, wait a sec, I'm a father. Cause I still think of myself as, as you know, a kid, for lack of a better word. I mean, I see twenty-one, I'm twenty-one years old now, and I'm going to school with a bunch of people, it's ninety-nine percent of the people in my classes don't, aren't fa–, aren't parents , but it has changed, because now, I'm, I know a lot more about it.

Apparently, Francisco has not yet adopted a definitive identity and a distinctively active consciousness as a man who has fathered a child. This is due in part to the unplanned nature of his paternity and the developmental phase he experiences as a person moving through late adolescence. So, even when a young man's child is born, he may not necessarily have an uninterrupted, distinctive awareness of his procreative abilities or paternal status.

Although unplanned pregnancy scenarios had a significant role in bringing the men's procreative consciousness to life, a few had relationship experiences that ultimately dampened their procreative consciousness and sense of responsibility. The experiences occurred over time and led the men to think about and reevaluate their fecundity. Two of the working-class divorced men, for example, began to question their fecundity after their former wives had failed to become pregnant during extended periods of unprotected intercourse. One, 27-year-old Jake, confides: ". . . I didn't think I could get anybody pregnant . . . because of my past relationship with my ex-wife and everything. She had been checked out by all the doctors and she was normal, was fine. And, you got to ask the question you know." After his divorce, Jake carried these doubts with him when he established a new cohabiting relationship. The new partner, by questioning his fecundity, also played a role in shaping the way he subsequently thought about his procreative difficulties:

> And it was a couple of months even after we went unprotected that she got pregnant. You know then it got real easy not to wrap up [use condoms] or whatever, you know so it got to a point where we weren't thinking one way or another. You know at the point that she got pregnant she was like maybe you need to go to a doctor and get checked out. . . . I was embarrassed to go down and get something like that done. It's hard to think that something's wrong with ya, but then a couple of weeks after that she was pregnant.

In this situation, Jake's and his partner's doubts about his fecundity lead them to downplay his procreative responsibility. Consistent with the symbolic interactionist tradition, once they began to think of Jake as potentially sterile, they began to "act" as if he were.

Procreative Consciousness Properties

Up to this point, we have used our interview data to look at how our young men initially become aware of their presumed ability to procreate and then apply that knowledge in their everyday lives. We now dissect the complex features associated with men's procreative consciousness. As we do this, we set our sights on advancing the conceptualization of how men are aware of and experience themselves as persons capable of creating human life. When we listened to the participants' stories, we thought about them inductively and deductively. This allowed us to discover four basic, interrelated properties (and their dimensions), including *knowledge* (direct/indirect, breadth, and depth), with an emphasis on fecundity perceptions (awareness of others' and one's own potential, degree of potency, and confirmed status); *emotional response* (type and intensity); *temporal orientation* (duration and frequency of episodes); and *child visions* (presence and type). By exploring these properties, we are able to achieve a more refined understanding of young men's inner worlds as they relate to their procreative identities.

Knowledge (Fecundity Perceptions)

Obviously, for men to be aware of or to express the subjective aspects of their procreative identity, they must possess ideas, a base of knowledge. What men "know" about their own procreative abilities and more general issues related to contraception and fertility is probably the most fundamental property of men's procreative consciousness. Knowing captures a range of subjective experiences, including awareness of certain things; ability to recognize facets of a situation; certainty or understanding of something; ability to distinguish between features of a phenomenon; and familiarity with characteristics of an experience or setting. Men's knowledge may or may not be accurate in a technical sense, but their ideas about procreative issues often lead them to behave in particular ways. In some instances, they will have formulated clear thoughts about particular issues, whereas in other instances they have a vague, perhaps muddled set of images. Taken together, these lucid and obscure thoughts represent the backbone of men's awareness of different aspects of sex and procreation. This knowledge has several key dimensions, including the breadth of what is known, how deep and refined the knowledge is, whether the knowledge has been acquired directly though personal experience or witnessed as an outcome for someone else, and whether the information is primarily technical in nature or emotionally laden. Before we discuss these four dimensions, it is useful to explore the most significant form of knowledge, which we call "fecundity perceptions."

Fecundity perceptions refer to several features of men's lives including their knowledge of others' and their own ability to procreate, their perceived degree of potency, and whether they have confirmed their ability to procreate. Perceptions about others' and one's own fecundity, by definition, represent the core facet of men's procreative consciousness. This type of awareness is impossible without an appreciation for the link between sexual intercourse and conception. As discussed earlier, males typically develop this awareness in their early teens. A fundamental feature of it is the knowledge that men in general can impregnate their female sex partners. On a personal level, men learn that they are individually capable of creating human life. Once acquired, this rudimentary knowledge or awareness remains with them throughout their lives in either an active or dormant state—ready to be called to the forefront if the situation dictates. This does not, however, preclude at some point men's changing their perspective to believe that they are no longer capable of procreating.

Another dimension associated with fecundity perceptions includes men's assessment of their own sperm's viability, their perceived degree of potency as it were. Some men may have a rather vivid self-image in this regard, but many simply assume that they're fertile and do not give much thought to quantifying or assessing their potency.[7]

As mentioned above, some men's image of their degree of fecundity may change over time as they encounter different types of situations. Recall Jake's earlier comments. He assumed that he was fertile originally, then altered his perceptions about his fecundity after attempting unsuccessfully to impregnate his partners, and finally developed a more definitive perception of himself as fertile when he impregnated his current partner.

Jake's experience illustrates that men can use their firsthand knowledge of "successfully" impregnating a woman as a means to verify their fecundity status—to confirm that they are capable of impregnating someone. This type of confirmation is not permanent, but experiential knowledge of one's own fertility is likely to shape men's subjective understanding of their ability to create human life and to reinforce the most fundamental feature of men's procreative consciousness. Men's firsthand knowledge, in the vast majority of cases, is based on their willingness to trust that their partner's pregnancy is not due to a sexual liaison she might have had with another partner. The men in our sample typically felt confident that they were responsible for the pregnancies attributed to them, but this was not always the case. For example, Reginald, a 20-year-old participant who recently moved to the United States from the Bahamas, had gone through the pregnancy and birth of his partner's infant child, acknowledging the child as his own. Nevertheless, he continues to wrestle with the idea that the child might not be his biological offspring.

> I feel like it ain't, and sometimes then, I don't know why. But, then, it show little mannerisms, and a little of my charisma sometimes, as young as it is, but maybe it just might be that the baby is bein' like that, so it might not be my mannerisms. . . . [S]he [partner] say if I want to take a blood test, take it, but she might be usin' reverse psychology on me though when I say it. . . . I wish some type of way of blood test, come up

free, I'll take that right there and then, but I just ain't go through all them procedures and stuff. I don't want to go tell her parents or her family that I do that. You know, I livin' there, too, you see?

A little later in the interview, Reginald elaborates on his reasoning for doubting his paternity status in this instance. Part of his uncertainty is due to the infant child's physical appearance; he comments that the child does not look anything like him, unlike an older child he fathered who lives in the Bahamas. Reginald remains skeptical about his current paternity status, then, because he uses his older child's resemblance to him as a point of comparison. Despite this uncertainty, he is not eager to go through the hassles of a paternity test and expresses a willingness to be involved in the infant's life and assume his status as father. However, he admits that his connection to this child would probably be strengthened if he knew for sure that he is the genetic father. His account also illustrates how his decisions concerning his infant child are affected by his partner and her parents, both directly and indirectly. A number of individuals, therefore, may contribute to the negotiation processes that affect when and how men assume or establish paternity.

An even more intriguing example of how others can play a role in this informal process of establishing paternity involves a 22-year-old participant and his mother. As far as he knows, Ed has fathered five children with three different women. When asked if he were sure that the children he was discussing during an earlier segment of the interview are his biological children, Ed indicates that they are and provides this explanation:

> Because, see me, when it's about a baby, the first thing I say is take it [to] my mama's, . . . cuz my mama, she'll know, she'll look at the baby an, she'll just say, "Yeah" and if that ain't my baby, and she'll look at it, like this one girl tried to say I, she [made] my baby, my mama looked at her, looked at the baby, and told her, "Girl, if you don't get up out my house bout this my damn son child, this ain't my son child, this one 'em nigger child, either you just don't know who you baby daddy is, or this is mine," she'll tell you. My mama, she look at the nose, the eyes, and the ears, and sometimes she look at the set of teeth because she, I don't know what it is, but she be knowing. She know all along though.

Ed goes on to clarify that each time one of his sexual partners has a baby that she asserts is his, he invites her to show the baby to his mother. In effect, this arrangement places his mother in an informal gatekeeper role to establishing paternity. So, while growing numbers of individuals are resorting to voluntary as well as court-ordered DNA tests to establish paternity,[8] most individuals still rely on "good faith" assumptions and others' judgments. The informal means by which paternity is established, including those countless occasions where a challenge is not made, implies that individuals in the course of their everyday living socially construct and negotiate men's emotional and legal connections to children.

Technically, for men who actually impregnate a woman, their sperm represents their only essential contribution to the pregnancy. Given its importance, we were curious to know whether our young men had any particular thoughts or attachments to their sperm that might expand our understanding of how they think about themselves as procreative beings.

Although most of the participants responded that they did not think about their sperm very often or in any particular way, they typically said that it was very important to be able to father their own children. We explore this point further in chapter 6 when we consider men's perceptions about their readiness to become fathers and their perceptions about what would constitute an ideal fathering situation. Here, we simply mention that only a few participants had any unusual or noteworthy perceptions of their sperm. Sean, a 23-year-old, mentions not really having any thoughts about his sperm but adds, "I don't endear my sperm to myself, I guess I do have a sentimental attachment to them cause I don't want a vasectomy, and I know that with a vasectomy you still ejaculate but there's no sperm coming out. Only in that sense do I feel—I guess they're my boys, I don't want them cut off." Desmond uses different language, but provides an equally colorful account of how he recently started to think of his sperm.

> Well let me tell you how I've been thinking about it lately just cause I've talked to other guys on the phone and I had a guy tell me, he was telling me that his, ah, one of his friends, his wife was, they're young, they were married young in their twenties, and his wife was cheating on him. An, then I said, "Well how do you know?" He said, "Well he knew his wife was cheating because he had suspected his wife was with somebody else." I said, "Well, did he, his wife allow him to have sex with her?" He said, "Yeah, but, she wouldn't allow him to sperm in her." I said, "What do you mean?" "Well, she wouldn't allow him to put his load in her." I said, "My goodness." And so, that's the way I think about it now, you know, when you're I guess sperming in somebody. It's like a load of sperm, you know,

ah, load of soap, or a boatload of something, but that's what it is, it's a load. I guess that's what you're releasing, a load.

And another participant, Reynaldo, actually dreamed about his sperm. ". . . I saw the sperm just swimming with my face on them and, it's just—you're thinking that each one of them is a possibility to have a child. And it just takes one and there's millions. . . ." Reynaldo's reflection on his dream aptly conveys his sense that procreation is amazing.

Although it is useful to appreciate the different aspects of men's fecundity perceptions and their significance to men's procreative consciousness, there is also value in exploring several dimensions to men's procreative consciousness. One dimension involves the distinction between experiential knowledge and indirect ways of knowing. Others include the breadth and depth of men's knowledge regarding procreative issues, as well as whether the knowledge is technical in nature or emotionally laden.

As we listened to the participants who had encountered specific fertility events, such as an abortion, pregnancy, or childbirth, the commonsensical phrase "knowing through doing" rang true. Men often obtained experiential knowledge and an understanding of procreative issues from playing a direct role in some type of event or discussion about sex and procreation. Some of our participants, for example, played an active role in helping a partner make arrangements for an abortion. Their help consisted of calling clinics, arranging exams and procedures, driving a partner to a clinic, and being present during the procedure and/or recovery phases. Some of them also acknowledged that some of their indirect experiences, observing others or talking to them, played a role in shaping their procreative identities. A number mentioned that they became more attentive to their own procreative abilities, at least momentarily, when they saw children playing or noticed someone who was pregnant. It may be useful, therefore, to differentiate men's experiential knowledge from knowledge based solely on secondhand sources such as friends, parents, TV, and school experiences.

Both direct and indirect forms of knowing can be studied by first considering whether a particular type of knowledge exists, and if it does, the degree to which a man has developed it and how it has affected him. We learned in chapter 1 that Sean has folk knowledge about preejaculatory fluids that leads him to believe that he may be putting himself at risk of impregnating his partner when he's lying naked next to her. Even though that "knowledge" is consistent with what has been reported in various popular and clinical literatures, it is not supported by studies that have found no viable sperm in preejaculatory fluid. Indeed, two researchers who reviewed the available evidence concluded, "The generally accepted wisdom that the presence of sperm in pre-ejaculatory fluid makes withdrawal an ineffective method of contraception—an opinion widely cited in the literature and echoed by clinicians world wide—has little scientific support."[9] However, from a symbolic interactionist perspective, the accuracy of men's stock of knowledge may be irrelevant. What is most important is the degree to which they possess "knowledge" and have feelings about something relevant to their procreative consciousness, including a sense of responsibility. If they believe something to be true, even if it is incorrect, then this belief can have consequences for the choices they make. From this vantage point, Sean may experience his procreative consciousness more deeply, and apparently more often, while he's involved in intimate moments with his sexual partner than do men who do not share his ideas. Despite the fact that his understanding of "pre-cum" is not supported by scientific evidence, Sean's comments suggest that his procreative consciousness has some degree of depth.

The participants who had lived through different types of fertility events seemed able to express their procreative consciousness in a broader fashion. Some had a range of experiences, including some combination of the following: multiple opportunities to negotiate birth control, experiencing one or more pregnancy scares, one or more abortions/miscarriages, and going through pregnancies and childbirth. Some whose histories included one or more of these events sometimes did so with the same partner during the course of the relationship with her; others tended to have undergone different events with various partners over the course of their young adult lives. Thus, much of the men's knowledge was in some cases derived from a particular relationship, whereas other knowledge was discovered, developed, and perpetuated with a variety of partners and sometimes friends or family.

The types of ideas men relate to their procreative abilities differ not only in terms of the particular issues they address, for example, abortion or pregnancy, but some are emotionally laden and others refer more to technical kinds of information. To the extent that ideas are emotionally charged, they may take on unique meaning because they intensify how men think about something. If men are emotionally invested in thinking a certain way or having a particular type of thought, they are likely to do so more deeply. As we will illustrate shortly, men who have pro-life views are likely to have an emotionally laden perspective on a partner's fetus, viewing it as their child. It is an orientation that can influence how men experience the unexpected resolution of a pregnancy by abortion.

Men also harbor a number of less emotionally laden ideas as well. For example, some understand that their potential for impregnating a sex partner who is on the pill is higher if she is also taking antibiotics. Or, they may think, as Marcus did after he had a pregnancy scare at age 15, that particular condom practices are more effective: "I started to use two condoms. And I was like I feel pretty safe or crazy? I didn't look at it as being as crazy, I just looked at it as being smart. . . . But after a while, I stopped doing that and I just started using one condom again. But it [was] just more, I [was] just more responsible."

Aside from their direct sexual and fertility-related experiences, men's procreative consciousness can be activated when they are exposed to conversations with family and friends. Desmond talks about how some in his family pressure him about having kids. They say things like

> "Well, you better have a kid before you get too old" or some of my other relatives that have families you know, "Well, see, you could have a family like that." So you get all this pressure coming from different areas. Ah you know, because I choose school and things like that, you know, then I have to sacrifice those things. Ah, but that's what caused me to really think about it because its always constant, and you hear those things. "Well you better have some kids. You get old. You're going to need somebody to take care of you." So it's a battle.

Family members can also expose sons to individuals who may offer these young men insights about their procreative abilities. For example, a few days after Sean had received a sex lecture from his dad, he was the beneficiary of yet a second lecture from his dad's friend, who used a metaphor to get his point across. Sean recalls his saying: "[A guy who works in the iron yard] you know he has to put the iron in and take it out of an oven. And that while the iron is sitting in the oven it's hot and if you are not wearing a glove you could get burned." Sean goes on to say that "he left it at that and they were just sitting there looking at me waiting for me to get what he was saying and I was like oh, OK, I see. This conversation was much more helpful [than my dad's]."

Harper, a 29-year-old, recalled that his "running mates" talked about the possibility of unplanned pregnancy among themselves. Re-creating a sample of these exchanges, Harper says,

"Oh, man, you finna have a kid," like it was cool and I'm like, "Naw, man, I ain't, you know, I ain't trying like to, like its, you know its fun to go out and have a kid." I just trip out on some of my friends you know. It's almost like, man "Her dad is going to kill you, man." I'm like, "Whatever, man. You know, I ain't worried about that." And some, man it'll be all right, like "She ain't really pregnant, man, it'll be all right and you worry yourself over nothing."

Here we have responses ranging from congratulatory praise, to warnings about parental responses, to expressions of denial that the woman is really pregnant. Harper describes being unmoved by listening to his friends, saying that he didn't "really think too much of it."

In a similar vein, Desmond tells the interviewer that guys did acknowledge among themselves the possibility of impregnating a woman but that the focus of the conversations was on "scoring." "Are you keeping a tally, how much have you scored. You know, if you haven't scored, what's wrong with you. It was the girl who reminded the guy that there were consequences for this. I remember one young lady telling me, 'why are we always playing these adult games?'. . . I still think about that."

Emotional Response

Not surprisingly, there are often important emotional overtones to the way men are aware of and react to their procreative abilities or involvements in different facets of the procreative realm. The men in our study often spoke in ways that revealed that their procreative consciousness, including fecundity perceptions, involved an emotional response of varying type and intensity. The men's consciousness was activated in various contexts, ranging from thinking about the ability to father a child, to miscarriages and abortions, to experiences during the pregnancy and childbirth process, to opportunities for being involved with children. Numerous participants reported having emotions such as amazement, pride, sadness, anger, fear, powerlessness, insecurity, ambivalence, attachment, and joy when circumstances triggered some facet of their procreative consciousness. They differed in the intensity of their feelings, and the intensity varied depending upon the nature of the circumstances they encountered.

Because the sample of men we interviewed tended to be responsible primarily for unplanned pregnancies, few had occasion to tell of upbeat, emotional messages about their procreative experiences. Other researchers who have focused on men who have become fathers under more desirable circumstances have documented men's positive feelings about their fathering experiences.[10] Although feelings about these paternal experiences can in some ways be viewed as conceptually distinct from men's orientation toward procreative issues, they are related in a broader sense.

Men can and do have feelings about procreation that do not require them to have firsthand experience with impregnating someone. In the abstract, such feelings among the participants tended to be rather positive. For example, when asked to comment on his thoughts about his ability to get a girl pregnant, Marcus provides a colorful account of the amazement and perhaps masculine pride he feels.

> Shoot, I could make a nation if I could, if I had my own land [Int: laughs] and a bunch a girls I could make my own country. That's something, that's something cool. I mean we hold the power to create kids. WE do, males do! That's how I look at it. I like that's, pretty cool. I ain't gonna say it's cool, but I mean it's nature. [I: It sounds like it's a powerful thing to you?]. . . . Yeah, it's a very powerful thing.

Here, Marcus displays an emotional tone that captures his sense of awe about males in general and his own presumed procreative abilities more specifically. When the interviewer initially proffers the word "powerful" to describe his feelings, he quickly confirms this observation. Marcus's narrative conveys his excitement about his presumed procreative abilities, but the hypothetical nature of the scenario suggests that Marcus and others like him probably have few occasions to experience these good feelings. The feelings may come to the fore more forcefully, though, when men find themselves in situations where they are trying to impregnate someone, a rare occurrence in our sample, or they practice contraception half-heartedly because they may have some latent desires to father children. We found that although most of the men want this power, some do not. Carlos, a 21-year-old emphatically asserted, "I don't want the power to get people pregnant ever! . . . Like I'm ready for a vasectomy. Like, I've talked to my friends about getting a vasectomy. They said that was crazy though. I'm not joking."

Some of the participants recalled their emotional reactions when they thought about the prospects of getting a partner pregnant. Tim shared a story about his junior year in high school when he was involved with a girlfriend who lived with him at his parents' house. As someone who at times had sex without the benefit of contraception, Tim describes how he reacted to scenarios when his partner was late with her period: "You start freaking out and you don't know what to do and you get nervous." Despite such strong feelings, and being fully aware that he could get her pregnant, Tim admits that making "mistakes doesn't mean that you necessarily use protection or that you say, yeah, you should get on the pill." Similarly, Marcel mentions that early on with one of his partners he had "a wild panicky fear that perhaps I would torpedo my own life course and things I wanted to do by getting a woman pregnant." For some participants, then, contemplating the prospects of unplanned paternity led them to wrestle with strong negative emotions. However, the grappling did not guarantee that the men would use contraceptives effectively.

Some of the men freely admitted to having been driven by other emotional forces that suppressed their procreative consciousness. In Tim's words, he was "swept away, involved with the passion of the moment."

We found that despite the presence in our sample of men who either had no procreative experience or had unplanned events, a few reported positive emotions in connection with their paternal awareness. Francisco, one of the fathers in the study shares his excitement about spending time with his 10-week-old infant:". . . [W]hen I'm not at the house, all I think about is being home, going home and holding her, and playing with her and being there, and that's what I look forward to." Even so, Francisco actually sometimes had to remind himself that he was a father. Nevertheless, throughout his second interview, Francisco made it clear that he was enjoying the early months of being a father.

In addition to the good feelings, men can feel deep sadness when their procreative consciousness is activated. For example, Tom, a 22-year-old participant aptly expressed his sadness over the loss of his fiancée's pregnancy. He describes the intensity of what he felt when he accompanied her to the hospital to deliver a 2-month-old fetus that had been dead for at least two weeks: "[B]efore that [trip to the hospital] it was like oh the baby's dead, not that many emotions coming out. But when I saw [my fiancée] on the cart going into the emergency room, it just hit me. . . . [T]he entire time I was just outside, bawling my eyes out." He likens his sense of loss due to the miscarriage to how he felt about losing his child through a previous divorce. Tom's account shows that reproductive physiology effectively removes men from the direct physiological experience of a miscarriage, but men can still be distraught over a pregnancy loss.

Miller, a 28-year-old single man, came to the interview having just recently discovered his girlfriend was pregnant in spite of being on the pill. That she was married to another man, and had broken up with a live-in partner who retained ties to her 4-year-old complicated the issue and contributed to Miller's "nightmare." Miller wanted to be a father but not at this time. Shortly after the interview, his partner had a miscarriage that proved devastating to Miller in spite of his extreme anxiety about the timing of the pregnancy. Miller then intentionally got her pregnant again within several months.

Tom's and Miller's accounts are consistent with the limited research that has explored how men respond emotionally to a partner's having a miscarriage. One recent in-depth interview study of twenty men aged 19-35 living in England found that being involved with a miscarriage stimulated deep emotional reactions, including "grief, confusion, blame, anger and disgust."[11] A number of the Englishmen acknowledged having strong feelings about the miscarriage; most believed that they had few if any interpersonal outlets to express them. Male friends were generally unsympathetic and the men themselves felt that they were expected to be strong for a grieving partner.

We interviewed only five participants who had learned that their partner had a miscarriage but conducted twelve main interviews and three supplemental interviews with men whose partner had aborted a pregnancy for which they believed themselves responsible. The abortion scenarios described were quite diverse, as were the feelings men recalled having had when they learned of the abortion. The detailed descriptions we obtained are rather rare because little research has focused on men's responses to abortion.

Though perhaps a bit dated, a study published in 1984 of one thousand men who accompanied a partner to one of thirty abortion clinics located across the United States is the most extensive treatment of men's emotional reactions to abortion in the research literature.[12] The study reports that 29 percent of the men had frequent thoughts about the fetus, and some continued to ruminate about the fetus after the abortion. Many were upset with a partner's abortion, with some indicating as sense of deep loss; many others were largely indifferent or relieved. How men respond to an abortion appears to depend on several factors, including their attitudes about becoming a father at the time, their religious and/or moral beliefs about abortion, and feelings toward a partner. These factors may be interrelated, sometimes creating internal conflict. For example, a pro-choice man may express love for his partner and the baby-to-be, yet believe it is not an appropriate time for him to become a father. Likewise, a man who is pro-life and believes abortion in any context is unacceptable may still feel anxiety if his partner is pregnant by him, and he believes he is ill-prepared to assume fatherhood responsibilities at this time. Finally, men who impregnate a woman during a one-night stand or who feel emotionally distant from a partner are more likely to be indifferent or even relieved by an abortion unless they are strongly pro-life.

Men's emotional responses to the initial decision about abortion should be considered within the larger context of other possible decisions, all of which may create interpersonal conflict. For example, if the couple eschew abortion and the pregnancy comes to term, will they put the baby up for adoption? Will they rear the child together or separately? Will only one person assume parental responsibility?

Some men may feel unready for fatherhood and view abortion as the only way out of an untenable situation. However, if a partner chooses to give birth and to keep the baby, the men then have to consider issues of financial support and the role they will assume with the child, and negotiate these with the partners. The relationship with a partner is critical. Doing what a partner wants may not be in keeping with what they prefer, but some men may choose to look good in a partner's eyes rather than privileging their own desires.

Men who feel ready for fatherhood may embrace the idea of a child, and ultimately the child. These visions of themselves as fathers and of the child may or may not be related to their relationship with the partner. Some men may almost exclude a partner from their thoughts about the child; others may permit the mother to mediate their relationship.

Our abortion veterans, though limited in number, give voice to the dynamic nature of men's procreative consciousness and the inherent complexities. For some we interviewed, dealing with an abortion meant that they had to wrestle with painful feelings associated with their sense of loss. Arthur, the young man we introduced briefly in chapter 1 whose partner terminated a pregnancy without his consent or knowledge that it was in the offing, describes his reaction after his partner informed him of her abortion. "And then the shit really hit the fan." Arthur speaks of himself as

> screaming mad, smashing pictures and it ended up with me and my Avenger [a car] screamin' sideways out of the driveway. I said what do

you mean, you know. She said, I had an abortion, and then, that's when I went into that whole, that was my child too, how could you do this to me, just tirade. . . . [I]t hurt about as bad as it did when my grandpa died. Just at that moment, the combination between blind rage and just hating.

About the most difficult thing he had to confront, Arthur says: "Lose his life. I don't know, I was raised in a Catholic family. This was my baby. Bein' my first kid, my parents' first grand-baby, my grandfather's first great grandbaby, somethin'; it's always somethin' special. I was havin' a kid. Just took it all away, just like that." Arthur struggled to compose himself a few times during the interview as he recounted these memories, clearly affected by what had happened. The excerpt reveals that his difficulties appear to have been based on both his sense of loss and his interpretation of how specific family members were also losing a "baby" that would have been special to them. From Arthur's perspective, the loss was not just his but the extended family's as well. Viewing the "baby" in this symbolic way appears to have intensified Arthur's emotions as he was thinking about the pregnancy and abortion.

A few other participants with abortion experience talked about a sense of powerlessness and frustration. For example, the stories of two 18-year-old men reveal how various contextual factors affected their emotional responses to scenarios when a partner was considering abortion. Gavin describes feeling ineffective because he was not in a position to do anything to assist with his partner's pregnancy and eventual abortion. He lacked money, had educational and athletic goals to pursue, and was unwilling to tell his parents. At the same time, he recognized that he had obviously played a significant role in the pregnancy, so on some level he wanted to have a part in resolving the situation. Ricky talked about how his sense of helplessness was exacerbated because although he wanted his 16-year-old partner to bring the pregnancy to term so that he could keep and raise the child, she and her mother were committed to terminating it. In short, it seemed to him as though he had no choice but to defer to their wishes in that the mother threatened legal action because of their ages; she saw the pregnancy as an outcome of statutory rape.

Derrick, a 19-year-old abortion veteran (two times with the same girl at age 16 and age 19), describes his angry feelings toward his previous partner, whom he was not seeing anymore and who called him to tell him of the second pregnancy:

I mean, like, even though, sometimes I would use a condom, but you know, sometimes I didn't because she was on birth control pills. I would always talk to her every night and I'd be like, you know, "have you taken your pill today." . . . She was like "yeah," every day she would always tell me "yeah," but she was lying. You know, she lied even about that, so. Really she wasn't even taking her pills the way she was supposed to.

She also did not tell him she was pregnant until sometime after she found out, and she lied about when she had the abortion. Derrick would have liked to have avoided an abortion; he believed that he could have cared for the baby because he was older and that he would have been able to work and go to school, and he felt supported by his mother and sisters. He accused his previous partner of being irresponsible, "[Y]ou're not ready to take care of a baby, you know what I'm sayin. You can't even take care of yourself." Despite his anger, Derrick says he was able to accept the abortion decision after the abortion "cause we weren't together."

Temporal Orientation

The temporal property is closely associated with our previous discussion about men's situated and global procreative consciousness. It refers to the duration of time in terms of both specific episodes and the more enduring periods in which men are attentive to their procreative consciousness. How frequently men experience themselves in this way is another feature of the temporal dimension. We observed considerable variability in how often the procreative consciousness of the men in our study came alive. Contrast Raymond's earlier comment about not spending any time thinking about his procreative abilities with Desmond's response when asked how often he thought about his ability to impregnate females: ". . . [I]t probably comes into your [mind] daily. . . . So, yeah, I think about it often." Or, recall Derrick, who implied that he activated his procreative consciousness frequently when he asked his partner each night whether she had taken her pill. Tripp's comments about his regular but fleeting realizations about his procreative ability provide us with another layer of understanding of procreative consciousness: "I'm sure it crosses my mind everyday, but just in [an] instant, in and out, but nothing, I don't dwell on it or anything like that because I know it's a very remote possibility, very, very remote, 99.9 percent." Tripp bases his assessment of the probability that he would impregnate a partner on the partner's as well as his own regular contraceptive practices. Notice that whereas Derrick ties his procreative awareness to a particular time of day and event, Tripp verbally represents his understanding of his awareness to the interviewer as something that occurs on a more or less daily basis but not necessarily in connection with a particular situation.

Another aspect of the temporal dimension involves the timing of men's procreative consciousness in connection with a specific event such as an abortion or miscarriage. Learning about one of these experiences prior to it or as it is happening can be quite different from learning after the fact. The context and reasons for learning that an abortion or miscarriage has happened can diminish some men's sense of their procreative identity. One 29-year-old man in our study, for instance, told of how a friend of his former partner divulged to him that the former partner had had a recent miscarriage. A lack of communication between Frank and the partner had led him to wonder, "Maybe she didn't tell me because she wasn't quite sure if it was me or not. I don't know! We're not staying together, she not coming home to me every night. She might be doin' something with someone else too."

In some instances, the men's procreative consciousness was heightened by multiple factors, recurring or overlapping in time. Drug rehabilitation classes, a case of gonorrhea, and too many children facilitated Ed's awareness. A recovering drug addict and pusher, Ed learned in drug rehabilitation about AIDS and STDS. He quoted local statistics and took the information to heart. "[T]hat's why I keep using [condoms] because I know, I ain't gonna be one of the ones, right, with no AIDS." Earlier, Ed had a painful case of gonorrhea that inspired him to use condoms "for the first time." In addition, he, his partner, and family members, believed that he did not need any more children. This father of five with three different women says:

> I don't want no more chirren [children]. And she (partner) don't want no chirren so we keep 'em (condoms), my cousin she's a RN, and my Auntie, she's the head person of the business and they give me a box of them, I talking bout a real big box I have sitting in the house on the dresser. Then she gave me rubbers for like, female rubbers, the lubricatin cream for it an all that too. . . . I keep 'em in my trunk, got about nine of 'em in my trunk. . . . I got a little black thing, it's square, like that, in my car it looks so small, like a little wallet. But it's plastic and it keeps three condoms.

Child Visions

The final property we encountered in our data involved the men's visions of children they might eventually sire. The visions that seem most relevant to procreative consciousness include the mental images the men constructed of specific future children, which included references to gender, personality, and physical features. To a lesser extent, their general references to children were significant. Additionally, the men expressed child visions by talking excitedly about sharing activities with their future children. For instance, Austin, 21-years-old, implies that his procreative consciousness was often activated when some event or experience put him on a "high": "[I]f I see something really amazing, that just moves me. If I see something like that, I'll be, god, if I ever have a child or, I'd want them to experience this."

Francisco, describes, as an expectant-father, elaborate visions of the still-to-be-born Emma as a child in the future: "Well, I wonder a lot about what she's gonna look like. . . . I know exactly what she's going to look like, but, I can see her being very outgoing. Moving a lot, you know. Always wanting to go everywhere. . . . I can see myself coaching her . . . I ran in high school and I was always very active in sports when I was younger." Francisco not only predicts her personality and sees himself in a role as her athletic coach but also envisions the relationship Emma, her mother, and he will have with one another:

> I could see her being very close to me. . . . I can see she probably coming to me probably when mom's been mean or mom won't let her do something . . . not that I won't be strict, cause I'll be strict later on in life. But I'm very, I mean, my dad was always very pretty much let me do what I want. He knew that I was a good kid. He gave me a lot of freedom and that's what I'm gonna do. She'll know what's right and what's wrong.

Francisco thinks Emma will be "extroverted," not a "shy, shy kid"; she will be "happy" and "popular"; "have nice toys" and "good clothes"; and like "to travel." "I see us enjoying her love . . . you know I think we're going to enjoy that baby a lot. I think we both are." Francisco fantasizes about what people will think because he is such a young father, "I can see people being shocked." He even thinks about taking Emma to his college classes if there is no one else to care for her. Francisco expends much mental energy on Emma.

In contrast to Francisco, Reginald, a 20-year-old father-in-waiting and the nonresident father of a 4-year-old boy, describes more limited and more general child visions that emphasize gender. He expresses satisfaction that his new baby would be a boy. "Rather a boy than a girl. I feel that girls are more problems and more, uh, more money. . . . I know if we had a girl, I always look on ahead. . . . So I know with a girl, the girl more than likely gonna end up meeting up with some other few promiscuous girls." Reginald, instead of focusing on the child as a baby, looked ahead, anticipating that he might have to deal with his daughter's becoming sexually active as a teenager. He went on to reason that it would be easier to be parents of a boy than of a girl who, because of her gender, would experience more stress. Francisco's visions revealed the hope and beauty that are often associated with a new child, whereas Reginald's visions foresaw future problems for her parents. Francisco's close and loving relationship with his partner and Reginald's highly fragile relationship may have affected the nature of their child visions.

Gender preferences were prevalent for a few of the men. Most of the participants who expressed a gender preference for their future child wanted a son. Harper, a 29-year-old, wants "a cute, bright red big boy . . . I want a son." Miller, a 28-year-old, reflects: "Oh, I don't know. I could go either way. When I was younger I had thought that I would want a daughter. But I guess now that it all boils down to it, I want a little boy." Ricky, an 18-year-old participant, presents a unique view: ". . . I always said I wanted a girl, because I guess uh, there was someone, . . . I can give my love to, that wouldn't try to run over me or something, just as I'm giving them all my love, they appreciate all my love, and that would be my little girl, my pretty lil girl, that I can call mine, that's all I really want is a little girl, so I can just love her."

Physical characteristics were the focus of conversations between some of our participants and their partners. Raymond, a 19-year-old, talks about what his children would look like with his present girlfriend. He has a wish list for his future baby: "I want my child to have her eyes, you know, my lips, stuff like that, but my smile. . . ." Kendal, a 24-year-old light-complectioned man, was engaged to a dark-complectioned woman. He describes their conversations: "We talk, you know, cause I mean I gotta lot o' different people in my background. You know, and she does too. So I mean our baby could come out, you know, dark or come out white as can be. So you know, blue eyes, green eyes, straight hair, nappy hair." However, Kendal fundamentally cared only that the baby was healthy.

Allen's Story

We have incorporated heretofore the stories of different participants to show how several key conceptual properties are associated with expressions of procreative consciousness. We now profile in greater detail Allen, a 27-year-old high school dropout who has a rather unique and complex history of relationships, sexual experiences, and procreative events. By looking at a few aspects of his procreative identity over the past decade, we can explore the nature of procreative consciousness and the interrelated properties we described above.

A phone call from a previous sex partner when Allen was about 17 years old provides a useful entry point to understanding his procreative identity. The girl informed him that she had aborted a pregnancy that had resulted from their sexual involvement. The message activated Allen's procreative consciousness, making him keenly aware at that moment that he in fact had the ability to procreate. He says he felt "gutless, or just like, you know, I didn't have any say-so. And I just felt crappy, like that I had something to do with this abortion even though I didn't help with the decision. And I felt like I had something to do with killing an innocent child." His emotional reaction was relatively short-lived, but he conveyed his immediate discomfort about having played a role in the pregnancy and abortion process. Allen placed his response in a larger personal context when he clarified that he became essentially indifferent after the initial wave of negative emotions. He acknowledges a nomadic lifestyle during his youth, admitting, "I just didn't care about a whole lot. I was just out seeing the country, and she obviously made her decision beforehand." Nevertheless, his narrative reveals that he had conflicting thoughts and feelings at the time of the revelation:

> I don't have any proof that it was mine, [but] no reason to believe that it wasn't because I was with her for a short period of time. . . . Maybe it was the right choice for her at the time, and probably for me too. I was far from being a responsible, ready-to-settle down father. But I was raised . . . My mom was right-to-life, raised Catholic, didn't believe in abortion. . . . I still believe that every child needs a father and should have a chance in life.

Allen also conveys having had confusing thoughts about the girl as well: "I'm not a girl, so I don't know how it would feel to, you know, be pregnant or you know, what goes through their minds . . . I don't know what she's gone through because I haven't stayed in touch with her." These remarks reveal that Allen is using a gender lens to comment on his limited inability to "know" what pregnancy and abortion feel like. He recognizes that because he is a man, his direct experiential knowledge of the physical, psychological, and emotional aspects of these events is nil. In addition, asked if that abortion experience changed the way he thought or acted, he says:

> I don't know that it did at that time. I partied a lot, drank a lot. And I didn't really care . . . I tried maybe to be a little more careful during sex, never really, you know AIDS wasn't a big scare at that point so I wasn't big on wearing condoms, and usually the girls I was with said they were on birth control, and you know, tried to be as cautious as you could. I guess I was probably lucky that I didn't get more girls pregnant. You never know.

Later he philosophizes that he wanted to "get over it and move on with life . . . I don't think it scared me that bad. Or I never even thought about it that much."

Allen describes another significant procreative event that occurred at a party when he was 20 years old. He "ended up sleeping with this girl [Jan]" who was engaged to a serviceman and they were preparing to move. He viewed the sex with her then as "fun," did not use protection, and "I had a gut feeling when we were together, you know, that last big moment, the thought ran through my head, 'Oh my God, I just got her pregnant.' . . . And I was hoping I didn't cause I wasn't ready to be a dad." Asked why he thought he got Jan pregnant, he says, "Maybe we both peaked at the same time . . . it was just a feeling and it came out of nowhere. . . ." When she asked, "Did you just have an orgasm in me?" he answered yes. Allen's account exemplifies how men can become aware of their procreative potential in a specific situation and for a relatively fleeting moment. It also shows that some do not fully understand reproductive physiology. He apparently felt that the chances of his impregnating Jan increased because they climaxed simultaneously.

Allen told the interviewer that he had heard that Jan wanted to have a baby. Even though he did not want to get her pregnant, he did not ask if she were using birth control but assumed she was. A while later, she told him that she was pregnant with his child. Her fiancé Norman, had been away on duty at the time of the tryst. Not feeling ready for a child and not being in love with Jan, Allen asked her what she wanted. They settled upon secrecy and that they would let her fiancé believe it was his child, and Allen therefore decided he would not assume procreative or paternal responsibility. He reasoned that he would not need to pay child support because the military had good benefits, but that he would be able to see pictures occasionally. The child, Donny, looked exactly like Allen according to Allen and the boy's mother.

Allen dealt with this somewhat unusual situation by adopting an altruistic explanation. He continues to deny the necessity of a DNA test because his son knows the other man [Norman] as his father. "I wouldn't want to take that away from anybody. . . . If he's being a good father and that's who Donny knows as his dad, why shatter his illusions?"

Later on, when Allen was living with another woman, she asked if he would have a DNA test to determine his paternity status relative to Donny. He responded that he viewed the test as "complicating everything," including "shattering—whatever Norman thinks he has going through his head." Additionally, "I might end up paying child support." He acknowledged, "It's kind of a strange situation, me knowing, but not doing anything about it, and maybe I'm not taking responsibility for it." Allen left it up to Jan to decide how she wanted to handle the "fact" that he was the biological father. He agreed to be "a friend of the family and that way at least I can see him [Donny]." Nonetheless, he thinks about the future: "Maybe one day when he gets older and maybe he'll look a lot like me and see me and say, 'What's up here?'"

Allen describes "knowing" Donny was his biological son: "[B]ecause I think when you look into your own eyes and you can tell, you know, that's my biological son." Allen first met Donny when Donny was 5 years old at a planned meeting with Jan after a chance encounter in a grocery store, and talks of having been scared. Asked why he was scared, he replied, "I don't know. Just seeing your own son, and you know, how are you going to deal with it if you can't help yourself but to, you know, be around him." Allen describes also having been struck by his beauty. He and Jan then discussed his health and family medical histories. Allen recalls that he had prayed for Donny's health throughout Jan's pregnancy, a worry because he himself "could have been classified as an alcoholic at that time" and he also used pot and cocaine "a little bit." He had previously used LSD and mushrooms. His praying in this fashion is another indicator that Allen was in one sense realizing his procreative consciousness even during the prenatal period.

Based on Allen's account, he has a unique procreative identity in that he is aware that he is Donny's biological father. It appears, however, that only Jan provides him any feedback to confirm this clandestine identity. Accordingly, Allen has a rudimentary sense of being a biological father, but his awareness of that identity is not directly fostered by Donny's treating him as his father. From a sociological perspective, then, he is merely a friend of the family, not a dad.

This set of circumstances was reinforced some time later when Allen dated Jan after she split with her first husband, Norman. Jan wanted Allen to become part of the family but he was reluctant: "I still wasn't in love with her. . . . Still wasn't ready to settle down." He did say he loved his son, "a beautiful little child," and that Jan was a great mother. During their dating period Allen spent time with Donny: "[H]e really liked me and . . . [was] totally attached to me." After the pair broke up he talked to Donny on the phone occasionally and was extremely moved when Donny said, "I love you Allen." At the time of the interview, Allen had not seen his son for a few years but said he is attached to him, wants to be his friend, and would like to see him, yet has trouble reconciling his desire with the possible consequences of an ongoing relationship. In his words: "But the reality of it is, he knows somebody else is his dad. . . . I don't want him . . . questioning who his dad is. I don't know how he would figure it out, but you never know. Kids are smart."

After the divorce and oblivious to his nongenetic relationship to Donny, Norman has continued child support payments to Jan for Donny. Allen told Jan she could call if she ever needed anything, and he sent some insurance money when asked. The transaction was complicated by the fact that Allen's mother was the middleman; Allen kept the funds secret from his current live-in-partner, Barbara, who pressed him to have a DNA test. The request angered and perplexed Allen: "I said, 'Why do you want to do that? Then the court's gonna get involved and it's going to break his father's heart.'"

Allen has also dealt with paternity issues with Barbara, "a trophy girl," with whom he fell in love on one of his extended cross-country journeys. He soon became aware that she was "spoiled" and self-centered: "I had lots of signs, but I didn't want to read 'em cause I just fell in love with this girl and I couldn't help it. Maybe 'cause she was so beautiful [physically] to me, anyway, still is." Allen also found out that she was hooked on prescription medication and was getting worse. He continued to see her off and on and wanted to be with her in spite of her assertion, "I don't want to see you no more." Her smile made him "the happiest guy in the whole world," yet because of her pain and because she was "walking around like a zombie," she "broke [my] heart." While in drug rehab, she reinitiated the relationship but nothing came of it until, still in love, he returned to the West Coast some time later and found her "hooked on crack." "I just wanted to help her," he declares. However, Barbara, was not ready for help and refused his invitations to travel with him while he worked.

Allen believed that Barbara would end up dead or be a lifelong drug addict, so he "was actually hoping that she would get pregnant. I said maybe if she gets pregnant and has a baby, she'll straighten her shit out. . . . I didn't intentionally try to get her pregnant. I asked her, 'Are you on birth control?' We were not safe with sex at all. She said she was on birth control."

Allen returned to the East Coast, and a few months later Barbara called to tell him that she had married but was separated. "It kind of broke my heart hearing that she was married because I always had plans. I had envisioned our wedding." After a few months passed, she called again to tell him that she was pregnant. He immediately asked if the baby were his and tried to figure out the chronology involved, thinking he might be the father and hoping that was the case. He was concerned because she had continued with drugs until she realized she was pregnant. Inspired largely by his feelings for her, he and Barbara reunited when she was six months pregnant. His aim was "to be her friend and help her through her pregnancy." "She did not want to get into a close-knit relationship because she knew that it might not have been my baby." They moved into an apartment; he paid half their bills; and he accompanied her to prenatal-care appointments.

As Allen tells the story, when Barbara went to the hospital to give birth, she was "snappy" and "mean" and caused "hurt feelings" by not inviting him into the labor room with her parents and sister, even though both the family and he were hoping the baby was his. When "little Ricky was born,"

> I went in the room and the nurse let me hold him. And I looked at him and he's this beautiful baby. He had dark—he was white at first you know, kind of pruney-looking, but, in Barbara's mind, what I found out, and her parents', they're like, "This might not be Allen's baby." . . . I gave him his first bath like dads do in the hospital . . . I knew that he might not be [mine], but I looked at him and swore that he was because he had those toes, little crooked toes, like everyone in my family has. I thought that

might've been a for-sure mark, but a lot of babies could maybe have those toes, that are kind of folded up a little bit. [During his bath] "his skin looked to me really dark-complected, dark hair. He looked like a little Sicilian baby, like I remember my brothers and sisters looking. . . . And I said, "Man he's mine." You know, that's great. The possibility was still there that it wasn't. I didn't, at that point, even see a reason to do a DNA test . . . you know, look at him.

Allen's search for physical cues to compensate for his inability to presume paternity with confidence attests to his strong desire to bond with the baby. Soon thereafter, however, Allen acknowledged that "babies change so quickly" and that maybe he could not be sure Ricky was his child.

Largely because Barbara "wanted peace of mind," they requested a DNA test when the baby was a few months old. Allen didn't care and knew that Barbara did not trust him. "I don't know what she thought. Maybe she thought I'd leave if I found out. I made it clear to her. I said, 'Barbara, even if he's not my baby, it won't matter. I love you, and I love him to death.'" Nevertheless, he was saddened one day as he was holding Ricky, when Barbara told him that the DNA test was negative. "I started to cry a little bit cause it kind of hurt. . . . I said, 'You know I cried because I was hoping so bad that he would be my baby.'" He asked how she felt, and she admitted she was thinking he would leave as soon as he heard the result. He said, "Barbara, I love Ricky no matter what." Allen acknowledged that he was sad but in the interview comments, "It was just an emotional time. . . . I got over it the same day." Barbara's family praised him: "'Man, you're a bigger man than we all thought you were.'" To this Allen replied, "It ain't about being a big man, it's I love him, and that's the bottom line . . . it doesn't matter to me that he is somebody else's. Every baby deserves a father. . . . I've got a choice to do what I'm gonna do and I did it out of pure love."

When we look at Allen's latest fertility experience, it appears that his physical attraction and "rescue" orientation toward Barbara affected his level of attachment to "his" prenatal and postnatal child. In some ways, this reflects the "package deal" arrangement many men employ toward their children and a romantic partner.[13] It occurs when men's bonds with their children are sustained or severed dependent upon their level of attachment to the mother of the children. When men love and are involved with a woman they are more likely to embrace their children; when love and involvement wane, they too often distance themselves from their kids.

We also see that Barbara played an active role in altering Allen's biologically based procreative identity by encouraging the DNA test. Allen was content in accepting Ricky as his own child even though he had reason to doubt biological paternity. However, contrary to what happened with Allen's "biological" son, Donny, Allen was not successful in dissuading Barbara from insisting on a DNA test to clarify his paternity status relative to Ricky.

At present, Allen, who believes that he has gotten two women pregnant and is fearful of AIDS, says he wore a condom with Barbara every time they had intercourse after she had her baby:

> The whole time after her pregnancy [with another man] we wore condoms during sex, the whole time. And I will from here on out for the rest of my life until I'm ready to have another baby, mainly because of AIDS. And unless I know it's the right girl, and I do want to have another child later. You know, I got used to wearing condoms. Used to be it's like, they suck. . . . But it's something you do.

Allen's unusual story portrays how his knowledge of his procreative abilities evolved over time. From it, we also learn how the knowledge led to behavior that might not make sense to many people but, when understood in context, reveal a certain clarity or integrity of thought. Allen's knowledge is broad; he has had a range of experiences that have yielded firsthand knowledge. His experiences have taught him to presume that he is fertile; he now assumes that he can procreate even though no DNA test has confirmed this. He has also become more attentive to managing his procreative ability; he now uses condoms regularly. Allen's emotional narrative that depicted both his voluntary relinquishment of his biological child for the child's own good and his turbulent relationship with Barbara and her (his) child, exemplify that men's procreative experiences can be emotionally laden.

Allen feels strongly about children; he loves and wants them, biological or nonbiological. Coming from a family of ten helped him to "always get along with girlfriends' children." He describes some situations in which he missed the kids more than the partners when a relationship broke up. We can see his love for children in his being moved by the beauty of his biological and his nonbiological sons. Allen euphorically participated in the postnatal minutes and was excited by his biological son's expression of love for him. He was intimately involved in the birth of his nonbiological son, beginning in the delivery room, where he gave the baby his first bath. This involvement extended to his being a major caregiver during the infant's first few months. These experiences were critical to the heightening of Allen's procreative awareness. Allen searched for physical characteristics that reminded him of his family (crooked toes, Sicilian coloring) and, unlike many others, he delighted in the daily, though limited, care of a child. Perhaps it is his valuing of children and awareness of his emotionally laden experiences in that realm that led him to change his ways and commit himself to using protection.

Allen's narrative also helps our understanding of the temporal dimension of procreative consciousness. Initially, when Allen was younger, he seemed to be conscious only after a procreative event, an abortion or a pregnancy. Over time as he acquired procreative experiences, the consciousness became more global and enduring. Allen now attends to his procreative consciousness on a daily basis and believes in the importance of protection. He has both a retrospective and prospective consciousness, which means that aspects of his procreative identity have changed and are subject to further change.

Several key events in Allen's sexual and procreative life hint at the need to examine closely how and why men's subjective and experiential worlds change in the procreative realm. Embedded within Allen's personal stories about paternity and fatherhood issues was his turning point experience involving the baby he had with Barbara. According to his account, the pregnancy and subsequent birth influenced his awareness of his procreative ability and his diligent use of condoms. Other participants reported as well on how procreative experiences prompted them to change in particular ways. Likewise, diverse events led some participants to alter aspects of their procreative identity, their views about procreative issues, and their fertility-related behaviors. These types of changes speak directly to the dynamic nature of men's subjective lives as persons capable of creating human life. Given the importance of understanding how men transform themselves during their teenage and young-adult years, a systematic analysis is needed of how they undergo changes in the procreative realm.

4

Turning Points in Identity

For a variety of reasons, adolescence and young adulthood are dynamic, often turbulent times for boys and young men.[1] During these years males often experience life events that help them gain new insights into themselves, relationships, and other aspects of life. Because they are discovering their sexuality and becoming aware of their procreative potential, and in many instances are realizing this potential, sexual and procreative experiences are often central to their changing lives. These patterns call for an expansion of the discussion begun in chapter 3. We now look at the processes by which young single men undergo meaningful shifts in the way they think, feel, and act with respect to the procreative realm. Some of the shifts are tied to early paternity experiences.

As mentioned in chapter 1, we use the sensitizing concept of turning point[2] to guide our analysis of how young men's procreative identities evolve. We emphasize the fluid and subjective nature of men's procreative consciousness and identity while highlighting how the gendered nature of the procreative realm affects men's transitions.[3]

The insights we generate help us to understand and classify the types of procreative and nonprocreative events young men identify as significant turning points that relate to their potential to impregnate, procreate, or become social fathers. We extract key themes from the narratives of the men in our study that speak to how they changed as they reacted to diverse events such as military enrollment, a born-again religious experience, a baby's baptism, and a father's death. Likewise, we consider fertility-related and fathering experiences that deal with issues involving pregnancy scares, pregnancies, abortions, miscarriages, live births, and biological and stepfathering. Focusing on a range of procreative experiences rather than on, say, only abortion or paternity, provides us with an opportunity to explore turning points within the broad context of men's sexual/procreative careers and consider how some men may relate one experience to another. When the participants talk about why they did not perceive certain events as turning points, they furnish negative examples that add to our analysis as well. This approach—one that incorporates examples of distinctive turning points as well as negative illustrations—enables us to deepen and expand our understanding of the types of processes that prompt a critical shift in their procreative and paternal identities—or hinder them from it. Our primary interest is in how the men changed in consequential ways. But we are also concerned with the ways in which they changed gradually or subtly, as well as instances where they felt they did not change at all.

Finally, we explore the effect of various contextual factors on whether men experience and acknowledge specific turning points.[4] Although different men may have similar procreative experiences, not all perceive them as turning points. Similarly, various men may have comparable nonprocreative experiences but they lead to procreative turning points for only some men. Men's personal, social, and cultural resources can affect how receptive they are to changing in particular ways. Thus, in addition to identifying the types of turning points men experience relevant to the procreative realm, we strive to understand why some men and not others experience particular types of turning points and what types of consequences these turning points have for men's lives.

Personal Change and Types of Turning Points

The personal changes young men experience during their adolescent years and throughout their twenties occur in numerous ways and touch various aspects of their lives. For our purposes, we primarily seek to understand the types of experiences that make a significant difference in shaping their procreative identities. Accordingly, we explore how men define these experiences and look at how they affect their lives.

Recall the brief description of turning points in chapter 1. They are instrumental transitional moments in men's lives when men come to see themselves in a new light or to adopt a significantly different perspective on some aspect of life. In one sense, this new light or perspective enables them to evolve, to become different persons. For some, this may represent a radical departure from their former selves; for others, the change may not be dramatic but is significant nonetheless.

As we examine the events that mark these key transitional experiences, we are attentive to the slow, gradual process whereby the self is modified because individuals present a certain identity frequently enough over time. This process has been labeled ossification.[5] It is relevant to our analysis of the participants' accounts of how they have changed with the passage of years and the possible relationship between situated and more global expressions of procreative consciousness or identity. Instances in which they underwent slow, gradual change may provide a useful contrast to transitional processes that incorporate a more distinctive turning point. By studying these issues we can flesh out the parameters of the turning point concept as it applies to men's procreative and paternal consciousness. We can ask, for example, what distinguishes turning point experiences from less dramatic experiences that incorporate change, and what differentiates among turning point experiences?

Theorist Anselm Strauss, developed a typology of turning points,[6] and we kept it in mind in reading the participants' narratives. Some of his types were not relevant to the accounts, but variations of five of them provided us with a starting point for exploring processes associated with change having to do with the procreative realm.

The first turning point, *milestone*, represents an incident that hammers home a message to men that they have experienced some type of change and developed a new perspective. It enables them to see that they are in another place in life and have different ideas. They recognize that their shift in identity is marked by this experience. The shift may be due to acknowledgment by the men that they have achieved a goal or acquired a new status. Or perhaps the incident crept up on them, alerting them that something is not as it was, even though they may not have been fully aware that a transformation was under way.

Second, sometimes men are exposed to an alternative way of seeing or assessing personal changes. Other folks often come into play here by foretelling what is likely to happen and may even provide a vocabulary to make sense of it. Their input may or may not be accepted, but it is often remembered in some form. This approach is referred to as *forecasting*.

Third, there are occasions when men engage in a *ceremonial announcement* whereby they make a public proclamation or are acknowledged for acquiring a role in an institutional setting. There may also be occasions when men make a private avowal to friends or others. By declaring that they believe this or that (e.g., identifying themselves as pro-life), or plan to pursue a particular line of action (e.g., wanting to father a child), their statements signal a significant alteration in direction and focus.

Fourth, men engage in *experimental role dramas* in which they handle a strange but important role. These situations typically occur when men perform roles that they and perhaps others have believed were beyond their grasp. Their self-appraisals often take into account others' assessments and their own appraisals of others' performances in similar roles. In most cases of this type of turning point, men are somewhat surprised that they have been able to "pull off" the performance. They may have even viewed the role with disdain and suspicion. Now, with the turning point experience under their belt, they begin to realize that the role is within their repertoire and may even begin to see it more positively. They begin to recognize that they had this potential even though they did not recognize it.

The role performances just described refer to situations in which men successfully perform particular roles, but they may also experience this type of turning point when they perceive themselves as being inept in certain roles. Some of the roles may have been ones performed effectively in the past; others may be roles that they have viewed as within their reach. Once men discover that they are not capable of fulfilling a role so as to match some informal or formal standard, they may experience a turning point in identity as they begin to see themselves differently. They may revamp their thinking and accentuate or downplay their self-perceived shortcomings.

Fifth, men can experience one of several basic forms of *betrayal*. One form relevant to our study includes instances when men feel let down by a particular role model. They may or may not know the model personally but have identified closely with and patterned themselves after the model. Another form includes instances when men experience betrayal as rejection felt to be personal. Such instances often occur over time, with multiple incidents along the way, although on some occasions a single event, such as a girlfriend's having sex with someone else, may be viewed as the decisive and in some cases the only impetus for a sense of feeling betrayed.

In our study, these turning-point categories are used in a manner called "emergent fit." This is a strategy for verifying the utility of existing concepts or theories by comparing them with the data.[7] The aim is not to distort or force data but, rather, to assess the application of theoretical concepts to our data. We are interested in concepts that are both analytic and sensitizing. Employing a symbolic interactionist perspective, we work to deepen our understanding of the social psychological processes associated with how the participants identify and experience turning points. We also consider the turning points' dynamic features and the meanings the men attach to them, but we do not attempt to catalogue the relative frequency of particular turning points. Instead, by means of our data, we explore how the processes associated with the selected turning points from Strauss's typology are relevant to procreative issues. We want to enhance our conceptual understanding of turning points, not focus on their social demography.

Previous Research on Transitions

Research on the transition to becoming a prospective father, establishing paternity, assuming responsibilities as a father, or being involved with a partner who has a miscarriage or abortion is relevant to what we want to learn in regard to turning points in men's lives as procreative beings.[8] Unfortunately, little of the research deals with the transitions relevant to our interests here. Much of it has dealt with new fathers' inner worlds. Research on young fathers is particularly apropos to our study of young men because their transitions to fatherhood are also connected to their more general transition from adolescence into adulthood.

Scholars who have talked about transitions to fatherhood have suggested that they sometimes involve a type of "fatherhood click"[9] or "perceptual snap."[10] These concepts highlight the process by which men become invested in their roles as fathers and internalize their commitment to being fathers. The process involves men's developing new ways of thinking about themselves that are connected to their social relationships. How this "snap" occurs varies widely (for example, it might include one clear and significant experience or a series of much smaller, protracted changes over time). When this "snap" occurs memorably and discretely, it may be seen as a type of turning point experience. Some of the changes can take place during a partner's pregnancy or around the time of a child's birth; some, occasionally occur long after the birth. For some men, there may also be differences in whether these changes occur with the firstborn or with subsequent offspring.

Researchers who have worked with the "fatherhood click" notion in particular have suggested that it refers to the "translation of paternal identity into paternal generativity."[11] When it happens, fathers develop a distinct child-rearing philosophy that reflects their commitment to care for and lead the next generation. It is this phase of human development that enables fathers to invest in their children in a way that is more than a responsibility or obligation. It also goes beyond men's basic awareness that they have produced children who are genetically related to them. For men who become fathers during their adolescent years, this kind of generative desire is less likely to emerge because of their stage of socioemotional development. When it does, however, it can accelerate their transition out of adolescence.[12]

Some research has shown how the transitions men (and women) make as new parents are gendered; mothers typically engage in far more mental labor than fathers. One study of twenty-five white couples with newborns is of particular interest because it centers on "parental consciousness . . . how babies fill parent's minds."[13] It does not deal explicitly with parents' self-proclaimed turning points, but the data imply that men may be less likely than women to experience turning points in connection with their parental status, and to view them as less pronounced when they do. Compared to women, they spend less time thinking about their children. Men's transitional experiences as fathers also appear to be mediated more often by their partners than vice versa. Given gendered differences in reproductive physiology, this process begins prenatally and is reinforced postnatally by gendered cultural expectations about family life and gender-biased employment patterns. The "aligning actions" parents use to justify fathers' limited care of their infant children are likely also to hinder fathers from seeing parenting as a turning point experience.[14]

Men's experiences with miscarriage and abortion, though studied less than male involvement in pregnancy and fatherhood, can have profound consequences for some men. Although researchers have studied women's personal thoughts and feelings after having a miscarriage[15] or abortion,[16] much less is known about men who have been involved in either. The Shostak and colleagues study of men and abortion mentioned earlier found that some men's experiences with the aftermath of an abortion altered the way they thought about their procreative potential, contraception, babies, human life, and romantic relationships. For some, then, miscarriage and abortion represented key experiences that affected how they thought about themselves, their partners, and other matters relevant to their daily lives. We know little though about when and why these types of experiences may become turning points that affect the way men perceive themselves as sexual and procreative persons.

Participants' Turning Points

Most of our study's participants could identify turning points or critical junctures that played a significant role in their lives with respect to having sex, procreating, or developing a father identity. We were interested in understanding the men's own sense of these key transitional experiences in their everyday lives prior to the interview, and our interviewing strategy and subsequent interpretation of the data reflect this goal.

We focus primarily on the fertility-related experiences that some men report have altered their procreative identity and more general sense of self, as well as their dating, sexual, and contraceptive attitudes and behavior. In particular, we deal with the young men's pregnancy scares, miscarriage and abortion experiences, pregnancies, births, and experiences as stepfathers. We also show how turning point experiences outside the procreative realm can sometimes affect how men think about procreative issues. As we consider these issues we comment on why some men do not perceive particular experiences as turning points.

Procreative Turning Points

In chapter 3 we showed how discovering their fecundity was a significant experience for some of the participants, although most did not assign much meaning to it. It essentially was a minor turning point for those who were frightened or felt more adult-like when they learned that they could procreate. What more of them found significant was being confronted with some type of pregnancy scare or fertility experience. The personal pregnancy scares encountered, by definition, turned out to be false alarms, but some of the men viewed them as significant events that thereafter colored, to varying degree, how they viewed themselves, the prospect of fatherhood, and their contraceptive habits. As we noted earlier, Marcus recalled that he was forcefully affected by a pregnancy scare when he was 15. His heightened procreative consciousness led him to use two condoms for a time, although he eventually used only one. Joseph declares that his experience with a pregnancy scare directly and immediately changed his contraceptive behavior: "I was like constantly thinking about it [that the partner might be pregnant]. It just messed me up completely . . . I was just nonstop thinking about it. . . . Afterwards we realized it was time to just get on the pill and just alleviate most of the doubt." He tells of "worrying about everything" from parents knowing, to "having an abortion or having a kid." Although they had talked about having an abortion if a pregnancy occurred, he says that "that would just hurt me immensely."

The most typical pattern, though, was for the men to report that the pregnancy scares they encountered did not have a dramatic and lasting impact on their views or actions. In some instances, they were not put off at all by the prospect of a partner's disclosing a possible pregnancy. Philip took his cue from his partner. Her period was late, but he declares, "I wasn't nervous. Because she said that there was no reason to be . . . I guess she knows her body pretty well, and she could tell. Everything felt the same. She said it's happened to her before in the past." Having been told by a previous girlfriend that she might be pregnant by him, Bakka, a 30-year-old native of Ghana who had been residing in the United States for four years, recalls that he quickly forgot about the experience when she later told him that she was not pregnant:

> At that point I just knew anything could happen. I mean, it could end up one day being true that she was pregnant, and sometime I like kinda accept things the way they are, like that's life, girls get pregnant all the time, so if she gets pregnant that's just part of life. . . . I don't think it's something out of the ordinary. If I got a girl pregnant, planned or unplanned, she's still pregnant and that's part of life, I mean, so I take it like that.

Bakka apparently did not perceive the pregnancy scare as a turning point because he possessed a philosophy of life that "things do happen" and sometimes girls/women get pregnant. When men with this philosophy pursue sexual relations, they may insulate themselves from interpreting a partner's late period as a real-life pregnancy scare. It appeared not to be common among the participants, although some did mention or allude to their belief that things often happen for a reason—which suggests that they adhere to a deterministic view of life.

Miscarriages, too, became turning points for several participants. When his fiancée miscarried after a car accident, Tom felt as though he had just lost a child, "[I]t was the worst thing I could ever imagine." He describes the pain he felt watching his partner being wheeled into the operating room two weeks later to have their dead baby "removed from her." Tom blamed her for being in the car with a foster sister known for driving "like a maniac." Tom espouses "different views on pregnancy . . . now"; he will be more selective in choosing a partner and will get to know his partner better before attempting to have another child. "[E]ven before I met her I,

I told myself I wanted to have a kid. And basically I guess I just found a person I could do it with." His reaction to the miscarriage caused him to reevaluate his desire for a child, the time for fatherhood, and how he chooses a partner.

In contrast, Philip's experience with a miscarriage in his late teens was "not a real big deal," not "a huge calamity"; it was more of "a shock" because neither he nor his partner knew she was pregnant until "she went to the bathroom, started bleeding really bad." A doctor diagnosed a miscarriage. "It wasn't to the point where she wasn't even late on her period," both were surprised. Philip criticizes himself in retrospect for his "cold feeling" and "negative attitude" but believed then that "everything happens for a reason" and that "there's not much we can do about it." Had they planned for the baby and if his partner had been further along in her pregnancy, he feels that "it would've been very bad." Philip and his partner went on to have a child together a year later.

Like Philip, Frank learned of both his partner's pregnancy and miscarriage at the same time from a friend of theirs. Although Frank's relationship with Sonya was "strictly physical," he still "felt bad . . . I still would've honored my [responsibility], you know." Reflecting on her silence about this important matter, he ruminates:

[M]aybe she didn't tell me because she wasn't quite sure if it was me or not. I don't know! We're not staying together, she's not coming home to me every night. She might be doin' something with someone else, too. And therefore, she's pregnant, she's not quite sure if it's me or if it's someone else, and God knows I didn't ask her that. And I'm glad, you know, looking in retrospect that probably could have been a possibility. You know what I'm sayin?

Miscarriages in a planned pregnancy or in the context of a loving relationship created the most pain and were more likely to be perceived as turning points. The men who were less involved with a partner and/or unaware of the unplanned pregnancy viewed the miscarriage experience as less troubling and as not affecting their procreative identity.

Although pregnancy scares resolve themselves, usually within a matter of days, and miscarriages are generally viewed as uncontrollable, some of the participants and their partners were confronted with an unplanned pregnancy that necessitated critical decisions. In one of the more dramatic turning point examples, 21-year-old working-class Arthur talks about his cohabiting partner having had a secretive abortion.[17] It not only infuriated him when she disclosed the news to him several weeks after the procedure but represented a highly charged turning point consistent with one variant of betrayal that we described above. Arthur swore that he would never again be involved with his former partner and professes that he would alter the way he pursued future relationships:

> I'm going to be a lot more careful about who I'm with. I think it's going to be a lot longer before I actually have sexual intercourse or anything like that with anybody. It's just going to be right there at the forefront, you know, what if she gets pregnant? What if the condom breaks again, or if you didn't use the foam right?

> I'm gonna start, if I want to get to know somebody a lot better, it's for what they're geared towards, what moral kinds of things they believe in . . . 'cause I'll never, ever date anyone who, any kind of pro-choice support at all. That will pretty much end it right there. I'll never make that mistake twice.

> Oh, I'll definitely ask'em, what are your views on, you know, sit down and have a nice long talk. How do you feel about abortion? If you got pregnant, would you have one? Would you put the child up for adoption, what would you do?

Arthur's experience heightened his consciousness of the gendered nature of the reproductive realm, both physiologically and legally. Even though Arthur reported that he had used condoms faithfully with this partner as well as the two others with whom he had had sex, he apparently had not considered how he might feel if he impregnated a woman and she chose to have an abortion. Consequently, the abortion experience provided Arthur with a novel set of circumstances and affirmed for him that the only way to protect himself in light of current law is to be more selective in choosing partners.

Because young men tend to spend little time thinking about their sexual partners' power to dictate their paternity status should a pregnancy occur, when a woman goes against a man's desire for how a particular pregnancy should be resolved, it often registers as a significant turning point for the man. This can occur when a pregnancy is either ended or brought to term contrary to the man's wishes. We heard of only a few instances of a woman's going against a partner's wishes as to the abortion decision, but some men may not have known that this happened if a partner had a secret abortion. Accurate national data are not available on the percentage of secret abortions, but a significant percentage of women do not tell the coconceiver of a pregnancy. One study of married women in Granite City, Illinois, documented that 10 percent did not tell the partner of their pregnancy and 17 percent did not reveal their decision to have an abortion.[18] We suspect that an even higher percentage of single women are not forthcoming in this regard.

Unlike Arthur, David, a 28-year-old unemployed abortion veteran, had an active role in terminating an unplanned pregnancy. He talks about how his abortion experience with Sarah eight months prior to the interview altered the relationship with her as well as his approach to birth control in subsequent casual sexual encounters. His preabortion relationship with Sarah was "pretty casual" because each had the "freedom to see other people," but David explains that going through the abortion experience made it impossible for both to handle such a casual relationship with the other. He feels that the abortion experience was a "serious situation" that forced both partners to "think about things more" and, consequently, realize that they needed to "either commit to each other, which both of us really didn't want to do, or just like leave each other." David comments that dealing with the abortion has also made him more conscientious about using a condom every time he has intercourse in a casual relationship. He takes this stance even if a new partner(s) is using the pill and asks him not to use a condom. David's experience with his partner and the abortion clearly illustrates the turning point we described as the experimental role drama. It provided an opportunity for him to evaluate his situation first-hand with Sarah and then acknowledge that he was incapable of dealing effectively with a serious relationship.

Arthur's and David's turning point experiences illustrate how others can shape the interactive processes surrounding a key event, thereby contributing to an individual's evolving perspective. In David's case, his view of himself as a single man rather than as someone in a committed relationship was solidified by Sarah when she affirmed for him that she was not ready for a committed relationship with him. David's pregnancy-resolution experience might have been a totally different type of turning point had Sarah responded in one of two ways: not had the abortion, forcing David to make decisions about how he wanted to relate to his child; or become more emotionally vulnerable to David because of the stressful experience. She might have even asked for a committed relationship. In any case, her decisions might have encouraged him to be more receptive to the idea of developing a committed relationship.

The above two abortion veterans describe their experiences with abortion as clear turning points for them. Some of the other participants who are abortion veterans had less dramatic, and in some instances more muddled, perceptions about how their experiences with abortion were related to their subsequent self-perceptions and behavior. One 19-year-old, Jerry, was interviewed about a month after his abortion experience; he says, "[M]aybe I've grown up a little bit, but not really a big change." Similarly, he gives a qualified reply when asked why he and his girlfriend are now taking "a little bit of time off" from their romantic dating relationship: "The pregnancy and abortion, and everything, I don't think directly affected everything, but in some ways I would say, probably. Like, just added on to some of the pressures and stuff."

Jerry's latter comments hint at issues concerning preabortion communication and relationship quality that may be relevant to some turning point experiences. If partners have previously clarified what they would do in case of an unplanned pregnancy and have agreed that abortion is the preferred option (as was the case with Jerry and his girlfriend), then men's reactions to abortion situations may have little influence on their self-perceptions. Indeed, by deciding in advance how a pregnancy will be resolved, men may reduce the anxiety typically associated with the period of time between discovering a pregnancy and aborting it. Minimizing anxiety ahead of time may actually mitigate men's seeing their abortion experience as a turning point. Even though many pregnancies may be unplanned, partners can still have planned for a response. Planning may result in fewer men intensely experiencing their procreative consciousness once they learn that a partner is pregnant. Initially, they may register what the situation means to them, but discussions with the partner are less likely to turn into gut-wrenching deliberation about the available options.

Other factors that may minimize the extent to which an abortion represents a distinctive turning point have to do with the man's degree of certainty as to his responsibility for a pregnancy attributed to him; the time lapse between the abortion and the man's knowledge of it; and his sense of involvement in the abortion decision making. These issues are apparent in Allen's story, presented in chapter 3. A 27-year-old high school dropout, he recalled an experience of about ten years earlier when he was traveling across the country. He had sex with a girl who later told him, on the phone, that she had aborted a pregnancy. When asked in the interview if the abortion has affected his life, he replies that it had not done much to change his perspective or behavior. Allen's story illustrates a type of abortion scenario that includes partners who are not involved in an ongoing relationship. In fact, he and the former partner were no longer seeing each other and were living in different states. Being estranged from the situation, as Allen was, appears to have limited the likelihood that he would walk away with a life-changing lesson. So, although both Arthur (whose story is presented earlier in this chapter) and Allen dealt with partners who disclosed their secret abortions, there may be several reasons that Arthur had a more volatile reaction: he was much more invested in his partner's pregnancy than she was; he confronted her face-to-face about her unilateral, secretive decision to abort; and his antiabortion views appear to have been stronger.

Fathering a child, in the biological and/or social sense can definitely represent a turning point experience for many men. In our sample, several participants commented on seeing a child or a stepchild as an incentive to become more serious about their education and work careers. These experiences can be viewed as *milestones*. When we first interviewed 20-year-old Francisco, whose partner was seven months pregnant, he talked then with his partner about the unplanned pregnancy as a "blessing," commenting, "I would have stopped what I was doing ['party and drink and doin' drugs'], it's just that it would have taken a little longer for me to realize, what's important in life and that I shouldn't take what I have for granted." Francisco reiterates the sentiment in a second interview three months after his daughter's birth, "[I]f ten, twenty years from now I sat down with my daughter and talked to her about how I was before we [his partner and he] got pregnant, I'd say, 'If it weren't for you, I probably wouldn't have finished college.' . . . [Or I] would have gone through a lot more obstacles before I finished." From Francisco's perspective, his daughter's presence in his life continues to shape his self-perception because he now sees himself as a much more responsible and focused individual who cares what others, especially his daughter, think about his work ethic and future professional accomplishments. His comments underscore how he has internalized the gendered norm for men to achieve status through their professional accomplishments and to value others' perceptions about the accomplishments.

In Ricky's case, a 25-year-old participant who had been an informal stepfather when he was 20, his milestone and experimental-role as a parental figure caused him to see himself in a different light. Referring to his experience as a "boost," he recalls: "I started looking at myself as a future parent and I saw that at the time I had nothing to offer, that's when it kinda like opened my eyes to that I gotta get serious in school. So yeah that did help me out a lot. I don't think I would have gotten that serious in school if it wasn't for that kid." Again, as with Francisco, we see that Ricky's commitment to being a competent economic provider plays a prominent role in accentuating his sense of his identity as a father figure.

Nonprocreative Turning Points

Although the thrust of our interviewing strategy was to encourage the participants to focus on their romantic relationships and procreative experiences, several males commented on experiences outside the procreative realm (e.g., military service, religious conversion, christening, father's death, engagement, female acquaintance with HIV) that can act as turning points and affect aspects of their procreative consciousness and identity. David, when reflecting on when he was 18 and thinking about marrying his girlfriend at the time, comments "[B]efore I left [for the service] I was thinkin' about it [having kids], you know. Bein' that I'm in the military, I can be stable, might even be able to have a family, and you know, be secure." The relationship ended prematurely, and once David left the service, he discarded his sentiment about actually establishing a "family-man" identity any time in the immediate future. Asked if he had thought about having a child with any other women, he replies:

> No . . . the thought might have flashed in my mind, but, most of the time, since I got out of the military, it wasn't, like a practical thing to do. You know, I might've thought about it for a second, but . . . I haven't had a lot of money since I got out of the military, so, that's a big damper on the family situation.

Lacking the financial resources necessary to provide for children as men are "expected" to do, David's visions of being a family man were severely thwarted and relegated to his latent consciousness. They may reemerge at some point when his financial situation improves but for now he deems them unrealistic.

Kyle, a 21-year-old devout Christian and one of our more intriguing participants, was enthusiastic about preparing himself to be a family man. Even so, he felt he was not yet developmentally ready to assume the status.

He recalled how his born-again religious experience turned him away from an anticipated life of sexual promiscuity, inspiring him to join the "True Love Waits" program and make a virginity pact until marriage. Being born again and joining the program can be seen as part of a ceremonial announcement, one that involves a public proclamation of sorts. Kyle's most recent romantic relationship has lasted a year, and he and his girlfriend went so far as to prepare a written contract outlining their relationship goals and the physical limitations they wanted to impose on their interaction.

Because Kyle's immersion in his faith has distracted him from thinking about his sexuality, he has not been motivated to think or worry about his procreative abilities either. He has, however, spent a considerable amount of time investigating what it means to be a good Christian husband and father. Using the Bible as a guide, he has worked to develop a personal inventory of the character qualities he believes he needs to acquire to fulfill the roles of husband and father. In Kyle's rather unique case, the roles seem to have been all but completely disengaged from any notion of a sexual or procreative self. His vows regarding premarital sex and his efforts to develop his spiritual capital as a Christian father can be looked upon as part of an institutionalized context with its own set of norms.

Though uncommon, Kyle's case suggests that young men are capable of putting a great deal of thought into their future responsibilities as fathers before they become fathers. In Kyle's words, the Bible is important because he believes he

need[s] to know what a husband and father needs to be and start working towards that. As I started realizing the character qualities that need to be there, and I realize I'm not anywhere near that and how much work is gonna need to be done on myself to prepare myself for that, the list keeps on getting longer and, you know, I'm tackling them one at a time or whatever ones I can handle at each moment, but I think by just having them in my thoughts, maybe it's just like a physical maturing now, when you're only twenty-one maybe some of these things come as I get older. But that's the way I can determine that—I want to be a good husband I want to be a father—I don't have any concept of what a husband or a good father is, but the Bible does. And it's all right there. So if I find it, and I find 'em, I mean, it's all over the place. I have notes of character qualities and then verse after verse that talks about it. Some of them are very difficult, you want to be, I need to be that? I need to be whatever, and, like, that's not easy. That's just not me, but it's clear, you know, there it is, so. Some things are easy, like, oh, yeah, that's no problem, you know, not giving too much wine. I don't drink. There I go, I got, I got one out of the way.

Another turning point fostered by an institutionalized context came when 25-year-old Harvey, accepted a brother's invitation to be the godfather of the brother's second child. Harvey remarked that the christening experience (a form of ceremonial announcement) prompted him to realize that he wanted to be a father too. Although the shift in perspective was technically not a procreative experience, it did deal directly with a related process. Reflecting on the christening, Harvey recalls when he initially recognized his desire to be a father:

> when I got to hold him [my godson] for the very first time, and pick him up and go, "This is my godson!" . . . looking in his eyes and seeing part of my brother and seeing part of his mother, a part of MY mother. It was that link. It's one thing to hold a baby and have a connection, but I hate to say this, but there is something to the genetic link. This is [the] same stuff that made me, made this child.

Harvey goes on to add that after the christening, he was less comfortable with where he was in terms of his lifestyle, which he describes as "living with three guys in an apartment that was smoke-filled, parties all weekend, and go to work hung over, just bachelor life." In his words, the christening "gave me a drive to better myself" and "gave me a perspective other than myself."

Andy, a well-educated 30-year-old participant, also talked about developing a perspective that stretched beyond himself and accentuated his desire to be a father. He refocused his perspective after his seemingly healthy 50-year-old father fell ill with an inoperable brain tumor and died within nine months. The death was a grievous life-course milestone for Andy, 28 at the time. In particular, it was memories of the "special father-son bond" that led him to adopt a more future-oriented outlook, replete with thoughts of long-term commitment, marriage, and fatherhood. Reflecting on his newfound appreciation for strong human connections, a type of self-generated forecasting, Andy comments, "I saw how important it was, and I realized that I didn't have it with anyone else, and he was going to die." He adds, "I wanted to have a son to replicate in many ways or replace the kind of relationship I had with my father, but instead of bottom up, it would be top down, generationally." Andy's desire for a child, a son in particular, was accentuated by his concerns about growing old without having someone to reciprocate the care for him that he had provided for his own father during the final months of his life. In sum, his hands-on caring for his sick father, losing him at an early age, and seeing the value of their committed relationship, Andy learned to become more vulnerable to his girlfriend at the time. They made arrangements to marry and have a child within the subsequent year.

Engagement, a ceremonial announcement, served as a nonprocreative turning point for Jack, a 21-year-old who was planning to marry in the summer. With his impending marriage came visions of fatherhood. Jack, who had experienced some pregnancy scares, noted that the engagement had essentially relieved him of the worry of impregnating his partner. Although he still did not feel financially ready for a child, he felt less frightened about the possibility, and even envisioned having children with his wife-to-be.

A 21-year-old college student, Paul, experienced an abrupt turning point when he learned with horror that Mary, "a really hot girl" at his university, was HIV-positive. She was the roommate of Paul's roommate's girlfriend. In the interview Paul links his awareness of her HIV status to his use of condoms, "Now I use [them] always." Paul appeared amazed that she "is HIV-positive and she's beautiful. . . . I never thought about it like this . . . it just goes to show that like looks in life aren't everything always because, like you could be a looker, you know, but like how far does that really get you?" He continues, "I'm petrified of the virus," and because of his fear, "I'm just not as sexually active as I could be." Knowing Mary, "makes me just not think that you don't have the virus . . . like you'll look at this girl and you'll be like, hmm, she doesn't have the virus and the next thing you know." Paul realized that appearances are deceiving, so he has to take control and always be careful. Recently, he has translated that prudence into abstinence, a dramatic change from his previous lifestyle, which emphasized recreational sex. Paul does not speak directly to how this experience has influenced his procreative identity, but his decisions first to use condoms and now to be abstinent have affected the likelihood that he will impregnate someone.

The above six examples represent the most prominent types of nonprocreative turning points that the men in our sample reported. Each example highlights how men's procreative identities are embedded within a complex web of life experience. Although we were able to locate several examples of nonprocreative turning points, we suspect that there are a variety of experiences that affect men's orientation toward procreative issues.[19]

Properties and Context of Turning Points

Now that we have identified some of the key turning points that the participants reported, we can direct our attention to a number of properties that distinguish their unique features. By identifying the properties, we are able to shed light on the conceptual complexity associated with turning point experiences relevant to men's procreative identities. The properties are treated as additional sensitizing concepts that involve aspects of the turning point event, as well as its consequences for men's subjective experiences and behavior. In other words, we use the properties as provisional, heuristic tools that suggest innovative ways to think about turning points and procreative identity issues.

The previous discussion was organized around one fundamental property that differentiates turning points: their procreative or nonprocreative nature. Some are based on a change that directly involves some type of procreative experience. Others index aspects of life not directly related to procreation but that affect men's procreative identities. Now, we draw selectively upon the types of turning point experiences we mentioned previously to illustrate additional properties, including (1) *degree of control*, (2) *duration*, (3) *presence of subjective and/or behavioral changes*, (4) *individual or shared experience*, (5) *vicarious or personal experience* (6) *type and degree of institutional context*, (7) *centrality*, and (8) *emotional response and evaluation*. When experienced as part of men's everyday lives, these properties are often interrelated and overlap. Although this makes it more difficult at times to treat the properties as wholly unique, we briefly point out why studying the nuances of the issues at hand should account for how the properties are interrelated. The participants' stories offer us opportunities to clarify our points by using their words. We are occasionally forced, however, to reach beyond the data and speculate on how the properties might be used to enhance our grasp of men's inner worlds in the procreative realm.

As we introduce the properties, bear in mind that the symbolic meanings associated with men's subjective experiences are social constructions that emerge within a value-laden social and cultural context. So although the subjective experiences involving turning points are by definition personal, they are embedded within and shaped by a larger context. Men's inclination to judge personal experiences in specific ways, that is, to see them as turning points that affect their sense of identity and perspective, is likely to be affected by their willingness to embrace certain types of broader social and cultural messages. The gendered nature of the reproductive realm, in concert with perceptions about gender relations, may also influence whether men perceive certain events as turning points in their lives. Because men are largely detached from the physiological aspects of reproduction, it is reasonable to suspect that particular events for many may not be included in what Alfred Schutz refers to as their relevance structures—the set of circumstances or symbols that alert a person to view an aspect of reality in a particular fashion.[20] Likewise, men's perceptions about procreative and parenting issues may be filtered at times through a gender lens that frames individuals' explicit and implicit understanding of parenting expectations.[21] Taken together, these considerations draw attention to the contextual factors that can influence men's subjective experiences.

Degree of Control

Turning point events and their consequences for men (and others) can unfold in a variety of ways. For instance, these experiences vary widely in the degree to which men are able to plan and control them. The process by which turning points occur covers both the extent to which men control the onset and evolution of the event itself, as well as the consequential impact it has on individuals' lives. Men may or may not believe they have much control over the onset of an event (e.g., a pregnancy scare, pregnancy, job loss, a father's death), but sometimes they can shape the way the event unfolds once begun. This is much less likely to be the case, though, for short-lived and discrete events. Whereas men may spend considerable time planning and anticipating certain events that later turn out to be turning points, such as the conception and birth of a child, other turning point experiences like miscarriages occur unexpectedly. The experience may end in a matter of minutes; its consequences may linger for years. Turning points of this type are largely beyond men's ability to plan and control. Having had previous experience with a miscarriage, especially with the same partner, may alert men to pay attention for indicators that signal problems. However, men in these situations are still not in a position to control the process. Even if they have learned certain things that enable them to minimize the chances that a miscarriage might happen, its occurrence is outside their domain of control.

Men may also have the means to control some or all of the ways a particular turning point experience continues to affect people's thoughts, feelings, and behavior. For example, although Francisco initially was not particularly excited about his partner's unplanned pregnancy, he embraced the idea of becoming a father as the pregnancy progressed. He eventually began to redirect his partying energies into being a more responsible student, and then into being an attentive new father as well. Likewise, David's abortion experience, "a serious situation," helped him decide with his partner to dissolve the relationship and, on his own, to be far more careful in his future sexual activities. Upon considerable soul searching, David took control of the aftermath of a painful event.

Because our sampling design did not include married men, it is not surprising that most of the procreative turning points we heard about provided the participants with little or no control and were very often unplanned. Although most were unplanned, some of the events and the consequences associated with the experiences were less of a surprise than others. For instance, some of the men had anticipated prior to a partner's pregnancy that they would be frustrated and anxious if she were to become pregnant. The unplanned experiences were sometimes perceived in a less than favorable light, at least initially. The men often assigned new meaning to their experiences, though, and began to emphasize their positive aspects later on, as was the case with Francisco.

Duration

The degree of control men have over their turning point experiences is sometimes closely related to their duration. Some turning points occur quite quickly and engender immediate consequences. Others present themselves not so much as specific moments but more in the form of unfolding processes that can be interpreted in different ways over time. As the participants look back on their lives, they may mentally collapse their turning point experience into one general category of experience, alluding to it as a "relationship breakup," a "pregnancy scare," or a "childbirth resulting from an unplanned pregnancy." But this shorthand referencing of an experience as a turning point can downplay the nature and value of the process that significantly changes men's procreative identities. There may be a variety of identifiable moments, issues, conflicts, ideas, discussions, and other aspects of interaction that are a part of the larger process that comes to be referred to as the turning point experience.

The duration property can also be useful when considering the consequences of turning points. How long do the consequences associated with particular turning points continue to affect people's lives? For 21-year-old Stewart, his experience with a notable pregnancy scare supposedly brought on by his partner's poor diet, prompted him to abstain from sex for a considerable period. As he says, "[M]y sex life kinda slowed down for a while after I hear about that. . . . [H]eld off for like a long time, probably about six months to another year . . . pretty much a decision on my part. . . . I just wanted to make sure she was the one [someone he loved]." Stewart eventually did resume having sexual intercourse with the same girlfriend, but his lengthy celibacy suggests that the pregnancy scare affected him intensely. It represented a turning point for him. As we saw in our previous discussion, not all the men experienced lasting, dramatic changes when they encountered a turning point. Several were affected in significant ways by pregnancy scares, but their diligence in altering their condom use lasted for a much shorter period.

Duration issues also come into play when considering how men sometimes periodically use a turning point experience as a motivational reference point. Some men keep important experiences, and the feelings they associate with them, in the back of their minds—ready to call upon whenever they feel they need direction and guidance. At one extreme, men regularly bring into their wideawake consciousness particular experiences that left an imprint on them. They may even mull over these experiences while they remember the associated good and bad consequences, a practice that reinforces men's new identity and perspective.

Antoine's painful experience more than three years ago remains with him today, affecting his daily choices and long-term dreams. When Antoine was 16 years old, he impregnated his 16-year-old girlfriend. He learned that she had been pregnant when she told him she had had an abortion two months later. Previously, they had discussed that she might be pregnant due to a "bust" condom, but "she told me [the results of a pregnancy test] were negative when later I found out that they were positive." In their conversations about the possible pregnancy, they predicted that her parents "would have flipped out" and that the baby would be a "danger . . . to her body . . . because she's very petite." They believed that having a baby would dictate a move, prolong high school, and ensure an uncertain future. These prospects troubled both because "she had a promising future and, I thought I was going somewhere." Upon discovering the pregnancy the girl's parents isolated her from Antoine: "no contact, taking her car, her phone." Some months later she confessed to the abortion and even later, "after everything died down," they became a couple again. Antoine viewed this as "a new beginning." Over time, they revisited their experience, playing out various scenarios in their minds that involved their education and the baby.

Today when Antoine "is in deep thought," he still thinks about the complexities and possibilities of the situation, the "what ifs." He fantasizes the child that could have been; he laments that he never had a father. "I always said I'd never want my child to go without a father." Antoine feels strongly that now "if I was to get someone pregnant, we'd keep it, you know, even though I'm not where I would want to be at financially . . . I'd go ahead and take care of the child." Since his abortion experience, his feelings have changed. He realizes that he cannot be certain now about what he would have done then, had he had a degree of control, but he does know he would keep the child. Antoine has become a strong advocate of protection; he and his partner use birth control pills and condoms. He also wants to be married before he becomes a father. When men like Stewart and Antoine use a turning point as a springboard for thought and action, the experiences may intermittently find their way into the men's inner worlds as the years come and go.

In other instances the meaning of a turning point experience may be woven in a subtle way into men's fresh perspectives of themselves and aspects of life. When this happens, the experience becomes invisible and men may seldom fully appreciate its significance because they do not actively think about it. In other words, a turning point experience can change men's sense of identity and perspective fundamentally without men's reflecting on the experience directly. Here, the turning point, though present and significant in impact, remains hidden from men's everyday conscious awareness. It may be no less significant but simply different from an experience that is referenced directly.

Presence of Subjective and/or Behavioral Changes

Turning point experiences can bring about subjective as well as behavioral changes, each of which may be associated with significant consequences. Many of the turning points the participants experienced produced a shift in how they perceived themselves (or relevant situations), as well as how they behaved. In a few instances, though, the men talked about their turning point experiences only in terms of how the experiences changed the way they perceived themselves and situations.

Gilbert, a 20-year-old, was profoundly changed after an abortion experience when he was 14 and his partner was 20. He learned of the abortion only after the fact. In describing the experience, "[I]t hurt me more than any damn thing," he acknowledges his love for the woman, his desire to have children with her, and his naivete and or/ignorance concerning paternal responsibility. He reevaluates his ideas about the woman who would be suitable for him: "That really made me think about the type of woman I want to be with. And she sure enough wasn't the type of woman. . . . [The] type of woman I want to be with is the type that would be open with me. Be honest—that will discuss things with me and she didn't." Gilbert believes that he had been honest and forthcoming with her, sharing his most intimate secrets: "Shit like, [I] told [her] about a kid I killed in a drive-by." Revelations such as this from his days as a drug dealer led him to expect her to be as open. That she was not "makes me feel like I'm less a man, knowing that she was afraid to talk to me. I don't know what I did to make her feel that way though." Gilbert does not mention any specific behavioral changes that resulted from this noteworthy experience, only that he had revised his thinking about the important qualities in a woman and in a relationship. In fact, Gilbert went on to impregnate a 15-year-old girl during a one-night stand when he was 17. Both were drunk. Gilbert loves her, his daughter, and being a father, although his time in prison has prevented him from being present much of the time.

Turning points that lead to a change in outlook and behavior are likely to have the greatest impact on men's and others' lives. Experiences can begin to resemble turning points because they encourage men to pose fundamentally different questions and interpret their reality through a new lens. Though a change in attitude may be useful, attitudinal changes by themselves do little to affect men's lives. Behavior ultimately influences men's and others' lives.

The primary behavioral change the participants talked about that affected their actions in the procreative realm was being more conscientious about using condoms after a pregnancy scare or an unplanned conception. As we have mentioned, however, these events served as turning points for only a small number of men.

It was much more common for the men to talk about how procreative experiences led to behavioral changes. Francisco, for example, discussed both when his partner was pregnant and then, after his daughter was born, that he was partying much less and taking his education more seriously. Attending classes and completing assignments took on new meaning for Francisco as he sought to prepare himself to be a conscientious family man and breadwinner. The behavioral changes were accompanied by a gradual shift in the way he thought about himself. We learned earlier that he was still in the process of growing accustomed to thinking of himself as a father, though he did see himself in this light much of the time. Part of the transformation included his evolving view of himself as a more responsible adult looking toward the future.

Paul's situation is somewhat different from Francisco's although he, too, executed behavioral changes as a result of his turning points. Hurt and fear propelled him to withdraw from close relationships and recreational sex. His beliefs about sex and relationships have also changed. Paul voices having experienced a radical shift in thinking and behavior after two turning point events: being betrayed by a longtime girlfriend and, as discussed earlier, learning that a beautiful co-ed, a friend of a friend, was HIV-positive. Sex has all of a sudden become "a very serious thing" for Paul, and his new perspective suggests a dramatic departure from the focus of co-ed life at college. He describes relationships there as "at this stage of your life it's all sex orientated and everybody's, you know, there's no way to get around that." He also volunteers that he has had sex with about fifteen young women over the seven-year period since he was 14. More recently, however, Paul admits to not liking a girl "anymore after she like slept over at my house." Conceding that "I guess I might be weird," he doesn't "wanta have sex with anyone that I don't wanta like . . . marry . . . I don't think most guys my age are like that." Paul essentially wants to re-create his family of origin. He wants his wife's parents not to be divorced, his wife to be like his mother: "See, my mother's like a diamond, you know what I mean. Like she doesn't drink and she doesn't smoke and she just like drinks coffee sometimes. . . . And I think it would be a lot easier [for him] for a person [his wife-to-be] to have those morals."

Individual or Shared Experience

Some of the participants experienced their turning points largely on their own, altering their perspective through self-reflection. Some tended to work through their turning points with the help of others, typically a partner who herself was involved in the process.

One 20-year-old, Barney, mentions how his perspective on relationships changed once he had a serious talk with a girlfriend after having sex. He began to imagine that "I could possibly be with this girl for the rest of my life, and I mean after we had sex and we talked about maybe possibly having kids or having a family or getting married that that was probably a turning point where I realized that I could maybe be with this girl for the rest of my life." Although he only had a few hypothetical, casual discussions with this girlfriend about his becoming a father, Barney realized that the prospects of being with this one girl for the rest of his life "scared" him because he was so young. Even though Barney does not explicitly say so, thoughts of becoming a family man with kids appear to have accentuated his fears about being with the same woman indefinitely. In one sense, then, the initial phase of Barney's individual turning point experience was facilitated by his having a discussion with his girlfriend. Although Barney's interview does not reveal that his girlfriend had a similar reaction, the impetus for his change in perspective incorporated his experiences with her.

Tom and his partner experienced a shared turning point after his partner miscarried their child due to a car accident, a child they both wanted. The miscarriage appeared to be a turning point for both, but they responded to it differently. His partner chose to exit the relationship because she believed that they were too young to consider marriage; Tom decided to be more selective in his choice of women and to emphasize good communication in his relationships.

Vicarious or Personal Experience

Seeing friends or acquaintances deal with particular situations affected men in some instances. Witnessing other young people struggling to deal with the consequences of a pregnancy scare, a miscarriage, or an unplanned pregnancy is one type of experience, a vicarious experience. Cal's friend's miscarriage served as a cautionary tale for Cal. At 15 years of age he vicariously experienced the pain of miscarriage with a 15-year-old friend, who became pregnant the first time she had sex. They hung out together, confided in each other, and discussed options for the pregnancy, including abortion. At two months pregnant, she miscarried. The experience prompted Cal's increased sexual caution, and he reflects on it: "You know like when you just get into that kind of situation [where sex is possible] you kind of tell her to back off a little bit you know. Slow down." Now 16, Cal has not had sex since this situation and says he is "saving myself I guess—secondhand virgin . . . just live without it until you get married."

Cal and a few others describe vicarious experiences that linger in their memories, but it was the men's own experiences that affected them the most. It is one thing to learn indirectly about someone's having a miscarriage or abortion; quite another to be confronted directly with the difficult decisions, emotional turmoil, and psychological anguish that are often associated with a "crisis" experience. A similar pattern distinguishing the power of vicarious versus personal events is likely to exist for pregnancy and birth circumstances that are greeted with welcomed anticipation and joy.

Type and Degree of Institutional Context

We also found that although most of the experiences the men brought to our attention evolved outside clear-cut institutional borders, men sometimes undergo transformations in identity or perspective while they are associated in some way with formal groups and institutions (e.g., family, religious organization). As more pregnancy-prevention and sexual-health programs are developed to target young men's needs, those in them may also begin to experience more turning points involving their procreative identity within an institutionalized context. Presumably, men who are associated with these programs and who experience procreative events with their partners will have a unique forum to discuss with others in the program what they are going through. In this type of situation, young men's involvement with the program facilitator and other participants may accentuate and crystalize the way they are processing a particular experience. Their involvement may also influence their discussions with their partners. Thus, the turning point experience may include both the event and men's handling of it within the context of the program.

Ed, the 22-year-old father of five we introduced in chapter 3, entered drug rehab after years of being a dealer and addict. He attended classes and learned, among other things, about STDs, AIDS, drugs, and alcohol, and their physical and psychosocial consequences. He did so well that he became a teacher in the program, receiving a certificate from the sheriff's department. He radiates excitement and pride about his own changes that involved being clean and sober and about assuming responsibility for himself and his children:

I try so hard now to change my ways, that's how come I got a job now, I'm trying to get myself back on the right road because the way I was headed, it ain't but two ways, prison or death, and the third way . . . an' I choose to go the third way and I walk down this narrow road . . . I pray that every night that God take over . . . because I can't do it by myself, I realize that. I tried so hard to do it by myself; it won't work.

One of Ed's new behaviors involved not wanting to have any more children and ensuring that he does not impregnate anyone. At present, Ed is living with his girlfriend and they use condoms "all the time." Ed also says he uses condoms with any other women with whom he has sex. He credits the program for changing his life, "So now I'm really enjoying my life . . . my life perfect now."

Centrality

Not all turning points are alike in how deeply they affect men's lives. Some reach to the core of how men see themselves; others are largely peripheral to men's key identities. It appears that although young single men's sexuality may be an important feature of how they define themselves, their perception of their procreative ability is far less important to their sense of self in their everyday life. However, we saw that fears associated with a pregnancy scare or unplanned pregnancy can prompt some men to reevaluate how central their potential procreative identity could be to their overall sense of self. The shift sometimes has a lasting effect. Men become more aware of their ability to procreate and concerned about the possible consequences they would encounter if they were to become fathers before they are ready. Likewise, some events can encourage men to reevaluate their life priorities in a way that fatherhood becomes a highly salient and positive identity. For example, we saw that the bonding Andy experienced with his dying father as he cared for him and that Harvey's connection with his godson during his christening helped alter these young men's perceptions of self and their direction in life.

Andy's and Harvey's stories illustrate that the "centrality" property associated with procreative turning points has at least two aspects that should be taken into account; first, the extent to which a turning point taps into an already prominently featured part of men's procreative identity and changes it in some way; and second, whether the turning point fundamentally affects a more secondary aspect of men's procreative identity and enables it to become a more significant feature in men's overall sense of self.

Philip's unplanned paternity and betrayal by his fiancée (she left him for another man) initiated profound changes in him that involved a new way of thinking about himself and his world. He has reprioritized: "I'm in a situation now where I've got more of my priorities straight and I'm not as worried about dating different women as I am [about] taking care of my son and finishing my education. And, that's my main priority. The rest of it can wait."

Philip has also chosen a new kind of woman for an intimate relationship:

> As I look back on it now, my ex-wife didn't have as much motivation. . . . My girlfriend is a hard worker, she's much more like me. She's willing to work for whatever's she's got. She won't take any handouts. It's one of the first relationships that I can ever remember being in that I . . . wasn't counted on as being the provider . . . I mean it's nice to be able to do extra things for somebody but not have to . . . do it because you want to.

This harmonious relationship, coupled with lifestyle changes including forgoing "drinking beer and going out with friends," and an intense focus on caring for his son, indicate the centrality of Philip's turning point.

In contrast to Philip, Marcus's pregnancy scare when he was 17 affected him in a more peripheral way; he chose to cut off the relationship:

> It was a big enough scare for me where we stopped messing around. We just friends right now . . . she still wanted to be with me but I was like no. I gotta stop that. Cause I know how I am. I get, I ain't trying to say I'm a crazy sex person but I know myself, right? If I'm around somebody, if we're constantly around each other, and you know you like her, she knows that she likes you. It's always gonna be that static where you want to do something when you're around her . . . So . . . we just gonna be friends.

Marcus severed the romantic ties that perhaps could have irreparably altered his young life and moved on, minimally changed by the experience.

Emotional Response and Evaluation

Because turning points stimulate individuals to see themselves, others, and situations in new ways, they are often associated with emotional responses. When men encounter, either personally or indirectly, events such as pregnancy scares, pregnancies, abortions, miscarriages, and child-bearing, they often experience some kind of emotion. The intensity of that response appears to be a critical factor in determining whether men view a particular event as a turning point. Not surprisingly, when men are affected in a profound way, they are more likely to remember the precipitating event. The event, too, is more likely to have a lasting impact on the way men see their life and those of others.

Sid, a 25-year-old father-in-waiting, believes his feeling "nervous" about the six-week-old pregnancy was because of his partner's miscarriage three years ago at three months into her pregnancy, an event that had been exquisitely painful for Sid:

> And I was hurting . . . a real bad feeling . . . about the worse feelin I've had, that I can say I ever experienced. That was a pretty rough time but that's why I'm like, excited this time but I'm not too excited because of what happened the last time, so I don't want to get all built up again, end up getting hurt again, so I just, waitin it out.

Sid anticipated that when his partner was about four to five months along that he would "be more relaxed" and "probably be real, real excited. . . . But right now I'm just a little excited, with a little bit scared [about the possibility of miscarriage]."

Tom, likewise, had an intense emotional response to his miscarriage turning point, described earlier in this chapter, saying it was "hard . . . it devastates everything."

Although many men, like our study's Sid and Tom, experience strong emotions in connection with their procreative experiences, whether it be a miscarriage, abortion, pregnancy scare, pregnancy, or birth, some do not. To experience any of these events personally, however, means that men will be involved in some way with a female sexual partner in terms of a friendship, a romantic partnership, or a casual sexual rendezvous. How men characterize these types of sexual involvements to themselves will directly or indirectly be related to how they see themselves, their connections with others (typically their partners and children), their ability to procreate, and their feelings about various fertility-related events. Consequently, understanding the social psychology of men's procreative identities requires that we consider men's romantic relationships and sexual involvements more closely.

5

Romantic Involvements

Young men typically discover that they have the potential to create human life when they take sex education courses or talk to friends and family. Once they have acquired this knowledge, their procreative identities evolve, in part, through the romantic relationships they manage during adolescence and young adulthood.[1] Men can and do cultivate ideas and feelings about procreation and related matters outside these relationships, but procreation is intimately tied to the availability of a sex partner. Exploring men's romantic involvements with females is therefore essential if we wish to understand the larger context within which men form, express, and transform their procreative identities.

Although various strategies can be used to examine the issues and processes associated with men's romantic involvements, we focus primarily on how the involvements are related to procreative identities.[2] Because the participants were solely males, we look only at males' perspectives on the evolution of their relationships. We recognize that this is just one piece of the heterosexual dating equation and is poorly understood.

One would be hard-pressed to overstate the complexity of romantic involvements. Men's involvements are quite diverse, ranging from one-night stands to casual friendships to committed relationships. Some are fleeting, some endure years of special moments, sentimental rituals, heated arguments, difficult negotiations, and life-course transitions. Some involvements with particular partners evolve without interruption for decades. Some are monogamous and intermittent, here one moment, gone the next. Some are concurrent involvements with several women and may be defined by similar or different boundaries. Partners in "on again/off again," "sex with the ex," and multiple relationships may have negotiated agreements about sex, contraception, pregnancy, abortion, and children that were once clear but may or may not apply when a relationship is rekindled or redefined. The spectrum of involvements evokes a potpourri of emotions from men, ranging from the wonderful feelings of love, respect, and passion to the darker sides of anger, jealousy, and sadness.

The symbolic meanings men and women assign to the arrangements they have experienced, the romantic partners participating in them, and the sex that takes place can affect how men think and feel about themselves as persons capable of making babies. For most, envisioning the prospects of fathering a child or negotiating the resolution of an unplanned pregnancy is likely to be quite different when a partner is a fiancée or long-term girlfriend rather than a partner who is a casual acquaintance.

Men have a wide range of personal relationship histories varying among the number of partners, depth and length of relationships, simultaneous or monogamous arrangements, and sequencing of types of relationship and fertility experiences. The vast majority of adult males have dated or been involved with different partners over their lifetimes. Some of the involvements are sexual; others not. Those in which vaginal intercourse occurs are particularly important because of the pregnancy possibility. Men can still grapple, though, with procreation issues in the context of other types of nonsexual, romantic involvements. We saw this with Kyle, our born-again Christian participant who prepared and signed a formal relationship contract with his girlfriend that stipulated they would not have sex before marriage. Some men's moral concerns about having sex and procreating outside marriage may prompt those with an active procreative consciousness to avoid vaginal intercourse—perhaps all forms of sex for that matter.

In addition to having different partners over a lifetime, some men have concurrent multiple partners and may thereby find themselves facing an awkward set of circumstances. At the very least, maintaining relationships may prompt them to think about procreative issues in ways they would not were they in a more conventional, monogamous relationship. Men may have a more active procreative consciousness and sense of responsibility with some partners. Those who do may evaluate the consequences of an unplanned pregnancy with particular partners differently. Further, when men's partners have multiple partners themselves, men may be compelled to worry about having their paternity status falsely presumed or ignored if another man (or men) is a viable candidate for assuming paternity.

Having multiple partners can complicate matters, but we do know that popular perceptions about young males' rampant sexual partnering are somewhat overstated. Data from the 1995 National Survey of Adolescent Males show that 54 percent of the respondents aged 15-19 had had only one sexual partner in the previous year; 26 percent, two partners; 14 percent, three to four; and 6 percent, five or more.[3] Data from the 1991 National Survey of Men, which includes a sample of both married and single men, document that the median number of partners with whom its respondents aged 20-24 and 25-29 had had vaginal intercourse was 6.2 and 6.8, respectively.[4] Eighteen percent of the younger cohort and 21 percent of the older cohort reported having had twenty or more lifetime partners. Median figures for the eighteen months prior to the average interview date were 1.4 and 1.1 for the two cohorts.

We did not specifically ask our 16 to 30-year-old participants to report the number of relationships or sexual partners they had had, however, the overwhelming majority talked about having had multiple partners. Being aware of men's previous relationships is important because they often influence how men approach current relationships or anticipate becoming involved in new ones.

Men's relationships with individual partners are uniquely colored by a personal history of discussions, negotiations, and decisions related to sexual and procreative issues, each of which can be quite complex and encompass a number of transitional experiences (e.g., agreeing to become sexually involved; having an exclusive or open relationship; deciding whether to use contraception; experiencing a pregnancy and miscarriage; having a child together; deciding not to have children). Consequently, any snapshot of a relationship at a given time probably oversimplifies and is not likely to capture the antecedent phases or types of involvements that have shaped the current relationship. Even though partners' sentiments and relationship circumstances can change drastically over the course of an involvement, the partners may sometimes still rely on definitions or images that once guided how they perceive and deal with each other. If, for example, a man is aware that his partner has had sex with other men during their "exclusive" relationship, he may be more prone to challenge his paternity when his partner has an unplanned and unwanted pregnancy.

Men's romantic involvements or relationships are fundamental to our main focus because they provide men opportunities to work through a range of interpersonal issues and processes in their everyday lives. These include sex and family planning talks and negotiations, commitment, cooperation, decision making, trust, betrayal, conflict resolution, and various types of personal disclosures. For our purposes, one challenge related to the study is to explore the possible connections between the practical features of men's romantic lives and their experiences within the procreative realm. By their very natures, the sexual and procreative domains overlap. Men's sexual desires and concerns about the potential consequences of impregnating a partner are often directly linked to their awareness of their procreative abilities and views about a variety of procreative issues. These thoughts, feelings, and experiences are sometimes pleasant, sometimes painful. Some deal explicitly with procreative issues, others with sex-related concerns such as preventing STDs. Even sexuality issues that are not directly tied to procreative concerns are often a part of a larger relationship scenario within which fertility-related matters find meaning.

Defining Partners, Relationships, and Sex

Even though our interviewers typically did not ask the participants to explain how their definitions of their romantic involvements and relationships were related to their procreative experiences, their detailed stories shed light on the connections. They talked at some length about their feelings for particular romantic partners, using language that characterized these partners in distinctive ways (e.g., fiancée, serious girlfriend, best friend, casual friend, female, fuck buddy, one-night stand). A few referred to one-night stands as "hi and bye" and "bend 'em and send 'em." Harvey extended the concept a bit, "one-month stands." Desmond, the participant who we presented in chapter 3 as having offered a colorful description of his recent thoughts about sperm, disparages the women in casual arrangements: "sperm buckets" and "sperm dumpsters." In a parallel fashion, Reginald describes his thoughts on the subject: "They don't be girlfriend. They has to be females. If they just a female, you know what I mean, they know they only want one thing and they know I only want one thing, so they don't need no relationship." In contrast, women with whom men were involved in a more serious type of relationship are generally called by name, "girlfriend," or "fiancée."

Mario, a 20-year-old participant, is particularly attuned to how he differentiates potential partners: sex partners and relationship partners. Additionally, he sees women as "trashy," "decent," or "religious" and tailors his behavior accordingly. He is particularly self-aware that he deals with procreative issues according to his perceptions of a sex partner. Asked if he talks to his sex partners about whether they would abort an unplanned pregnancy, Mario replies, "Only if it is something more than just a sexual relationship. If it's an actual relationship in the terms of girlfriend-boyfriend, then I would. The other girls that I've had sex with haven't had that title." Mario goes on to clarify that he would not want to be a part of a woman's life, or his child's, if the child were born as a result of a pregnancy he did not want brought to term.

> Unless the girl wasn't trashy, cause I believe that any girl that wants to keep the child other than a really religious girl which I wouldn't have sex with because I know she would definitely not have an abortion. . . . [A]nother type of girl who I would think wouldn't have an abortion would be a trashy girl, I would not want to be a part of a girl's life, of a fathering of a child of a mother who's trashy, but if it so happens that the female is a nice good decent girl then I would try to be part of the child's life.

Mario defines a "trashy" girl as someone "who is promiscuous or usually sometimes they come from a low socioeconomic background and are not very well educated above and beyond the point of a high school education." He wants to pursue a serious relationship and concludes that when he finally does, "[I] will definitely want my girlfriend to be on a pill, even though I wouldn't take one myself because I heard the male pill makes your eyeballs go yellow." Mario's penchant for categorizing potential partners is significant because it helps him to integrate his views about relationships, sex, procreation, and fatherhood, to make sense of his sexual involvements.

Overall, the men's stories reaffirm the commonsensical notion that not all relationships are created equal, and a few of the men, contrary to popular belief, admit to finding sex "overrated."[5] Although the stories highlight unique ways some men interpret relationships and sex, they still underscore the well-established differences between body- and person-centered sexuality.[6] The former refers to a type of sex that occurs without emotional commitment and because it feels good physically; the latter refers to a kind of sexual experience that takes place between people who genuinely are concerned with a partner as a person beyond the sexual episode. Some participants chose person-centered sexuality from the beginning; others, especially those who felt betrayed by a previous partner, now choose impersonal sex or abstinence. They want to move away from psychological intimacy, at least for the time being.

Our participants' perceptions of different types of partners reflect the variety of relationship contexts within which they have experienced sex. Some of the men are quite adamant about having sex only with a partner whom they love; others have no qualms about having casual sex, including sex with friends. This stark distinction is illustrated nicely by three of our participants: Barney, age 20; Josh, 22; and Tripp, 23. Barney explains: "I don't think I should have sex unless I really care about the person and that I'm basically in love. . . ." Jeffrey gloats about his experience during an "off-post pass" between basic and advanced military training: [A] "wild three days . . . it was like a wild sex feast." Tripp, who talks about having sex with friends, found relationships confining and had to make what he describes as a conscious decision about whether or not to invest emotional energy in a relationship. For Tripp, sex can be fun or emotional, though it is emotional only in the context of a relationship.[7]

Some of the men also remarked that as they got older they had altered their preferences for the types of sexual relationships they sought, becoming more interested in serious relationships. Jeffrey, now 21, says he is changing how he thinks about women:

> I don't do this as much as I used to, but you know guys, they look at women as inanimate kinds of sex objects. And . . . I'll tell ya, I turned eighteen, I went to the nudie bars, and I'll tell ya, even then, you didn't look at them as people. You know, it was kind of like you were in a theme park and those were, you know, the rides. . . . That's not the best analogy but [laughs] those were the sights.

Marcel, as do some of the other participants, incorporates both forms of sexual experience (casual and relationship-based) into his current sexual lifestyle. He describes his pattern of serial monogamy punctuated by one-night stands: "Generally, I move through serial monogamous relationships that typically last three to four years, and then, between those, there's often one-night stands or a couple of one-night stands before the next serial monogamy pattern begins again." He talks of his urge for "wanton promiscuity" but notes that his "respect for women" prevents this from happening:

> Every time I have a break up I always think that this is my opportunity now to sort of play the field and . . . I usually start off with that and I meet one person and end up starting to develop a relationship. So I never actu-

ally act out that possibility of wanton promiscuity that I'd so like to. Something about respecting women somewhere along the line traps me.

He explains his behavioral pattern by emphasizing how he grows "increasingly interested in [the women]" once he gets into the sexual relationships. "And, as I get to know a person's personality then [she becomes] more appealing to me. So I don't have a certain desire to consume women in a body form except in some abstract way. Like when I'm single and I think about women I think well of course I want to sleep with them all." Marcel appears to have put his finger on a process whereby he is driven to sample many women's sexuality, but the practical and emotional realities associated with getting to know and like one restrict his sexual experimentation. He also mentions elsewhere in the interview that he spends a good deal of time comparing women he meets to women he's known. Using a scheme to categorize women can facilitate this type of comparative process. Although he appears to have some minor reservations with the way things work out for him, he is largely content with the way he gravitates to serious relationships.

The men's firsthand romantic experiences, combined with their awareness of stereotypical cultural images of girls and women, left them with plenty of insights useful in forming their own images of females, sex, and relationships. At a crude level, the narratives reveal several potentially overlapping features that distinguish the types of relationships they describe. These include: feelings for the partner; perception of relationship seriousness; degree of sexual exclusivity; length of time together; marriage expectations; living-together status; and presence of biological or stepchildren.

Another feature, virginity status of the sex partner, came into play for two of the men. For them, virginity status has more to do with the woman as a sexual partner or potential mother than with the relationship per se. Marcus found the virginity of a partner to be relevant at times because, he observed it was less pleasurable to use a condom with virgins; he was more self-conscious and he worried about condom reliability. When using condoms with sexually experienced partners who expressed less physical pain than virgins, Marcus was less likely to think about the mechanics of use.

Another participant, Paul, describes his thoughts on the kind of woman he wants to marry and be the mother of his child. He wants a virgin, in part because he thinks his mother was, but he doubts any virgins exist in today's world: "I don't know any girls that are virgins, and I know a lot of beautiful, beautiful girls in this world and I do not know one of them that's a virgin. I don't know anyone that's a virgin, beautiful or not beautiful."

The primacy of defining relationships was also apparent in several instances where the participants made decisions about how paternity should be established. Gavin, for example, had nonchalantly responded to a girl who told him that she might be pregnant with his child by saying that she should assume that the pregnancy was the responsibility of her steady boyfriend, irrespective of any potential genetic tie he may have to the child. "Because it was like, it was me and this other guy. She had a steady boyfriend but I was kinda like . . . a superstar. . . . I got those extra perks . . . I think she ended up getting an abortion or a miscarriage, one of those, but . . . it wasn't my conversation to have with her." Gavin indicates that because he was "on the side" he felt he was not responsible for her pregnancy because she had a "steady boyfriend" to whom he assigned the paternity issue. Allen, described at length in chapter 3, responded similarly after his sex partner, who was engaged to someone else, told him she was pregnant with his (Allen's) child. Thus, when faced with self-serving avoidance reasons, men in general are sometimes willing to ignore their physical involvement with a partner and biological connectedness to a fetus in favor of an arrangement that relieves them of potential paternal responsibilities. Allen, however, did make a case for doing what was best for the child. He believed that given the circumstances, his purported son would be better off with the husband of Donny's mother, who believed himself to be the biological father.

Relationship Context and Procreative Consciousness

Compared to men who are spending time with casual partners, men involved in more serious relationships seem more likely to think about having a child in order to bond with a partner, and to visualize their potential children. At the same time, men who find themselves in romantic casual arrangements may tend to be more aware of trying to avoid paternity with a woman with whom they do not want to be permanently involved or have as the mother of their child. Although the men's thoughts about procreative issues may differ according to the type of romantic involvement being experienced, their procreative consciousness may at times be equally active.

For Butch, a father-in-waiting, safe sex had been important in unimportant relationships; his important relationship freed him from worries about pregnancy.[8] Within that relationship, talking about marriage had been and still was part of his reality. About the talks he's had with his partner of three years, Butch remarks,

> When I was younger and didn't really know if I was going to be with a girl for a while, of course, I would practice safe sex. Because I didn't want to have the responsibility of them having my kid and me having to be tied up with them because they had my kid. But, the girl I'm with now, I've been with her for quite a long time, about three years now. And we pretty much talked about getting married and everything, settling down and everything. That's why we kinda stopped having safe sex and we . . . didn't not try not to have a kid or we didn't try to have a kid. If it happened it happened or if it didn't, you know, it didn't.

It appears, then, that as Butch and his partner became more comfortable with the fact that their relationship was indeed serious and heading toward marriage, they began to redefine what a pregnancy and child would mean to them. They were less put off by prospective parenthood. In Butch's eyes, his willingness not to practice "safe sex" with his partner was a departure from the way he had interacted with previous partners; then he had been uncertain about how long the relationships would last.

Butch's description of the way the relationship changed over time highlights an important feature of romantic relationships. As we saw in chapter 3, various processes affect how men's procreative identity changes. Just as young men undergo individual changes because of developmental or circumstantial processes, men may redefine their ongoing romantic relationships. When men assign new meaning to their relationships, as Butch did, this may in turn affect aspects of their procreative identity. Likewise, men's changing outlook on specific procreative issues may prompt a shift in how they interpret their romantic relationship(s). Recall how Andy's budding desire to become a father in the near future, spurred on by his father's untimely death, led him to intensify his commitment to his casual dating partner at the time. His change of heart precipitated an engagement, a marriage, and a pregnancy. Prior to his father's illness, Andy had been reluctant to define any of his dating relationships as serious, so he took a leap when he made himself vulnerable to his partner and committed himself to a long-term relationship.

Some of the men, like Butch and Andy, describe experiences that directly linked their relationship and procreative experiences; a number talk about their relationships in a manner that hints at the connection. Take, for example, Jeffrey, who, when he felt the promise of a good relationship, was quite sensitive to his partner.

> [K]nowing her past, I'm very hesitant because I don't want to put her in positions that will make her feel uncomfortable. Having said that, I usually, you know, maybe will hold off [from having sex], whereas in past relationships I'd say, let's go ahead and do this or whatever, and . . . so I'm very sensitive to her emotions and want to make sure. . . . [T]his is one I don't want to screw up.

Jeffrey's approach in his current relationship illustrates that although men may have a relatively set pattern in trying to foster the evolution of an involvement or relationship, they can opt to try a different strategy when they deem it appropriate. Jeffrey does not speak to the point directly, but this type of sensitivity can affect how men and women relate to each other, and alter their discussions about contraception, pregnancy, and children.

As we've seen earlier, Kyle took a very deliberate approach to how he allowed his current relationship to develop. He recalls having been especially aware of how relationships evolve and how he could enhance his by learning about his partner:

> I learned a lot about guys, how they respond to girls and I don't think we try for the most part to understand where they're coming from. We don't realize that they come from such a different point of view. I don't know if there's some chemical thing that goes on in there or something, but I know situations, how to react. And I know when to run, when to get away. I know when to give a hug and . . . it just kind of flows now, like as I learn and I definitely ask them questions all the time.

Kyle is quick to check in with his girlfriend, asking what's on her mind, and to figure out ways for them to meet their jointly defined needs so long as they remain true to their Christian values. In developing the relationship, Kyle is well aware that it is part of a jointly defined, continuous process that may lead to marriage and family. Still, he does not spend much time thinking about those long-term issues as they relate to her. Instead, he thinks about them as abstract life stages for which he is preparing himself. Kyle's respect for his girlfriend, and his willingness to go slow, set the tone for how he approaches life-course issues. He believes there's an appropriate sequence for life-course events; children and sex before marriage are out of the question. Thus, this type of Christian family-man orientation can have profound consequences for how men like Kyle orient themselves to the procreative realm.

Sid, like Kyle, speaks of the importance of his current relationship. He describes how it evolved from friendship into something more intense; he and his partner became a couple and, most important, soul mates:

> [A]fter we were friends for a while we got like, just so in sync with each other it was just like, like dis, my soul mate. She just know everything about me, she know exactly what I want when I want, she can look at me and see like, well, he in a bad mood so I know something, or he had a bad day or he's upset. And I do the same with her, I can tell like when she's sad, she don't even have to say nothing. I can just look at her and see like, well she sad, um, I do something nice for her, make her feel better.

At the time of the interview Sid's girlfriend was six weeks pregnant, causing Sid to view their future together as a family with great joy.

The men who talked to a partner in these types of close, evolving relationships sometimes discussed the importance of educational goals, financial stability, and psychological well-being for themselves and a partner. Not surprisingly, difficulties arise in these and less serious types of relationships because not all partners in these pairs have similar feelings for each other or compatible aspirations for their individual lives and relationships. Individuals may also be confused about their feelings for a partner or what they want out of life, or if they do know these things, they may be less than candid in that regard. To illustrate some of these ideas, we turn to Austin, who tells us that he realized after a period of time that he and his partner had different views about their relationship. During the interview, he again faces the painful reality that he does not want to be with her forever:

> She tells me that she wants me to be there [and she says things like], "I want to wake up in ten years and have you there" . . . and she would say things like that kinda frequently and I would never really know how to respond because I don't think I feel that way. She doesn't know that, but she's like, "Well, why don't you say anything when I say this sort of thing?" Cause you know, I love her but I don't think I'm in love with her. I don't . . . want to spend the rest of my life with her. It's really strange saying it

out loud. I don't think I've ever said that out loud. . . . She has talked about moving out somewhere with me and spending the rest of our lives together. But honestly, and I'm not just saying this because I don't feel that way but because I know her very well and I think that it isn't so much that she feels that way, sincerely, but I think she wants to feel that way. And so she tries to convince herself that she feels that way . . . I know her kinda well and I think that she wants to be in love and she wants to live a fairy tale, you know.

As relationships like Austin's unfold, men sometimes become more clear about what they want, what they and a partner can offer each other, and their interpersonal fit. With time, men begin to bond with or distance themselves from a partner as they maneuver within evolving relationships, dealing with procreative issues and events along the way.

In all relationships, sooner or later, contraception became an issue. The men share their varying approaches in their interviews, revealing how the nature of a relationship directly affected their thinking about contraception. Several of the participants, including Tom, Sean, and Arthur, describe consistent condom use. In the words of one, "I would never ever sleep with anybody without using condoms, at least nowadays." With a casual-sex partner, there was no discussion, just routine condom use. For these men, when a partner requested that they not use a condom because "it feels good," they refused. The possibilities for disease and pregnancy weighed heavily on their minds.

Enrique, a 20-year-old, reveals a sexual pattern quite different from the others. During the early years when he was sexually active in three close relationships, he routinely used condoms or his partner was on birth control. Since the dissolution of his last relationship, Enrique has participated in a series of one-night stands or short relationships in which he did not use a condom and did not ask if the girl was on birth control. He admits not caring too much about his sexual partners:

> I assume that if they are not going to be protected then, not that it's not my place to worry, ya know, they are just the same as I am and not caring like that, I'm assuming that they are, not that I wouldn't take the responsibility, but they are not going to be calling me back, being like "You're going to be the father of my baby and all this, because I need a partner," and all that ya know. Since it's a one night stand, they are probably feeling the same way I am.

In the context of a nonrelationship Enrique does not talk about his views on birth control or even ask his partner about contraception or protection. He throws caution to the wind; he has his own ground rules for one-night stands. From his perspective, protection/contraception is up to the woman; he is not responsible for what happens. Unlike many of our participants he also seems unconcerned about himself and the possibility that he could acquire STDs/HIV. Enrique lives in the moment, which is in marked contrast to how he describes his contraceptive talk and behavior with the women with whom he had long-term relationships. It appears that Enrique and others like him who consistently used condoms or birth control within a close relationship tried to control their shared future with their partners.

Relationship Issues and Processes

Bonding

Men and women in relationships can establish, express, and intensify their emotional commitment to each other in various ways. Many of our participants' stories illustrate that they and their partners have powerful bonding opportunities when they jointly face sexual, procreative, and parenting issues. *Bonding* means attaching psychologically to another, having that person in the forefront of one's mind and hence the object of considerable mental energy. It refers more to the energy of and commitment to a relationship than how the relationship looks to outsiders or even how the partner responds.

Many participants talked about occasions when they felt close to their partners, when they dealt with issues involving relationships, sex, contraception, miscarriage, abortion, and pregnancy, as well as when they envisioned future children and parenting opportunities. Some of the occasions had to do with emotionally laden, traumatic events and occurred in committed relationships as well as in meaningful friendships or dating relationships that were not exclusive. Most of our participants mentioned that they are currently either in an exclusive relationship or have been involved in at least one such relationship.

A number of the men also emphasized the importance of sexual attraction and friendship as foundational to a relationship. Not surprisingly, they are more likely to have bonded with women attractive to them and whom they perceived as friends. Harper observes that "most of my relationships with women correspond to my relationship with my best male friends. But it just doesn't take that long to get to that level of comfort with them." He speaks of seeing women as friends. He does not have to have sex with them but enjoys both the sexual and the communicative relationships. Sex, he notes, "supercharges" the friendship. Tom differentiates between being physically attracted to a woman and having her as a friend. "If it's someone who I am physically attracted to, I think that my feelings toward her might be different than they would be toward someone I would consider more as a friend. In as a potential lover, but in both cases I consider friendship to be the basis of any relationship I have with any woman."

Jeffrey, whose sensitivity to his partner we spoke of earlier, describes his exclusive relationship in an enthusiastic review of his unique two-month-old involvement. Though sharing a bed with his partner at night, sometimes sleeping naked at her request, Jeffrey had not yet had intercourse with her. Unlike his previous relationships, "it doesn't feel like cheap, playing around. It feels like two people who really care about each other." Jeffrey is comfortable waiting to have intercourse because he does not want to jeopardize his relationship. He even admits to the interviewer, "I could see myself marrying her . . . I feel a very close emotional bond . . . there's not ten minutes that go by that I don't think of her. In that regard, that to me is about as real as it can get, especially at this age [21]."

As Jeffrey's interview unfolds, it is clear that he is quite happy with and proud of the emotional space he has created with his partner. They have successfully brought about a relaxed and safe space to talk about important issues related to sex, contraception, and procreation, and do so in an open, mature fashion. For instance, they have talked about such things as waiting to have intercourse, their limited sexual histories, concerns about STDs and HIV testing, Jeffrey's preference for wearing a condom until he is married, and their respective preferences of what to do to resolve an unplanned pregnancy. These talks are noteworthy because many persons never speak of such issues until after they have had sexual intercourse, and many don't talk about them then. As he reflects, Jeffrey accentuates his connection with his current partner by commenting on how his approach to her and their potential child would be much different than it would have been in any of his previous relationships.

In a similar vein, Sean, a 23-year-old, talks about his current relationship, which he characterizes as unusual because "[he and his partner] don't do anything that people our age are supposed to do, like party and stuff like that." The relationship is one where they "mostly talk and read together." They do not live together, but see each other every day they are both in town. Sean comments that he and his partner "constantly" talk about birth control and pregnancy issues even though they have not had sexual intercourse. Many of their conversations about these issues deal with what they plan to do after they're married, and after they have had all the children they want. For example, he told her that he was okay with using condoms, but she said that they were not 100 percent reliable, and that he should consider a vasectomy after they completed their family. Part of Sean's rationale for considering condoms grew out of health classes where he learned about the side effects of female birth control options. His concern for his partner's well-being is apparent in his quick dismissal of medicalized forms of female birth control. Overall, his description of their conversations suggests that, like Jeffrey, Sean has played a role in creating an interpersonal environment that is conducive to communicating about personal issues including sex and fertility.

Ricky, a 25-year-old, is another example of a young man who actively discusses future family life issues, including marriage and raising children, with his current long-distance romantic partner, even though he has never had intercourse with her. After years of being a self-proclaimed "male chauvinist" who was willing to be romantic if he saw that doing so would enable him to "get the sex out of them," Ricky has dramatically altered his approach. He vividly recalls that this transformation began once a platonic female friend challenged him for being disrespectful for swearing in her presence. One of the long-term consequences of his shift toward greater gender sensitivity has been his willingness to honor his virgin partner's wishes to not have sex. Ricky professes that he respects her more than his previous partners and that sex is less of an issue than it was with others he dated. He recognizes, though, that his less determined approach to sex may be different partially because he doesn't see his girlfriend often.

Kyle's story, which we discussed earlier, is a noteworthy example of how partners can solidify their emotional bond through attention to sexuality issues. Recall that he and his girlfriend diligently worked to prepare their own detailed written agreement outlining how they were to treat each other in their romantic friendship. In this case though, Kyle and his girlfriend were not basing their emotional connection on sexual attraction; rather, they were intentionally trying to become closer by acknowledging that they needed to be careful not to jeopardize their relationship. They both feared that they could damage the relationship if they ventured too far down what they perceived as the precipitous sexual path. Kyle talks about how he had reflected on the sexual foreplay experiences he had with his girlfriend early in their relationship and the possibility of becoming more sexually intimate:

> [We] definitely talked about the emotional impact of what would happen. I hate to say it, it was hardly anything for me. You know like it [sexual foreplay] didn't really affect me at all. It took me a long time to figure out why this affected her so much, and I still don't know really. I just know to stay the heck away from it because it doesn't make her happy in the long run, and I want her to be happy. . . . I think we realized that at the time we thought that it was making the relationship stronger but when you're looking back, . . .[it] just put up more walls.

Armed with these concerns, Kyle developed his unique relationship contract to demonstrate his commitment to his girlfriend and religious beliefs. His behavior shows that it is possible for men to invest time and energy into a relationship, and to deal indirectly with the possibility of fatherhood issues, even if the relationship is not yet sexual.

Contraception

A handful of the men demonstrated affection for a partner by expressing concern for the partner's well-being when it came to using hormonal forms of birth control. Kendal, for instance, notes that once he learned that his partner, whom he planned to marry, was having problems with using birth control he told her to "just forget it. . . . Forget 'em, I mean they messin' with you like that, forget 'em." Reginald advocates condoms over female pills because

> I know that there are certain side effects that they give you because I read up on them because I read a lot of magazines. And learn a lot of stuff . . . cause women work with me . . . and they show me all this stuff of what birth controls can do to you in the end. Could develop certain things in your body and . . . if I love the woman, I wouldn't want [her] to be on [the pill].

And Desmond describes how his girlfriend took the pill only intermittently:

> I guess they do something to her system. It was like there was always some side effects or, you know, getting swellings in certain areas, maybe headaches and things like that. And . . . so, we would take breaks from them. . . . And really, I don't think it's fair for women always to be taking contraceptives because that stuff does come back and side effect their bodies . . . I was actually for her stopping.

Discussions such as these can open opportunities for a man to let a partner know that he cares about her health and, more generally, about her. We did not talk to the participants' partners, so we did not hear directly from them about their feelings in response to the discussions. It seems safe, however, to assume that women would appreciate a partner's saying that he does not want her to jeopardize her health. For some couples, though, these discussions are unlikely to occur and are irrelevant because both partners are comfortable using hormonal birth control.

We found one of the men willing to describe a more egocentric, possessive form of "bonding" reflected in birth control discussions with his partner. Harper explains why he did not want one of his former girlfriends to go on the pill when they were dating: "I just feel like she had no need to be. If I'm her boyfriend and the only one she was sleeping with was me and if we using protection [condoms], then she didn't have no need to be on birth control." He admits that because he wanted to limit her chances to have sexual relations with other men, he would not give her permission [which she asked for] to go on the pill. His reasoning: sex with other guys would be too easy if she were on the pill.

Harper was also quick to restrict the use of birth control by a former partner because he wanted to ensure her commitment to him. He mentioned as well that when he was young his sexual involvement with women, which presumably included some degree of bonding on occasion, did not mean that he would be willing to assume paternal responsibility if they said they were using birth control. Essentially, he believed that when his partner was on birth control, he was exonerated from paternal responsibilities if the birth control failed. In Harper's words: "It was like if you told me you were on birth control then if we have sex and you get pregnant . . . it's not mine. Because you told me you were on birth control. So, it was like, oh well, you get pregnant, you get pregnant it's not mine. . . . That's how I used to think; that's not how I think now."

Harper's approach, when compared to previous research with national data,[9] is unusual. Generally speaking, men are more likely to stop using condoms as a relationship with a particular partner evolves, often because they know the partner is beginning to use or is already using a hormonal form of birth control. Numerous participants in our study reported some variation on this pattern. For Austin, feelings of closeness to a partner had led him to stop using condoms even though several of his partners were not using birth control. Austin describes how he changed his contraceptive behavior within three "long-term relationships": he gave up using condoms after feeling "a level of comfort," reasoning that the partners had been tested for STDs so they felt "safe in that sense." However, unlike many of the men who stopped using condoms because they knew that a partner was using modern forms of contraception, Austin and his partners relied on withdrawal, which they believed was preferable.

Abortion

Abortion, for most people, is a stressful experience. It can offer couples a chance to grow closer as they support each other or help to push them apart.[10] The men's stories illustrate both patterns. After he ineffectively practiced withdrawal with a partner whom he had been dating for fourteen months, Austin recalls, he felt that supporting her during the abortion was the thing to do. They had discussed and decided long before the conception that they would abort a pregnancy if it occurred. Despite the understanding, Austin remembers quickly reassuring his partner after she told him that she was pregnant that "no matter what she decided to do, . . . I would be there to stand by her." He captures how he dealt with his partner during the crisis:

> I knew she was going to be really upset, and I knew that she was going to be, really fragile and what not. And I knew that I would have to be the one, and I didn't mind that. That's my job. I just, as the male, as the boyfriend, as the mate, you know. I mean nothin' really made me decide. It was just, I knew this is what I had to do. There wasn't really an instance where I said, okay, this is it. I mean, I knew the whole thing was going to be hard, to deal with.

As Austin describes it, he clearly understood that he had an obligation as a man and partner to stand steadfastly by her throughout the experience. Implicit in his description is that he could and would show his concern by supporting her through this crisis. He goes on to explain how their relationship improved: "[S]ince it happened [about a week ago], I don't think we've argued once. Since it happened we've just been very, very close and understanding, put aside all the petty differences." There is little doubt that Austin's reassuring behavior enabled the two to feel closer as they jointly struggled to come to terms with the situation.

The gendered realities of reproductive physiology and the social dimensions of gender relations played a role in shaping the expectations Austin and his partner had about their interaction during the pregnancy-resolution and abortion process. They reasoned that because she was the one who was physically pregnant, she would be the one who would have a more intense emotional reaction. Though less obviously, it also appeared that perceptions about men's and women's emotional dispositions led Austin to believe that it was his role as a man to keep his composure. With this kind of implicit understanding, it seems that Austin and his partner developed a form of uncontested interaction that provided them with a sense of direction.

Reginald, a 20-year-old, offers another example of how partners can feel connected to each other as they take steps to abort a pregnancy. His story highlights what can be seen as a short-lived bonding, during which he and his partner confronted what he perceived to be extremely troublesome circumstances. He was particularly fearful because this was happening as he was finishing high school and preparing to attend college on a scholarship. His partner was also finishing high school. Reginald's interview tells of how they tried to induce an abortion when she became pregnant. They sought the services of someone who tried without success to use "medicine, like alcohol and stuff like that" to terminate the pregnancy. They were also "gettin' a lot of alcoholic beverages, Guinness, all kind of strange stuff, trying to kill it." He describes last how "she let me hit her stomach to lose the baby, too, I used to hit it and stuff, [she] used to tell me, say, hit harder, open it up, and the baby come out healthy and strong as hell, and smart. It's like, this baby must be supposed to be born." Though unconventional, Reginald's story highlights how partners have the potential to feel connected when they confront a fertility crisis of some sort, even if the type of bonding that results may not be long-lasting, based on love, or appealing in the eyes of many individuals.

Pregnancy

We interviewed only a limited number of men who had knowingly experienced a partner's pregnancy and most spoke of wanting to connect with and support the partner. Albert, for example, says: "[I] read books on bein' pregnant and stuff to help me better understand what she's going through. And she exhibits everything that them books talk about, about her hormones, paranoid." When asked how he dealt with his partner's changes due to her pregnancy, Albert declares:

> Oh, she just gets mad at me, for no reason. She's insecure. My job requires me to be gone till, sometimes till ten o'clock at night. The jealousy, and accusing me of cheatin' on her. And, "Am I ugly? Do you think I'm ugly?" And, "Have I gained weight?" Stuff like that, but, I mean, like I said I've read those books. I understand it. If I wasn't such a strong person, I probably would've already left by now 'cause I, I mean, sometimes it really gets to me. It really bothers that she'd accuse me of doing, wrongdoing. But I understand, like I said. I understand that's to be expected and because their body's going through changes, they're gonna act that way.

Albert concludes his comments about how he has dealt with his partner's moods during the pregnancy by reminding the interviewer that the way his girlfriend was acting was out of character for her: "[S]he never done that when, before she got pregnant . . . everything was picture perfect, no problems." The set of circumstances Albert describes illustrates that even when partners are not having an ideal pregnancy experience, the nature of the event can still provide men a chance to demonstrate their commitment to a partner. His glowing remark about how wonderful he felt their relationship to be before the pregnancy suggests that he anticipated that his efforts to support his partner would sustain that high-quality relationship.

In another vein, Frank talks about his "animal instinct" aroused during his partner's pregnancy, "that den thing" where he "felt more protective of home . . . and more committed." He struggles to put his feelings into words:

> I'm not even coming close to what it make me feel like. I could tell you I was as high as I ever was doing any type of drugs. I could tell you that, um [I had] a sense of accomplishment but then that's not doing it no justice

... it was just like ... one of the greatest feelings I've ever felt ... just being around her during her pregnancy ... it aroused things in me from a male point of view ... it turnt me on, excited me.

The pregnancy accounted for the most intense emotions and most enjoyable time of Frank's life. It also gave him a singular opportunity to feel connected to his partner while tapping into his sense of masculinity.

Previous research on how men respond to a partner's pregnancy has shown that a significant proportion experience pregnancy-like symptoms similar to those that pregnant women describe. The most common include gastrointestinal disorders (nausea and vomiting, abdominal bloating/pain, heartburn), aches and pains (toothaches, leg cramps, backaches, urogenital irritations) and behavioral manifestations (change in appetite, change in sleep habits, anxiety, restlessness). These types of responses, referred to collectively by anthropologists as the couvade syndrome,[11] illustrate various ways some men bond with a partner during her pregnancy.[12] The term *Couvade* was coined in 1865 and derives from the French verb *couver*, meaning "to brew, hatch, or sit on eggs." As it is broadly used in the literature, *couvade* "refers to the male experience of pregnancy whether this is manifested in the form of behavioral changes that may or may not be socially sanctioned [approved], or somatic symptoms for which there is no apparent physiological cause."[13]

A few of our participants expressed in part their deep identification with a pregnant partner through couvade. When 24-year-old Kendal, who was living with his fiancée, found out she was pregnant, he says, "I was happy. 'Cause I knew ..., I realized what I want to be [laughs] ... when I would be around her I'd just get sick ... you know, stomach would start turning ... couple o' times I threw up. ... [W]e did the test. I said, 'Okay. That's the problem.'" Later, he was surprised by his newly discovered food dislikes and cravings: "[F]or some reason, I used to, couldn't eat that Jolly Ranchers, the apple kind, that type of hard candy like the Blow Pop ... I have to have it. You know, pickles." Kendal also says he "slept a lot."

Francisco links not only his cravings but also his thoughts to those of his pregnant partner:

It was kind of like when I was eating. ... She had a lot of cravings and so did I. Weird cravings and we'd wake up ... with like stomach aches and things like that. Like lately ... we've both been craving chocolate ...

maybe 'cause I've been sick . . . I haven't had much of an appetite, but chocolate just sounds really good. And the same for her and . . . we've had a lot of similar things, not just physical, but like, similar thinkings. Both wanting to listen to music at the same time. We're finding ourselves both reaching the radio at the same time, or you know, wanting to watch the same thing on TV or thinking the same thing. . . . We're like, "Oh my God! I was thinking just like the exact same thing."

Although Kendal and Francisco were both excited about becoming fathers, Kendal says he felt "a bit scared" about his fiancée's pregnancy and he thought that "things could get complicated and she might lose her life . . . that's one of the things, or losing a child," although the promise of pregnancy was equally compelling. Francisco relates that he focused on how his partner was dealing with the pregnancy and their relationship:

I understand that you know, she's pregnant and I understand you go through changes, but at the same time I don't believe in a lot of the things, I believe that she should you know . . . the whole thing about being very insecure, I know she's very insecure about how she looks physically and, but she, I believe that she should be more outgoing, and she should-n't think that everyone is out to get her, everyone's against her you know, because she has this thing with all of my friends, she thinks everyone hates her . . . thinks people talk about her.

Francisco also describes his partner's fears that he would leave her and acknowledges her physical and psychological distance from her father and mother. He attributes her "insecurity" mostly to "the whole pregnancy thing . . . it makes you more depressed as a person and she has those thoughts a lot." He attempted to counteract her anxiety by reassuring her verbally and offering alternative explanations for his behavior. For example, he might explain to her that he was irritable because he had received a poor grade on a test rather than because he was aggravated with her.

Both Kendal and Francisco could easily be called sensitive and introspective; they each spent a great deal of mental energy on the pregnancy, the partner, and impending fatherhood. Sharing physical symptoms and unique experiences with a partner inspired each to be aware of his feelings for his partner and his procreative role. Once again, these types of stories bear witness to how men's emotions can influence the way they experience themselves as persons capable of creating human life.[14]

Even men who have not yet experienced a pregnancy firsthand with a partner can delve into a close emotional space with her as they anticipate the prospects of what it would feel like to have a child together. These kinds of experiences were not common among our sample of single men, but some did share how affection for a partner encouraged them to embrace the idea that having a child together could enhance the romantic relationship and increase the partner's attachment.

Miscarriage

Having a bonding experience based on the joy of sharing a pregnancy can be contrasted to the type of bonding that stems from the shared pain of a miscarriage. As we noted earlier, we interviewed only a handful of men whose partner had a miscarriage. The likelihood that a miscarriage will serve as an impetus for the partners to bond is affected by a number of factors, including how each feels about losing the pregnancy. In instances where the pregnancy is planned, or at least wanted once it occurs, partners may find that the associated strong emotions strengthen their interpersonal bond, at least for a while. Sid, a 25-year-old father-in-waiting, experienced a miscarriage with his partner three years ago. They remained together, sharing the pain of their loss, the joy of their present pregnancy, and dreams of future marriage when they were financially solvent. In Sid and his partner's case, their love grew out of friendship, sustaining them through their miscarriage and their subsequent anxiety about their current pregnancy.

Distancing

Although some participants talked about how their affections for and efforts to support a partner were related to their experiences with procreative issues, a significant number described distancing themselves from a partner for a variety of reasons. Some recognized they had different values, often highlighted in response to a procreative event. As described in chapter 2, Tim clarifies the ideological conflict between him and his partner about how to deal with their unplanned pregnancy:

> She didn't handle it very well either. It was something that came and something that was very unexpected. We spent most of that summer deciding what was going to happen. She was pretty much set on having [the

baby] from the beginning. She comes from a very strict Catholic family
. . . I mean it really is her decision really . . . I told her I want her to understand that abortion is an option. Okay, because if the child is born, do we
have the financial resources to support him and this is what the deal is. I
just said to her I gonna respect and I'm going to support any decision you
make. But don't just disregard abortion because you have to be a Catholic
and everything. She took offense to that and there were rocky times, man
we had a tough go at it. . . . [S]he wasn't even considering it. That's where
I got upset.

Tim's and his partner's beliefs about pregnancy resolution were so radically different that reconciliation proved impossible. Tim's son was born
and today Tim rarely talks to his previous partner or sees his son, in spite
of his wishes to do so.

Rudy's experience with distancing was less volatile and had fewer long-
term consequences than Tim's. However, as with Tim, his procreative
identity was involved. Rudy's slow realization that his present girlfriend
was not the right one for him indirectly implicated his procreative plans.
He wanted nothing more than to get married and have children to show
to his mother. Rudy had noticed how important grandchildren are for his
mother and the joy they bring. However, Rudy learned over time, that his
current partner would not work out as a mate and as a mother of his children. In his words:

It was just strictly she was not the one for me, and I knew that and all my
friends even saw it, but it wasn't even my friends that influenced me to go
off, you know, break with her, um, it's just, she was obsessed with me and
I had no obsession for her. . . . I really liked her in the beginning and
throughout all our little arguments and stuff, but, I mean, she would call
me every day, I mean, she still does. Um, as a friend. . . . I think she still
can't even let go of it. But [she's] gonna eventually have to, even end the
friendship, but, you know, I feel bad for her too.

Rudy sought to distance himself gradually so as not to hurt his former
girlfriend. He may have also taken a gradual route because of discomfort
and perhaps the fear he felt because of her obsessive feelings for him. It
appears that sometimes men like Rudy feel compelled to distance themselves from a partner whom they do not perceive to be ideal wife or
mother "material" in order to move on with their lives.

Some of the participants distanced themselves from a partner because they had been hurt emotionally by a partner in previous relationships.[15] These sentiments, though typically not closely linked to men's procreative identity, were sometimes indirectly relevant to the way men thought about matters pertaining to relationships, sex, procreation, and fatherhood. Fears of rejection, betrayal, and abandonment can influence how men pursue and manage their romantic involvements, which in turn can affect the context within which they develop and express aspects of their procreative identities.[16]

A significant number of the men voiced resentment over how particular girls and women had hurt them in the past, sometimes disrespecting them in the process. Feeling as though they had been abandoned and/or betrayed earlier in their lives, these participants were quick to point out that they often struggled to trust more recent partners. The sentiment caused some to have a jaundiced view of relationships, restricting their willingness to enter into serious, exclusive commitments. In a few cases, they made a conscious decision to turn the tables and to pursue sexual experiences with persons other than a girlfriend or current dating partner to minimize the possibility of being hurt. More generally, by cutting back on their willingness to pursue committed relationships, this small subset of participants circumscribed the interpersonal context within which they could think about their procreative identity.

The distrust felt by some men was linked directly to a specific partner; other men moved from distrust of a particular partner to full-blown distrust of all women. Desmond describes not trusting his partner's declarations that he had impregnated her: "It is possible, ah, but I'm unsure. I was told about a situation in the past but I'm not sure if I can believe her." Albert says his, "first girlfriend claimed she was pregnant and got an abortion, but I don't believe that, just the type person she is, and the situation, and how she said she got an abortion. It was impossible to go get an abortion, come back the next day and be all runnin' around happy." Such distrust of a partner often involves issues related to pregnancy, use of contraception, and fidelity. Occasionally, other people encouraged the partner distrust as being important for ensuring the man's health and control of his future. Garrett's mother advised such a course for him regarding sexual partners, and even women in general, when it comes to contraceptives: "[T]he one thing that my mom has talked about is, don't trust anybody, as far as if they say they're on the pill, then you should still use protection cause you know, a lot of girls will lie and stuff." Garrett remembers receiving much the same warning from an older male friend: "[A] lot of girls will think you're cute and they'll want to have your baby."

Paul offered an example of partner distrust that resulted, at least at the time of the interview, in gender distrust. His description of how one of his previous relationships affected his dating behavior provides a window into the long-term consequences related to how a number of the men felt about a previous relationship. His personal turning point involved his feeling betrayed by a girlfriend of almost three years who broke off their relationship in his senior year of high school. Because of the betrayal, Paul "won't trust . . . girls anymore." He still has sex with girls, but

> I'm not gonna sit here and like . . . definitely not gonna get hurt by 'em—that's the problem with relationships, right? I love girls, right . . . but I hate havin' relationships with people that like end . . . if you just have a girlfriend like that's just like whatever . . . you know it's definitely gonna end some day and somebody's definitely gonna get hurt.

Asked if his avoidance of relationships now was self-protective Paul replies, "And protecting the other person as well, like I don't know if it's gonna be me hurting them or if it's gonna be them hurting me . . . you can't tell until like the actual end happens." Paul aims in this fashion to avoid a recurrence of the pain "til I'm sure at least that I would never want to end the relationship." At least for the time being, Paul is limiting his sexual expression to situations that are not likely to inspire him to fantasize about children or about having them with any of his partners. The approach is likely to restrict some aspects of his procreative consciousness from being expressed while curtailing the chances that he will coconstruct his procreative identity through interactions with a romantic partner.

The surprisingly long-term implications for some men of a betrayal experience is illustrated by Harper's remarks about a long-ago event. To many, the incident might seem trivial; nonetheless, it has had a lasting effect on how he perceives women's trustworthiness:

> Well, I mean, I had this girl, this girlfriend, that's when I was young. We grew up in the church and I heard she liked this other guy. And I told her, if this is the guy you want to be with go ahead on I won't bother you. "No I want to be with you [girl's remark]." So then, like the next day at church the guy comes to the church and she run up and hugged up with him.

And I started like, I was like, you know that hurt there. It was like, I mean, that hurt me cause that's the girl I wanted to be with. You know, like I just don't trust women no more.

How men's distrust of women influences the way they think of them-selves as persons capable of creating life or dealing with practical decisions in the procreative realm is not always clear. Yet, we suspect that distrust in-fluences the relationship contexts in which many men deal with procre-ative issues. This was the case with Derrick's situation (described in chap-ter 3); he had grown reluctant to trust women because of his experiences with two abortions and because he felt his partner lied to him about using contraception. Derrick, like a few others, knows that he can trust only himself and his own contraceptive behavior.

During his interview, Desmond revisits a five-year former relationship by calling it a "long relationship" with a woman he really liked. He feels that he "got dumped," and confesses that as a result,

I do not trust women. I see them in a whole different light. Um, I know you shouldn't, you know, just judge, you know, [by] one bad experience but I think all women have that potential. And I think probably because some women they think men have the potential. I think now women are getting men back. . . . I think a decade or so ago men used to do all the dropping. I think these career-minded, educated women, they're starting to drop the men now. I think it's payback time, and, ah, and, ah, so that's the way I see them . . . I just do not trust them very much now.

As do Paul and Harper, Desmond links his specific betrayal experience and his distrust of women in general rather than looking to the details of the relationship and the two persons involved. From a sociological per-spective, Desmond believes that women as a group retaliate against men for their past betrayals.

Some of the men expressed unresolved psychic pain because of past re-lationships; others were able to look back on painful experiences intro-spectively, assessing their own responsibility in the uncouplings. Take for instance, Frank, who after an eighteen-month relationship saw no evi-dence of loyalty or commitment on the part of his partner. He believes she was interested in him only "when I was making really good money . . . as long as things were great." Frank accepts some blame for the breakup and admits that "drugs have played a part too," but, nonetheless, she "was drainin'" [him]. Suspicion grew when their home was robbed and only his things were missing. Also, she told him her tubes were tied but subsequently said she was pregnant. Because of a series of events perceived as lies and betrayals, he is now "not antiwoman but I'm more skeptical about who I let into my world. . . . I do believe that a man is not complete until he finds that woman that was meant for him . . . but at the same time if you sell yourself short it could do more damage in the long run."

Although he distanced himself from his partner, Frank is able to look at himself and see that he had problems with trust:

> That was probably something that I brought into the relationship, the baggage and shit that helped create some complications. I mean, by no means am I saying that, um, she was the villain totally in that 'cause I played some parts . . . some of the shit . . . my lack of trust, my questioning stuff you know. Probably created some animosity and some tension that normally wouldn't have been there. So by no means am I shirking my responsibility.

Frank's pain about the most recent relationship loss, and others before it, is palpable. He is quite open with his feelings: "It's hard to be vulnerable. It's hard to be open . . . and not to have as much control as you would like . . . right now I'm doing bad." Frank, like Rudy, wanted to have a family but had been unsuccessful in finding the right woman.

Recall Desmond's story, presented in chapter 3; he astutely describes a situation wherein he distanced himself from his partner. In doing so, he pinpoints how he has changed over time. Reflecting on his emotional reaction to learning, in his early twenties, that his partner might be pregnant, Desmond remembers saying to her,

> "Well you better you find out what's wrong" . . . it was just so immature. That's just not the right way to treat somebody. But I remember her breaking up with me after that, when she found out she wasn't. But then I remember her distancing herself when I tried to go back with her, after we found out everything was all right. She said, "All right, I've got your number," and I deserved that. Now, if somebody told me that now, I would handle it totally different. I'd say, "Okay, lets see what's going on." But back then, no. "What do you mean? Me? You've got the wrong person. You sure it was me?" It's, it's sad.

Desmond, like Frank, saw his part in the problematic relationship. He recognized that his youth prevented him from both communicating with his partner in a healthy way and accepting his procreative responsibilities. Although the ability to be introspective and self-critical is frequently not directly linked to procreative issues, such qualities are fundamental to good relationships, and it is within the context of relationships that procreative issues are often confronted. Absent self-knowledge and the willingness to reflect on their needs and responsibilities, men's approach to procreative issues is likely to be rather superficial.

During the distancing process, some of the men who were not reflective or self-critical sought retaliation against a partner or women in general. Some retrospectively recognized their retaliatory behavior; others vented their anger at women. Cecil remembers the pain of losing his first girlfriend:

> I really liked her. I don't know why. It was like weird. I mean she wasn't that good-looking or anything but I really liked her. And then she dumped me and I think that sort of affected the way I feel about women . . . I had to take it out on the next twenty, right? And so I did. . . . I would have a quick relationship, but I pretty much would just want to get a girl to get her and then dump her, right?

The experience has had a lasting impact on Cecil, who resorted to retaliation against women generally. His conquests were faceless, only representatives of the female gender. With time, Cecil changed his behavior, distancing himself somewhat and minimizing the importance of sex in a relationship. Cecil, like Frank and several other participants, became more cautious with women, less willing to trust, more distant emotionally and often physically. He no longer viewed sex as having major importance; rather, a woman's personality, behavior, and goals took on greater meaning for him.

Talking

The participants' conversations with a romantic partner, both in content and style, often reflected the type of relationships they had.[17] Conversations also gave the men the chance to become aware of their procreative identity and experiences in this realm. When they talked to their partners about certain issues they set the stage for discoveries about themselves as persons capable of procreating. When they remained silent, they tended to miss out on possible opportunities to express their procreative awareness.

Generally speaking, the men in our study confirmed that the ability to express one's desires and dreams, negotiate personal interests, and resolve conflicts are essential features of a high-quality relationship. We saw this when Cecil described how his wife left him because of their radically different beliefs about having children. She wanted children dearly and soon after they had married; he was averse to having children at that point in his life. Unaware prior to their marriage of her desire for children, he realized in retrospectively that talking openly about the issue perhaps could have altered their relationship in a way that would have minimized their pain. Had he chosen to speak candidly about children earlier, Cecil would have forced himself to sharpen his procreative consciousness.

Some of the men recognized how difficult talking about some subjects could be and that timing is important.[18] Marcel laments that

> the one person that it's difficult to talk with sometimes is the person you're in the relationship with. Because you got a situation where you're both self-interested . . . not that I have difficulty talking to them in general but specifically about the dynamics of the relationship. For instance, with the current relationship we haven't discussed the fact that we both anticipate it ending. I think that it's understood by both of us that there's no possibility of it going on. Since she'll be moving away and I'll be moving away.

For Marcel, the idea of their talking explicitly about their relationship and a future together was threatening to their current dating status.[19] They implicitly understood that avoiding this type of talk and the tension they believed would result was the path of least resistance.

The issues were different for Kyle, but he and his girlfriend also had reason to avoid having certain conversations. They chose not to talk about sex, he says,

> because talking about it just keeps it in our thoughts, like it just brings it up and it's not, we don't, I don't want to think about it . . . the conversations that have come up have been, not awkward, just strange. We could talk about it all the heck we wanted to, but I think we both realize that it doesn't do our thoughts any good. We'll be concerned about that after we get married, but for now there's no reason messing with it.

Because Kyle and his partner decided not to have sexual intercourse until marriage, talking about it seemed to be counterproductive. From their perspective, the timing was inappropriate for that kind of conversation.

Jeffrey, too, felt that timing was important. For Jeffrey, it is best to talk about potentially sensitive subjects like children and sex early in a relationship. He told his partner that he will always use a condom until he is married. Having settled on a time that was not "in the heat of the moment," when he was able to "look her in the eyes," Jeffrey recollects saying to her, "'If you understand that, we can move forward. If not, we have to do something else.'"

As these excerpts suggest, decisions about what to talk about, when to talk about it, and how to talk about it challenged many of our participants. Clearly, those decisions affected, directly and indirectly, the way in which each of the men experienced himself as a romantic partner and as a person capable of procreating. Because how men define relationships is important to their procreative identities, and talk is essential to relationships, we need to appreciate how men talk to their romantic partners.

For many of the men, talk both increased closeness with a partner and resulted from the closeness. Earlier, we noted how participants like Jeffrey, Kyle, Sean, Ricky, and Tim grew closer to a partner by discussing issues having to do with relationships, sex, and procreation. Relatedly, the conversations helped the men at times to become more sensitive to a partner. Paul mentions that his partner "hated condoms" and that during their two-year-plus relationship he always used withdrawal. He says proudly, "I never came in her once. . . . She wouldn't let me cum in her—no way." He gladly honored his partner's wishes.

Desmond, reports a conversation between his girlfriend and himself about contraception because of the side effects she was having with the pill: "'Okay, you stop for awhile.' 'Yeah but are you going to feel comfortable using those condoms?' I said, 'I don't care about that. I mean . . . I don't want you getting sick, you know . . . using those things all the time.' So we're in agreement on it."

Some of the men found themselves preparing for the future as they explored a partner's thoughts and feelings. Tim explains how he greatly valued having "getting to know you" types of conversations with women, which he found to be a source of knowledge that enabled him to learn how women think. By questioning the women he met, Tim learned from and about them:

I really make it a point to talk to them about relationships, about their views on them, about how they think about things. . . . I can give them a scenario or situation and, well how would you react to that? I mean, what would you have done? . . . Because you want to be sensitive. Because when I was in high school and I was seriously . . . dating this woman, I wasn't really very sensitive, I took a lot of things for granted. And I wasn't always such a good boyfriend. And since then I've matured quite a bit and have become more sensitive, and in order to become more sensitive, you have to understand what's going through their mind, and in order to do that you have to ask questions, you have to quote scenarios, and you have to see what they have to say.

Thus, having gained a new perspective because of his earlier failed relationship, Tim sought to become a more concerned and interested listener because he wanted to learn more about his potential partner and himself.

Becoming a good communicator in a relationship was an achievement for some of the participants. Sean explicitly notes that learning how to talk about relevant issues took time and experience. It was not a natural skill; it took practice to cultivate. He recalls that when he lost his virginity at 16, "I didn't really feel comfortable enough to talk about it [contraceptives] with her. 'Cause, even though there was AIDS commercials, stuff like that on TV at the time, it just wasn't a subject that I was about to bring up. I could talk about sex, but I didn't know how to talk about contraceptives." Apparently, any procreative consciousness Sean possessed when he lost his virginity he had achieved on his own. Afraid to talk as a sexually inexperienced adolescent about contraception, he was unable to initiate a discussion that might have drawn his partner into his personal world. Though we have no way of knowing what his partner might have said or done if Sean had initiated a discussion, she may very well have talked to him in a way that would have accentuated his awareness of his procreative ability.

When the men did talk with a partner, the nature of their talks varied considerably. At times, it was free-flowing expressions of feelings and discussions of salient issues. At times it ranged from humorous verbal horseplay to heated arguments. The latter was most likely when the stakes were high. Take Sean, for example, who describes how he and his partner had discussed their future plans for children and contraception. He mentions that, contrary to his desires, his partner wanted him to have a vasectomy "when the time comes." Sean interpreted this conversation as argumentative because she was attempting to persuade him to have unwanted surgery. Cecil describes his former wife's mood as "angry" when they were discussing having children. Harper and his partner also exchanged angry words when, after a pregnancy scare, she refused to have sex with him if he did not use condoms: "We argued . . . I'd get mad. I mean, 'Why you doing me like this?' and she like, 'No, 'cause I almost got pregnant, so we not going to, you know.' I'm like, man, I get mad and we argue and that'll be it." Situations like these led to confrontations because one partner was trying to persuade the other to do something of significance that was inconsistent with his or her preferences. Although the men had had major disagreements about fertility-related matters with a partner, many had not yet encountered this kind of situation.

A good barometer of the strength of the men's relationships with a particular woman was the tone of conversations held with their partners. Jeffrey praises his relationship with his partner, emphasizing the importance of being able to discuss significant issues surrounding his partner's desire not to have children, at present, with some levity:

> [W]e can talk . . . and it doesn't sound so dire that you feel uncomfortable, feel like this is really a serious problem. I think the amazing thing is we can talk about it and at the same time kind of joke around a little bit about it. . . . I could've never done that before in a relationship. . . . It's a concerned tone but not a dire straits kinda tone.

The talks the men had with a partner sometimes dealt with procreative issues they were facing, sometimes with issues on the horizon. Conversations about birth control were relatively common in both time frames. Some of the conversations were quite brief; others were more extensive. Sean and his fiancée, with whom he had not yet had sex, made a decision to use condoms after their marriage because he declares, "I've taken a lot of health classes and I've heard there are like side effects to just about everything, so its like even though condoms aren't a hundred percent, they offer the least side effects." Sean remarks that he and his fiancée discuss birth control issues "constantly" and that she usually initiates their talks.

Rudy states that he discusses contraception only "after I have sex." He comments that when he was younger (16–18), he never talked about contraception but is glad that he is now in a new life stage and can freely discuss it. It is not ideal that such discussions occur for the first time after men have had sex with a partner, but better at some point than not at all.[20]

As we have discussed elsewhere in connection with such events as pregnancy scares and abortion, the participants' conversations with a partner were at times challenging and focused on problem solving. Desmond recounts that a partner told him emphatically early on, "'I cannot get pregnant.' Of course, I did everything in the world to reassure her that that would not happen." He showed her the condoms, one of which she opened and filled with water. She even checked one for a hole after they had had sex. When condoms broke, anxiety-ridden conversations sometimes followed. Marcus warned his partner to "keep an eye on your period for me. Tell me, keep me up-to-date what's going on and shit."

In contrast to the men who had bonded with a partner, some of the men describe not having had conversations or negotiations about birth control or protection with women who were casual sex partners or one-night stands.[21] Paul says, "You don't worry about trusting the woman. You just take control with the birth control [condoms]." Or, as in the earlier example of Harper, some men put the responsibility in the hands of the women. Reginald expresses his irritation with women who were one-night stands or wanted to be with him just to have sex but acted as if they wanted a relationship: "Sometime they'll try bring up conversations like be in a relationship. But I let 'em know right there and know we ain't seeing [each other] in a relationship, so don't even try asking no question about nothing. You know what this is, and I know what it is so that's that." Reginald wants "no conversations at all" with these "females."

Disclosures

The process of disclosing personal stories, secrets, preferences, and dreams is a central feature of romantic relationships. Much disclosure talk is of issues associated with relationships, sex, pregnancy, abortion, and children, and is typically a by-product of and an integral part of the bonding and distancing processes mentioned above. Speaking candidly, Marcel provides a detailed account of his own self-disclosures with the women he dates:

[O]nce I'm in a relationship and been with a woman two or three times and becoming closer friends and the relationship seems to develop. Then we'll usually, if it hadn't already occurred, initiate a talk on my sexual past in which I'll mention that I did have chlamydia and I have had crabs. I've encountered certain nasties along the way. And then, I'll tell them when

I've had my last blood work done and I'll tell if I had any risky experience between the blood work and the present. So they have full knowledge of what they're getting into with me. And then I expect that they'll do the same. I never really question it. So whatever that person tells me, I accepted it at face value.

As Marcel continues, it becomes clear that his conversations about sexual intimacy (including birth control and protection) and about sexual intercourse do not necessarily proceed in tandem. Again, he does not hedge when sharing his perspective:

I'm far more interested in getting through that sleeping-with-her-thing early. So, I guess, the point being once you can show her what you can do in bed, you can pretty much retain a woman for a long time. So the key is to get a chance to display your handiwork. And so this conversation [about contraceptives/birth control/condoms] doesn't usually come up until actually I'm in bed with them. Then I will insist on using some sort of protection. So it's not really a discussion; again, all the cases I've been with, there's never been a argument about this. The woman never said I'd rather that you didn't use a condom. Generally speaking, it's kind of a moment of relief. 'Cause she realizes that you are taking her safety into consideration as well as your own.

For Marcel, relationships appear to have an associated process that includes steps and rules: early sexual seduction opens the door to sexual history sharing, which is followed by a discussion about mechanics (e.g., condom use). Then the lab work can begin: his partner can evaluate his performance in bed. There seems to be an unwritten rule about when to do the condom talk:

Usually, the first date is far more of a seduction thing where you're out, it's clearly maybe you been out a few times, depending on which women you're talking about. Maybe second date or first date, whatever. Generally speaking my focus is on the woman and generally the sex sort of emerges out of a long evening of companionship. . . . So, the mechanics don't usually intrude into the conversation until immediately before some sort of sexual contact. Then it becomes unavoidable to mention them. It is almost as if it was some unwritten code that you're not going to discuss over dinner. You haven't had sex yet, so you don't have that liberty to bring up the whole conversation until she's naked in your bed and you're about to have sex. Then the barriers are already down and you can talk about things like that. If you talk about it over dinner, you probably wouldn't end up in bed with her after dinner.

Although Marcel apparently does not incorporate explicit discussions about pregnancy resolution into his initial seduction and discussion processes, a small percentage of the men do. From Marcel's perspective, talking about contraception and sexual histories requires a level of intimacy that is not easily obtained during the more practical aspects of a typical date. Fearing that he might jeopardize his chances for having sex, Marcel usually chooses to postpone such discussions until the very last minute. By doing so, he places himself in the position of having important discussions in a passionate situation where lucid, rational thinking is more difficult.

As we saw with Arthur and Gilbert in chapter 4, the participants' views about relationships, sex, abortion, and women can be altered radically by a partner who reveals a secret abortion. Although rare, Arthur's experience was not an isolated incidence. Recall Gilbert, the 20-year-old who described a situation in which he, at age 14, impregnated a 20-year-old woman who had had a secret abortion. He also used his former partner's poor handling of the abortion as the basis to judge, in a more general way, the type of partner he wanted.

Another intriguing example can be offered of how a personal disclosure about a pregnancy and abortion can be associated over time with bonding and distancing. In this case, the bonding and distancing processes have implications for, Alex and Kerry, friends who have moved back and forth between a platonic and a romantic friendship. Unlike the examples presented thus far, this disclosure involves a man not directly involved in the pregnancy. Alex, an 18-year-old, helps us interpret a disclosure about an unplanned pregnancy and abortion that was made to him within a larger context. He explains that Kerry had intercourse with two guys before she started to hang out with him for the first time, and then she had sex with one other person, Ernie, after she stopped seeing Alex. She confided in Alex as a friend that she was carrying Ernie's child and intended to abort the pregnancy. Ernie reassured her that he would be there for her as she went through the abortion and its aftermath; he did spend a couple hours with her at her home immediately after she had the abortion. She then ended her relationship with Ernie and eventually began to see Alex again. Kerry had never before expressed any serious interest in having sex with him but now told him that she was ready to do so if he wanted it. Alex told her that he was uncomfortable with the thought then, in part, he says, because "it was too soon after that whole thing with Ernie . . . I was just scared to go through that [an abortion] myself." His feelings were intensified because, he acknowledges, he had begun to realize that he had the potential to impregnate someone when he learned that Ernie had done so. Alex's procreative consciousness had been awakened and then developed as he helped Kerry. Although Alex never had to deal directly with a pregnancy and abortion, the experiences of someone he cared about left their mark on him. They were significant enough to discourage him from becoming sexually involved with a woman with whom he had wanted to have a relationship with in the not-too-distant past.

Generally speaking, men may have more limited options for sharing their experiences but they too have opportunities to make meaningful disclosures. Cecil, a 26-year-old participant, told of what happened a few years ago when he disclosed unexpectedly to his wife at the time that he was not enthusiastic about having children; prior to getting married, they "didn't really have specific plans for children." He had a sense that she wanted to be a mother, but that perception did not affect his thinking or their interactions for three years or so. By then Cecil had realized that he had "pretty much decided that I didn't want to have kids right away." After the issue of children was broached by his sister during an awkward conversation, he and his wife had two conversations on the subject on consecutive nights in bed. Cecil describes his wife's mood as "angry," his own as "conservative." She soon packed her bags and left. Cecil concludes, "I think the whole reason our marriage ended was because of disagreements on children and pregnancy and stuff like that." His experience showcases the dramatic consequences that disagreements about fertility issues can sometimes have for relationships.

By Cecil's own account, he was ill-prepared for fatherhood. As a bachelor, he had not thought much about children of his own; it was simply not on his radar. After a few years of marriage and discussions of the prospect with his wife, he became adamant that fatherhood was not for him at any time in the near future. His experience highlights the need to understand more fully how men think and feel about their "readiness" to become fathers.

6

Thinking about Fatherhood

Just as young men experience different types of romantic and sexual relationships, they can follow one of several paths to fatherhood. On the conventional path, they become fathers only after weighing the pros and cons associated with that status. Their desire antedates fatherhood, and they are prepared financially and emotionally. Most discuss the desire with a partner and perhaps even negotiate what being a father in practical terms means. The conventional path is well laid out.

On the path that is less straightforward, men unexpectedly head toward fatherhood because the preceding sexual relationship was marked by careless contraceptive practice, contraceptive failure, or partner deceit about contraceptive use. Many of these men initially feel ill-prepared to become fathers for financial, emotional, or developmental reasons. Some may take to the idea as a partner's pregnancy moves along; others may not, and grow uneasy about their unreadiness to assume a new status, or grow angry in particular with the partner. Many of the single men in our sample feared that they might find themselves on this path; and some were.

Much can be gained by studying men's evolving identities as persons who presumably have the potential to procreate. Men's procreative identities are linked to the sexual and contraceptive choices they make implicitly or explicitly. Do they have sexual intercourse? When do they have it? What is the nature of the relationships in which they have sex? Do they discuss pregnancy resolution options before having sex? Before conception? What, if anything, is decided about contraceptive use? The consequences of the choices ultimately place men on a path that is more or less likely to lead them to the land of procreation.

Men's identities are typically affected, too, by projected or actual commitments to their children. Understanding the personal and interpersonal processes associated with how men try to make sense of their prospective or new roles is vital.

The bulk of what we know about what young men think about father-hood comes from studies of acknowledged fathers and their partners.[1] From sampling young men, most of whom are not fathers, researchers have also delved into facets of their perceptions regarding sexual and con-traceptive responsibility, as well as pregnancy resolution.[2]

Additionally, some research has attempted to unravel how men of vary-ing ages think and feel during a partner's pregnancy and during the tran-sitional period to firsttime fatherhood.[3] Their analyses are grounded on men's personal experiences with pregnancy and childbirth processes. Much less is known about how young men who have not yet become fa-thers envision fatherhood and children.[4] Our study fills this gap in the lit-erature because most of our participants had not yet, to their knowledge, sired a child when we interviewed them, although twenty-two men in our main sample had impregnated a woman.

How do young single men represent their inner worlds as they contem-plate the prospect of becoming a father? We answer our question by build-ing upon our previous discussions that considered how males become aware of their perceived fecundity, experience themselves subsequently as procreative beings, and view responsibility issues while orienting them-selves toward their sexual and potential paternal roles. We focus here on several issues that relate more directly to the social psychology of father-hood, in particular, two interrelated concepts associated with visions of different aspects of fatherhood that emerged from our analysis of the par-ticipants' stories. First, we find that the men typically have a subjective sense of how prepared or ready they currently are to take on the responsi-bilities of being a father. For simplicity, we refer to that sense as *fatherhood readiness*, which, as we shall see shortly, has a number of associated prop-erties. Second, we look at the types of *fathering visions* the men report. These include views about the ideal fathering experience, images of the good or ideal father, and visions of future fathering experiences.

Because paternity and, in many instances, social fatherhood can be viewed as joint accomplishments of a man and woman, we build on our earlier discussion in chapter 5 to explore how the men's orientation to prospective fatherhood is sometimes influenced by involvement with a particular romantic partner. In this light, some men's relationship com-mitments can influence the way they perceive specific aspects of what it would be like to become fathers. To round out our analysis, we investigate how the young men generally think about the prospects of fatherhood separate from specific romantic relationships.

When we listened to the men's stories, we paid attention to the distinctive ways they shared their thoughts about procreation, social fathering, and children. Our analyses revealed, for instance, several properties that appear to cut across the two concepts (fatherhood readiness and fathering visions) that represent how men envision fatherhood. We introduce and define these properties when we analyze the men's sense of readiness for fatherhood.

Further, because we suspect that the men's sense of readiness is linked to their image of what represents a good or ideal father, we selectively use three of the properties to illuminate the men's views on fathering in general and, more specifically, their visions of how they themselves will act as fathers. In this context, we consider the significance and symbolic meaning underlying their desire to father a biological child someday, and discuss their perceptions of their own fathers and hypothetical children. Part of the discussion explores what the men have to say about whether they link their sense of manhood with their paternity or potential social fathering responsibilities.

Targeting for special consideration men who are not yet fathers is warranted because many such men who eventually become fathers begin to develop a paternal identity prior to a child's birth, and some do so even before a child is conceived. This focus is also consistent with recent initiatives to incorporate males into important policy debates and program interventions that address sex, pregnancy, paternity, and social fatherhood issues.[5] The initiatives embrace broader schemes for conceptualizing and promoting responsible fatherhood, especially among teens and young adults. In addition, many young men are hesitant to establish legal paternity or even report informally that they have fathered a child. Their reluctance stems from the stigma associated with teen pregnancy and unplanned paternity, as well as the fear of being held accountable for financial child support.[6] Others may not be aware that they have sired a child (or impregnated a female) if a partner kept this news from them. Consequently, typical information regarding young fathers comes only from those who acknowledge their paternity, a subset of the population responsible for the physical reproduction of children. This sampling pattern underscores the need to explore young men's perceptions about fatherhood and children before they experience paternity. Our analyses therefore generate insights relevant to both theory and program development for men with a wide range of experiences who are likely to become fathers someday.

For the most part, we used variants of eight interview questions to get at how the young men in our sample envision fatherhood. These questions allowed us to hear the thoughts of each participant on the following: (1) instances where he thought he may have impregnated a girl/woman; (2) instances where he talked to someone about impregnating a girl/woman or becoming a father; (3) situations or events that happened to him that changed how he thought about impregnating a girl/woman; (4) the importance for him to father his own biological child; (5) relationships in which he thought about what it would be like to have a child; (6) whether he anticipated having children in the future; (7) imagery he had of possible children and of himself as a father; and (8) his perceptions of the connection between being a man and being a father.

Our interpretation of the responses is guided by the symbolic interactionist and life-course perspectives we described in chapter 1. From an interactionist perspective, we are interested in the meanings men assign to situations, events, acts, others, and themselves as they relate to their potential experiences as fathers and the social psychological processes associated with their reactions. The processes include both the identity work men do by themselves as they attempt to define what they value for themselves and others, and the interactions they share with partners (and others) as they coconstruct their views on fathering and children. The life-course perspective reminds us that men's views on the timing of fatherhood are shaped by their ideas regarding the timing and sequencing of other critical life-course events, including education, work, and relationships (marriage in particular).

Envisioning Fatherhood

Because our sample included men between the ages of 16 and 30, it is not surprising that most had given at least passing thought to their ability to impregnate a sex partner. All of them recognized the connection between sexual intercourse and conception. Although we interviewed a few notable exceptions, the participants who were older and more experienced in having relationships, negotiating sex, contraception, and in some instances resolving a pregnancy typically had given more thought to being a father. However, some of the men, despite being sexually active, had not thought about the prospect of fatherhood or imagined what it would be like to be a father eventually. Understanding why the latter participants have remained oblivious is surely important, but given the scope of our efforts, we focus only on the men who have thought about fatherhood.

Fatherhood Readiness

Many of the participants commented on the nature of their preparedness to become fathers and assume the responsibilities associated with social fathering. Their remarks underscored the connection, as well as the subtle distinction, between desires to become fathers now or in the future and their sense of being ready now to do so. Another distinction can be made between being ready for fatherhood and being willing to deal with the consequences of paternity. Jeffrey highlights this distinction and interprets his response through a gendered lens:

> I see these young kids that are without fathers, and even if the fathers are supporting them, they don't live together, what not. And, it's just not the way I would, I could see myself. I'm not the type of person that, God forbid anything ever happened. I wouldn't run. I would stand up and take it like a man but you, you can't sit there and say that you're going to be, you know, a hundred percent gung ho into it because you're gonna, you're gonna regret it.

Jeffrey says that he would regret his unplanned fatherhood but would deal with it responsibly. He implies that he would be a live-in rather than an nonresident father.

The men's perceptions of an ideal fathering situation is closely tied to how they view the type of romantic relationship they want, as well as to their financial situation. For most but not all, being married first is critical. Terence, a 25-year-old, speaks for the majority: "I don't want my kid to come before my wife. I definitely want to fall in love, and find someone I want to spend the rest of my life with and then have a kid." For Terence, feeling ready to be a father would be contingent on his finding a partner who would "stay around . . . for the whole period." He describes how his worries about finding such a partner were accentuated because a girlfriend with whom he had a "very sexual relationship" during junior college did not return from summer vacation. In mourning his loss, Terence developed a stronger sense of the impermanence of most relationships. He expresses also the importance of devoting himself to his future children, a sentiment rooted in two life-changing experiences. First, he never knew his father. Second, he lost touch with his mother once he entered high school because of their strained relationship. Not surprisingly, concerns about abandonment were central to Terence's lifeview.

A few of the men seemed particularly eager to get on with their lives and make the transition to fatherhood. One 21-year-old, Terry, excitedly speaks of how it would be "pretty cool to raise like a son or a daughter and to teach them things and watch them grow and know that they're part, they're, I guess, half of them is you." Continuing: "I would rather start a family early, so I'm kind of young so I can relate more with the kids, rather than starting like later in life, that's kind of, I guess, why I wanna find a girl, settle down fairly soon, start a family." Although only a few of our participants share Terry's need to search immediately for a wife and the future mother of their children, most state that this type of family arrangement is something that they want eventually for themselves.

Becoming a father in the immediate future was real for Sid, a 24-year-old father-in-waiting who had had a painful experience dealing with a miscarriage involving the same partner three years ago. Like Terry, Sid thinks it would be good to be a relatively young father. Although he is not married and had impregnated his partner accidentally for the second time, Sid feels okay about becoming a father outside marriage:

> I feel like right now I'm at the age where, I know I don't know everything, and I probably never [will] know everything, but I know a good amount to where I can, give'm just, give my child knowledge so he won't get into too much trouble. I know he's gonna get in trouble, or she's gonna get in trouble, in the world, but I feel like I've enough knowledge to let him know what's right, what's wrong, or just certain things that I did that I don't want them to do, just pinpoint little experiences that I went through so they'll have a little knowledge, and at this time I'm still learning myself, so, when my child comes, I'll be learning what they're learning and I won't be like, too old to go out and play with them or to take'm places, I still got a little spunk left in me.

Sid appears to view his youthful standing as a parental asset that could enhance his ability to carry out his roles as ethical guide and playmate effectively. He also anticipates that his upcoming fathering experience is going to be a reciprocal process wherein he will be both a teacher and a student of life. He links his readiness to become a father to his perception that he is in an ideal place to be a teacher and a companion for his child. Though he is looking forward to his new status, Sid tempers his general sense of readiness because of his "rough time" with the previous miscarriage: "I'm not too excited because of what happened the last time, so I don't want to get built up again, end up getting hurt again, so I just, waitin' it out . . . I'll be more relaxed after like the fourth month."

Unlike Sid, who has personal experience to draw upon, Jared has not yet impregnated anyone. Nonetheless, he is quick to emphasize the importance of a romantic relationship when it comes to procreative issues by declaring that were he to impregnate a woman inadvertently,

> it would depend on the state of the relationship and if like love was a factor in the relationship, then by love I would just be assuming that if I was to have the baby, that I would have at least wanted it in the future, so there would be some want for it now. Even if I didn't necessarily wish it would have happened . . . and then I could see marrying the person because I love them already, so it would just be harder for us to live life because we did it at the wrong time or at you know, a harder time.

From Jared's perspective, children should ideally be an appendage to a relationship. "I don't have a child to, like, have a pet, I have a child to have an experience with the woman that I'm involved with." One reading of the perspective is that he sees his connection to his children as being closely tied to his involvement with a partner, a view consistent with the idea that men are more likely to see parenting and partnership as a "package deal."[7]

Some of the participants were receptive to the idea of paternity or fathering a child in an abstract sense but realized they were currently not inclined or prepared to embrace all aspects of being a father. Listen to Desmond, a 30-year-old:

> I do not mind being [becoming] a father . . . if I had a child, I could be ready to be a father. What I do not want to give up is the time. I'd like my son, well, let's just say son, may not be a son, might be a daughter, but I'd like my child to be very well educated, to have good advantages, to do well in life, to be all it can be, and I would support it as best I could. But, I wish there was a way to do that without, right now, without giving up the time.

Here, Desmond talks about his readiness for fatherhood in terms of a contradiction: he has high aspirations for his hypothetical (male) child and is willing to commit to supporting these aspirations, but at present he is unwilling to devote the time he believes necessary to raise a child. Part of his thinking about becoming a father is the seemingly irreconcilable benefits and disadvantages: helping a child "be all it can be" versus the time demands required to accomplish this. Desmond is also one of the handful of participants who because of gender distrust explicitly challenges the need to be married. As he embellishes a hypothetical story about women leaving men, he says:

> So, because you give her three babies and marry her doesn't mean that you can't get burned because you're going to neglect her somewhere along the line, and then she's going to burn you. And you're going to be stuck with the kids. So my question is now why get married? From what I, what I'm seeing happening now, these women are getting up and leaving, so why get married?

Although the interviewer did not ask Desmond to explain his thoughts about the potentiality of being "stuck with the kids," it appears from the larger context of Desmond's remarks that he sees children as burdensome if their father is not romantically involved with their mother. As with Jared, whom we just discussed, Desmond's perception of children's value to the father is intimately tied to his "package deal" philosophy.

As a father-in-waiting, Kendal has the advantage of hindsight to reflect on how ready he was to become a father before his child's conception. He does so in light of discussions he had with his partner when they stopped using birth control. Asked about the nature of those discussions, he replies:

> Well, it was just, we, we was hopin' that it, it would happen later but it happened sooner. So. You know, we often talked, we actually wanted kids a little bit later in life. But, like I told her, 'cause she kept askin me how did I feel about it. Like I told her, nobody's really ready. You know. Once you say you gonna do it, then you have to do it. But I mean, like she said, it was sort of a surprise. It, it really wasn't. I mean, if you don't, if you don't do somethin' to prevent it, then it's gonna happen.

By suggesting that "nobody's really ready," Kendal implicitly highlights the critical and novel transitions that first-time parents confront. He apparently espouses the philosophy that a person should accept the parenting challenge when faced with it and take care of the business at hand. With a cool logical demeanor, Kendal is quick to recognize that pregnancy is typically a consequence of unprotected sex.

When we considered how the young men shared their perceptions about becoming fathers and their visions or daydreams about prospective children, several interrelated properties emerged from their stories. We examined the properties to understand better what being "ready" for fatherhood means, how men perceive ideal fathering, and how they envision fathering for themselves. For simplicity, we labeled the more prominent properties *degree and form of collaboration*; *focus of attention* (relational and substantive); *temporal orientation*; *experience* (source and intensity); and *degree of clarity*. After using these properties to organize our analysis of fatherhood readiness, we incorporate three of them (focus of attention, temporal orientation, and degree of clarity) into our subsequent analysis of fatherhood ideals and visions. Where possible, we highlight how the relevant properties intersect.

Degree and Form of Collaboration

The men in our study acknowledged their sense of readiness by reflecting on it alone and by discussing it with others. Patterns of private reflection and more collaborative experiences have distinctive features but tend to reinforce one another over time. Both of these approaches may have been relevant intermittently to the men's sense of readiness as it varies over time within specific romantic relationships and between different romantic involvements. A few of the men recalled instances where they had acknowledged their sense of readiness to themselves without discussing it with someone; most reported at least fleeting conversations with others about their own sense of readiness. The conversations tended not to include truly collaborative exchanges in which the men were coconstructing and negotiating their sense of readiness with others. Rather, the conversations tended to reinforce the participants' orientations developed previously. Some of the men thought about their sense of readiness privately when they reflected on how others (e.g., family, friends, individuals in school or in public, persons on TV talk shows) were affected by the parental responsibilities they assumed before they were prepared to deal with them effectively. Seeing pregnant teenagers and young parents out in public had caught the attention of several of the participants, reminding them that they were ill-prepared at that point to have a child. A similar pattern existed for men, like

Arthur, who were raised in a poor rural area and have experienced close-up how family members had to struggle to deal with the financial hardships children often endure. In Arthur's case, he bases his sense of readiness and explicit preference to delay fatherhood until he is about 28 on his desire to improve upon the meager material life his father had provided for him: "[W]hen I grew up my dad, he didn't have nothin'. They [parents] had me when they were like eighteen, and they pretty much didn't have anything. We drove ol' beat-up cars, lived in an old mobile home, and I just don't want to be like that for the rest of my life." Arthur is also quick to add, "I want to be sure it's [having a child] with the person I'm going to be with for the rest of my life. Not just go and make a buncha kids." Although it appears that Arthur had not spent much time prior to the interview thinking about these issues, our reading of his responses suggests that he had given some thought to them away from his family and partner. In other portions of his interview, he makes clear that he had also been straightforward with his partner, mother, and grandmother about wanting to wait to have children until his late twenties.

Marcus, a 19-year-old participant, provides a specific example of a collaborative process when he recalls a conversation with one of his girlfriends: "And then we just talked about, she was like, I can't have no kids right now. I'm like, you. I can't have none neither. Too damn young." Although the excerpt illustrates a rather superficial exchange, talk of this sort can be important if it activates the man's sense of procreative responsibility and provides him an opportunity to establish, or reassert his own views on his fatherhood readiness.

In recalling a conversational exchange with a friend about a piece of folk wisdom, Desmond illustrates how men can collaborate to fashion their sense of readiness. Desmond began it by saying, "'You know, I could have a baby from this girl. I'd like to give this girl a baby.'" His friend responded, "'Well, you don't know that yet, until [you], look in her eyes.'" To which Desmond asked, "'Why?'" The friend, "'If you can look in her eyes and, when you look at her, see your children in her eyes, then that's when you know.'" Desmond goes on to tell the interviewer that he attempted to put his friend's advice into practice: "I tried to do that, and it kind of, I kind of saw what they [the friend and other friends] were talking about."

Harper remembers one friend who warned him:

"Oh yeah, Calvin became a father." He was telling me, oh, "[Y]ou gonna have to start doing this and doing that." I'm like, man, I ain't gonna have no kid, you know. He was about the only one who was—he talked a lot about changing diapers, you have to get up, you have to save money, buy diapers, you have to, the baby's crying at night, you getting up or you have to take it to the babysitter, you have to, a lot of stuff like that he was telling me.

The above examples highlight or allude to several ways that individuals intentionally or unintentionally affect men's sense of how prepared they are to become fathers. Some of these processes are interactive. Men can swap stories and ideas with family, friends, partners, and professionals. Although we found no clear examples where men vigorously negotiated or coconstructed their views on fatherhood readiness with their partners, we suspect that partners can and do affect men's thinking in this area. Likewise, had we interviewed men who had participated in fatherhood or pregnancy prevention programs we might have found that some of their perceptions of their readiness to become fathers had been influenced by their discussions with social service professionals.

As we saw in our interviews, not all forms of influence require men to be actively involved with others. Men can simply observe others from a distance, consider how these individuals' lives probably have been affected by their fertility experiences, and extrapolate the potential consequences for themselves if they were to father a child. They can also worry productively about how parents (and others) would respond after learning that a son would now become a father because of an unplanned pregnancy. For example, Jody, 21 years of age, explains that he felt it would have been "terrible" had he impregnated his girlfriend: "[O]ur families wouldn't really go for that because we hadn't known each other for a real long time at that point, and we would've been real young and not married." Even though the subject had never come up with his parents, the mere thought of how they would react would have led him to believe that he was not ready for fatherhood. Men can use reference groups or a "generalized other" as a basis for evaluating their behavior and options.

Not all the participants feared a negative parental reaction. Some who were in stable relationships anticipated receiving support from their parents or the partner's parents, or both. Andy, the man who became much more interested in getting married and having children after he took care of his ailing father, also believes that the Jewish community would be an asset for his future family. His partner is active in the Jewish community and he looks forward to his children's involvement in the religious environment:

It's a very stable, satisfying experience for children. . . . [I]t's sort of like a community awaiting the birth of a child . . . it's another support network . . . another way in which I feel that I'm ready to have children. . . . [W]e have her parents and grandparents living in town and we have a community that is supportive of what we are doing.

Focus of Attention

When the men talked about their degree of readiness to become fathers, they focused their attention in several ways. Their narratives involved both a relational object (self, partner, child) and substantive foci (e.g., financial and occupational stability, educational attainment, emotional and psychological well-being, time). Most looked primarily or exclusively on their own well-being or personal development. Typically, they reported fears about not being able to complete their education or follow career plans, and/or having their mobility or leisure activities unduly restricted. An 18-year-old, Alex, asserts: "There's a lot I want to do, a lot of things I want to see. A lot of things I want to accomplish before I want to settle down and have a family." Desmond, in recalling how he responded to a pregnancy scare in his early twenties says, "I did not look at myself as a father. No, that never, that part never entered, I never could see anyone calling me daddy or anything like that. No. It's, I just thought about the monetary impact." Simone, a 23-year-old, believes that an unplanned pregnancy would put his educational goals out of reach, that he would have to leave school and get a job. Even though he is quite sure that he is not ready to assume the responsibilities associated with fatherhood, and he and his girlfriend have agreed on an abortion if she were to become pregnant, Simone knows that he would do "anything" for the child were his partner to change her mind about an abortion. He adamantly asserts, "I do not want anybody to give me the money, nobody, except me. It's my job, my responsibility, it's what I have to do!"

A more elaborate and unique example is provided by Kyle, the 21-year-old devout Christian participant. Following on the heels of his comments about how little he has thought about girls and pregnancy, Kyle remarks:

I need to know what a husband and father needs to be and start working towards that. As I started realizing the character qualities that need to be there, and I realize I'm not anywhere near that and how much work is gonna need to be done on myself to prepare myself for that, the list

keep[s] on getting longer, and I'm tackling them one at a time or whatever ones I can handle at each moment, but I think by just having them in
my thoughts, maybe it's just like a physical maturing now . . . I want to be
a good husband, I want to be a good father—I don't have any concept of
what a husband or a good father is but, the Bible does. . . . I have notes of
character qualities and then verse after verse that talks about it.

Kyle may not have thought specifically about impregnating a girl, yet he
has thought extensively about his degree of readiness to become a father.
He is unique in our sample, and uncharacteristic of the more general population because of his commitment to prepare for fatherhood even before
becoming sexually active. Kyle is also one of a kind in that his preparation
centers primarily on his personal and moral development. Instead of worrying about how fatherhood would stand in the way of his personal life or
development, as we saw with Alex above, Kyle draws attention to how his
current stage of personal and moral development would restrict his ability
to be a good Christian father.

The orientation to self revealed in Kyle's narrative is instructive because
it illustrates how some of the men in our sample portrayed aspects of their
personal character and then linked them to their degree of readiness for
fatherhood. Such portrayals require self-awareness, the ability to articulate
it, and an understanding of how it may influence preparedness for being a
father. The men's orientation toward these portrayals sometimes grows
from their perception of how particular character traits have either helped
or hindered other men in expressing themselves as fathers. The men observe the way certain fathers' easygoing nature, loving kindness, temper, or
irresponsible tendencies translate into their enactment of their fathering
roles.

Kyle's narrative also demonstrates that it is possible for at least some
young men to recognize the connection between their personal or character development and their future fathering abilities. It shows that men can
take steps beyond capitalizing on educational and employment opportunities to prepare for their prospective roles as fathers.

Though men, like Kyle, can begin a self-reflective process without the
impetus of a pregnancy or birth, it is more likely to occur when they come
face-to-face with reality: a partner's breaking news of a possible or actual
pregnancy. As discussed in chapter 4, pregnancy scares and confirmed
pregnancies can be turning point experiences for some men or at least can
prompt some men to look more closely and through a slightly different

lens at their life, aspirations, and circumstances. Either way, they construct a sense of readiness as part of a larger process of trying to acclimate themselves to recently received information.

A smaller number of the men voiced concern about how an unplanned pregnancy and birth would affect the child's well-being. Such comments tended emphasize the financial aspects of providing for offspring. Reflecting on the money problems his single mother grappled with as she was raising him and two of his siblings, Jerry, a 19-year-old, draws his conclusion:

> [S]he always did what she had to do to get us what we wanted and what we needed, even if it was sacrificing stuff she needed at the time, but she couldn't get. She just wanted to make sure we had everything. Like come Christmas time she'd do whatever she could to give us presents and stuff. But then you see some people where their parents don't have enough money to even buy them things, and so [it's a] lot of things like that makes you want to, like makes you think that you need to have the money, and definitely want to be able to take care of your kids as well as you can.

Terence echoes Jerry's sentiments as he reflects on how his financial circumstances have improved over the years to the point where he thinks he now might be in a little better position to provide adequately for a child:

> [W]hen I was younger I didn't, definitely didn't, want to have one [a child], and it was like definitely no possibilities of me being able to take care of one, or supporting one, or teaching one, a baby, anything. But now I'm a little older, and I think that if I could support one, now would be, like 25 to 30 would be an excellent time to have, excellent time to have a kid. But only if I would, if I could give them anything I wanted to. If I could give my kid whatever I chose to give him, without a problem. If I saw something and I was like, "All right, I want you to have this," I could get it for him. I don't want to have one until I can definitely do that.

Terence, in elaborating on his current thinking, suggests that he believes he would have to be "able to take care of two other people," a wife and a child, before he could be ready for fatherhood. Hence, his perception of his financial status leads to his conclusion: "I'm definitely not ready."

Being ready was not only about adequate financial means or forgone educational opportunities for some of the men. A few spoke about whether it makes sense to bring a child into a troubled world. Sam, a 26-year-old who lives with his girlfriend and her six-year-old, admits that finances influenced his perception of his readiness for a child of his own right now but quickly goes on to say:

[A]nd a lot of things is you look at the radio and the news and you hear the Columbine shootings and a 13-year-old on trial for murder. What kind of place is it to bring a child into, though? It's getting worse and worse every time you turn around and watch the TV. It's about every day that goes by, you hear about a guy that, who ran his car into a preschool and killed kids because he wanted to "take them out." . . . If anything were to happen to Darin [stepson] by somebody else, I would probably be in jail for attempted murder on them.

Sam's emotional assessment of today's poor state of affairs for children is reinforced by his tour of duty as a 20-year-old MP in the army, where he saw many abused children. On one unforgettable occasion, he checked out a call from a neighbor reporting a crying baby next door. At the house, he learned that a soldier who had returned from thirty days in the field had killed his baby; the soldier "couldn't take his baby crying so he slammed him against all four walls." Having witnessed the "aftermath," Sam reasons that his MP assignments probably encourage him to be more restrained if and when he physically disciplines Darin. In a variety of ways, Sam's complete narrative shows how his observations and experiences have set the tone of his love for his stepson and children generally, and have resulted in mixed feelings about acting on his strong desire to become a biological father.

For men like Sam, their assessment of their readiness includes things beyond their immediate reach and control. They may feel that they can accommodate a child in their own lives but that it would be irresponsible to have a child whom they could not protect from the larger social environment.

Granted it was not common for the participants to factor in their concern about a partner as an individual or the future mother of their child, but a few, like Terence, explicitly mentioned or hinted at how their sense of readiness is, or would be, tied to a partner's circumstances. Not surprisingly, the men voiced concern for a partner in conjunction with their concern about their own well-being, sometimes saying, for example, that they were both still in school. After stating that he wanted kids someday, and then being asked his ideal age at which this might occur, Jerry declares: "[W]hen I'm through with college, and when I have a job, and my life's steady, and if I'm with someone that her life's steady, and just when we know the time's right, when you have the money that you're going to be able to take care of it and stuff."

One way men can focus on a partner is by considering the kind of mother she would be. If they are involved with a woman who they think would make a wonderful mother and support them in their efforts to be a good father, they may be more inclined to think that they are ready for fatherhood. However, if men sense that a current partner would not make a good mother, or perhaps is simply ill-suited to be a mother at this point in her life, they probably would feel as though they are themselves inadequately prepared to be a father, at least within the current relationship. Although the men seldom spontaneously talked about a partner's potential as a mother, a few did so. For example, asked if his partner's personality would affect him as a father, Ricky promptly responds that her "light" side would help. "She has a lot of patience, so that has kinda rubbed off on me. So yeah, I think that will help a lot."

The men related their degree of readiness to their concerns about themselves, a child, a partner, or some combination, but their views often implicated specific substantive concerns as well. Given prevailing gendered beliefs about fathering and breadwinning in the United States, it is not surprising that the men were most likely to mention financial considerations. Most typically recognized that they are not yet in a position to support children financially in a manner they deem acceptable. In a related vein, Tom, a 22-year-old, responds to a question about what being ready to have a child means to him:

> Steadiness, 'cause right now I've got a lifestyle that's like, I'll go work in a place for a while, and get set up. And get as much money saved up and then try to go off and move somewhere else a little better. I just haven't really found a place yet that I'm comfortable with staying.

The "steadiness" that Tom speaks of combines his work life and his living environment. Being settled in a place that he likes and where he is financially secure is important. In addition, some of the men identified the loss of time as a nonfinancial worry that affected the sense of fatherhood readiness, as is illustrated by Desmond's earlier remarks.[8]

The stories we heard consistently showed, implicitly or explicitly, that the men's focus of attention was usually multifaceted and combined both relational and substantive concerns. Kyle's earlier comments implicitly suggest, for instance, that although his focus of attention is on himself, he also believes his child and partner would suffer because he has yet to develop the traits that would allow him to express himself as a Christian father. Moreover, his comments reveal that he combines his explicit relational focus on self with his substantive interests regarding Christian fatherhood.

Temporal Orientation

Asked to reflect upon their fatherhood readiness, the men framed their description by contrasting the perceptions, experiences, and desires they associate with different periods in their lives. We saw this, for example, with Arthur, who linked fatherhood readiness with his desire to improve upon the financial circumstances he experienced as a child. In this manner, the men sometimes drew upon their previous familial or personal experiences to mold their message about their fatherhood readiness in the near future. In other words, the men assessed what in the past they had witnessed firsthand (e.g., living in poverty) and then speculated on how assuming or postponing father roles would influence them now and/or in the future. Having distinctive memories about their childhood and a parent's or parents' experiences may have provided the men with the impetus and means to assess their present prospects for fathering children in certain ways. Though young single men probably pay more attention to the difficulties that others have had or are having in relation to fertility experiences, they can notice more positive signs as well. Knowing someone of similar age and living in comparable conditions who speaks highly of his or her parenting experience could reassure some men that they are indeed ready to assume fatherhood responsibilities.

The men sometimes characterized their own transformations in terms of their readiness to have children. Miller, a 28-year-old, recalls that he "never even really gave much thought to it [having children]. You know, I like to travel. I like to work and take my time off and go and see and do. I never really made a place in that life for a, for a kid." He adds, "I'm getting to almost to the point where I should start settling down a little bit and actually, possibly looking for a house to live in and a job that I work at for more than a year or so." Here, Miller juxtaposes his previous and perhaps fading lifestyle with his emerging thoughts about a "nesting" strategy that would foster a more stable lifestyle, one that apparently would be more conducive to fathering a child. The narrative device he uses reveals how his identity slowly evolved and highlights the more continuous features of his procreative consciousness and sense of fatherhood readiness.

In other instances, the men privileged their current experience and did their best to avoid other time references. Marcus, for example, comments that he and his partner "wouldn't really talk about what if we have a kid because we were scared to talk about like, I didn't even want to look . . . at that. I just wanted to talk about things right now, didn't want to talk about the future."

Others among the men were comfortable comparing, implicitly or explicitly, their current situation with what they projected for themselves. A 17-year-old participant, Reynaldo, provides a useful example:

> I'm hoping to at least be out of college, have a steady job, be financially stable and be mature about things, and hopefully be married. And then I can think about being a father. But, right now I don't really think about myself being a father, it's just in the distant future. Like when I'm 26, 27, around there. But, I'm picturing myself being a good father.

Reynaldo, like some of the other participants, is able to visualize relatively long-term goals that he wants to accomplish before becoming a father.

Thus, in organizing their thoughts about their readiness, men reveal their manipulation of past, present, and future-oriented conceptions of self to interpret the meaning of becoming a father now. When they anchor their assessment in their image of a former or current self, they implicitly or explicitly convey an understanding of what the future would hold for them. They can also look into the relatively long-term future and imagine how their lives, and those of a child and a partner might be affected. Men who are inclined to construct a complex narrative can weave images from the three time periods into their narratives as they construct their sense of readiness.

Experience (Source and Intensity)

We earmark the men's firsthand experiences with aspects of the procreative realm and child care because some of the men viewed those experiences as salient to their degree of readiness to become fathers. They also warrant attention, given the men's limited exposure to certain types of experiences that result from the gendered nature of the procreative realm and child care. For several of the men, their sense of readiness has been affected by fertility-related experiences. Indeed, some of the men found the prospect of becoming a father to an unplanned child a wake-up call to think about fatherhood issues more seriously. Asked if his abortion experience affected the way he thought about children, 21-year-old Austin, explains "[I]t's definitely reminded me that I'm definitely not ready for that kind of responsibility. I knew that I wasn't before this happened, but if anything, it reminded me that I wasn't ready for that at all."

In Tom's case, his miscarriage experience deflated his desire and sense of readiness to have another child: "Before the miscarriage, I was more 'amped' to have a child, I guess you could say and more willing. And nowadays I'm going to be very selective, it's going to be a while till I have another, try to have another kid." He not only identifies the miscarriage as the source of his experiential connection to his sense of readiness, but his use of "amped" reveals that the intensity of the experience was such that it transformed his earlier willingness and readiness to have a second child. Thus, their fertility-related experiences were turning points in these men's perceptions of their readiness.

As we discussed in chapter 4, nonfertility experiences can also act as turning points in men's lives by affecting the way they think about fatherhood. In his response to a question about whether he sees children in his future, Marcus conveys how his sense of fatherhood readiness has been shaped by his frequent interaction with his niece, "the cutest thing on earth to me right now." His account of a typical day of baby-sitting her:

> I picked her up at twelve thirty, and I was with her . . . to like seven. . . . [J]ust constantly having to like give her bottles . . . and changing the diaper, and when I put her down, she cries, she wants to hold me, she wants me to walk around the house with her. She doesn't want to be put down. I can't watch TV, I mean, I can watch TV but I have to keep an eye on her. It's just things like that, that right there's being responsible. . . . I have a lot of other things in my life right now to take care of before I have children. So that's why I say that she [his niece] makes me want to have one [a child] . . . and, then again, she doesn't.

As Marcus observes, his exposure to the moral labor of child care is a dose of reality that convinces him that he's not quite ready to be a hands-on father, despite the possible appeal of having his own child. However, similar experiences may encourage some men to decide otherwise. Also, opportunities to be involved in the more playful aspects of children's lives may have a contrary effect. The following excerpts capture a sentiment shared by a number of the men:

> I've always liked kids, like my cousin had a little kid a couple of years ago and I just like messing, playing with them, and stuff. (Cal, age 16)

> Eventually I'd love to be a father. I mean, I love kids. I love playing with them. (Alex, age 18)

> I've always liked kids. You know, I have like nieces and nephews I love. I want to have me a kid, you know. (Harper, age 29)

Although the attraction to the playful aspects of spending time with kids may enhance Cal's and Alex's perceptions of their fatherhood readiness, it does not necessarily follow that they will challenge prevailing gendered patterns of parental involvement once they become fathers. In other words, their subjective sense of readiness may actually hinge on their willingness to express more traditional forms of father involvement that emphasize play, rather than attending to their children's more basic everyday needs.[9] A 25-year-old participant, Rudy, explicitly captures this sentiment when he talks of being ready to be a father if he finds the right woman:

> I'm ready to settle down but I'm also, I know I'm kind of, I don't know if you ever seen the movie *One Fine Day*, but that's probably the best example of what kind of father I'm gonna be. The mother's gonna be sitting there, yelling and screaming at everybody, and I'm gonna be running around like George Clooney playing with the kids.

Another type of experience that can alter men's perceptions of their degree of fatherhood readiness has to do with their comparisons: between themselves and their friends and family members who are parents. This type of appraisal process does not surface often in the men's narratives, but it is distinctive for 25-year-old Terence:

> I have friends that have kids, some my age, some younger. And, when they do a good job, and like I know where they come from and I know how much financial problems they already have. If they already doing a good

job and they're younger than me, from the knowledge I have and the background I have, I just assume that I could do just as good a job or even better, so it's seeing that, seeing someone younger than me, seeing someone probably in financial debt like me, be able, see them do it and complete it so well gives me faith to say that I probably could too. So it's not never knowing, you know, because when I was younger none of 'em had kids, so we were all just kids, so but now some of my friends can do it, it's like oh if he can do it, then I can do it type thing.

By being around and observing his friends whom he perceives as like him in many ways, Terence gains a useful perspective on his potential paternity. He sees the exposure as a "confidence builder" in regard to his taking on the responsibilities associated with fatherhood if necessary.

Degree of Clarity

Many of the excerpts thus far illustrate the men's level of clarity about their perceived fatherhood readiness. Given the age range of our sample, it is not surprising that most were relatively clear about not being ready to have a child. Still, as we just saw with Marcus, some expressed ambivalence about the prospect of fatherhood. And some, like 30-year-old Desmond, are straightforward about having been ready at various times to have a child. Desmond speaks of the possibility of having children with two recent partners:

It was all positive, just thinking about raising a child. Because, really, the last two, I probably could have married them in the wink of an eye. So I thought about how we would look in a house, raising a family, with a child being accepted, being loved, nurtured, cared for, and all of those things.

Desmond's ruminations suggest an active imagination that allows visualizing himself as a family man. His clarity about being ready for fatherhood in these relationships is evident when he contrasts his recent orientation with the way he reacted in his early twenties to a pregnancy scare. Desmond's narrative construction about his evolving fatherhood readiness over time is consistent with the "doubling of self" technique involving identity work.[10] Those who use the technique explicitly construct and present a current identity by comparing it to an identity they had previously expressed. We mentioned in chapter 5 Desmond's reaction a number of years ago to a partner's possible pregnancy: distancing himself because he was not ready to confront it. As he reflects on that experience, he talks of having hurt his partner and rationalizes that young people often do not have control over their feelings. Desmond's narrative is also instructive because it illustrates how an understanding of men's subjective experiences is fostered by attending to the intersection of multiple properties. The tapestry that captures men's subjective sense of being prepared to become fathers is most distinctly woven together as a result of men's focus of attention, temporal orientation, and degree of clarity.

Ideal Father and Fathering Visions

In our earlier analysis we implied that men's sense of readiness is related to their beliefs about how fathers should ideally express themselves as fathers. We now consider how our participants talk about the "ideal father" and their visions of how they will act as fathers. Some had given a great deal of thought to it; others had not. Here, we selectively emphasize several of the properties described earlier and broaden our analysis to highlight the men's penchant for biological fatherhood, their thinking about their fathers, and their views on how being a man is related to fathering a child.

Biological Paternity

Asked about the importance of fathering their own biological children, most of the men pointed out that being genetically related to any future children is an important feature of an ideal fathering experience. Marcus, for example, so indicates: "Cuz it's gonna be my seed. It's gonna be me. I made that being, that human being, that person. And I'm going to father it jis' like my father fathered me." Marcus says that he does not really need a kid but, he does want one "in terms of a sense of continuity." He adds, "That is, I come from a family that is aware of its existence as a family and the generations going backwards and I understand myself to be part of that continuum. I'm just a cog in that system. I in turn will naturally sire another generation which will sire another."

Relatedly, Rudy mentions that he is eager to have a child so as to "see" himself in a new generation and to share a son or daughter with family members. It is "how I view life, how I eventually want to have children so family members that I have now, they might die tomorrow and then I don't have a child or anything, I don't have a wife, so I don't, I can't show them [a descendant]." Rudy elaborates that it is important that he father a child for his mother's happiness; when she sees her grandchildren, she apparently reminisces about her children as youngsters.

Justin, too, stresses his affinity for the intergenerational connection by first commenting on how proud his parents were when he graduated high school, and then:

> I see children as, it's like you're passing on your genes, you're passing on your hereditary information. . . . [I]t's like you get to a certain point in your life where you're not going to achieve much more. You're just at a standstill and you can bring up a child who can achieve great things and continue on the family.

In his everyday words, Justin associates his desire for biological paternity and social fathering with what theorists of adult development refer to as generativity—the need to nurture and guide younger generations.[11] His affinity with contributing to his family's generational continuity is palpable.

Although most participants focused, as Justin did, on the relationship between themselves as father and potential children when evaluating the importance of biological paternity, Jerry accentuates the shared experience of the prospective parents that can accompany a pregnancy:

> Just the whole thing that you and your wife will go through. Just her becoming pregnant, going to the doctors with her, and when she has her checkups, and just the whole experience pretty much. Going to the hospital with her and being there in the delivery.

Jerry's comments reflected his appreciation for a type of collaborative approach to the prebirth process that he associates with the ideal fatherhood experience. In other words, fathering is made special by sharing the gestation process with the prospective mother.

For Desmond, biological paternity is also important and is accentuated by concern that his potential children carry his name, even if he were never with the partner. He describes that if he fathers a child with a woman who goes on to marry another man, he will still support the child but wants the child to have his name:

That's part of the deal. I need to have some stipulations along those lines, because if I'm going to pay and take care of it, then what's in it for me? You know, I'm telling the young lady, I'm gonna say, "Hey, look, you've got your freedom. You can go on and have another man, have another son if you want to, but this one is mine. So what's in it for me? I want the name" [banging the table].

Such a demand reveals how "ownership" may come into play as men think about their offspring and paternal obligations and rights. Absent the physiological connectedness that most women value because of pregnancy and childbirth, men look for other opportunities to establish a paternal bond. An awareness of the blood tie and/or sharing a surname can provide some with an alternative means to feel connected. The blood tie, along with the establishment of legal paternity, enables them to do so.

Images of the Good Father

Consistent with research that has sampled fathers,[12] our sample reported several key features of good fathering and indicated that men's own fathers can serve as positive or negative role models. Economic provisioning was mentioned by a number of the men; however, they stressed the importance of a father's time with his children and his desire to be actively involved in their lives.

Responding to what being a father means to him, 19-year-old Antoine reflects the sentiments of a number of the participants: "Always there, no matter what you do, right or wrong, thick and thin, whatever. Somebody that's not just a provider, not just put[ing] a roof over your head but taking care of you, gives you advice. Just your mentor and everything, friend, best friend." Reynoldo's glowing language, reinforces Antoine's comment by noting how his father is a good father no matter the circumstances: "[M]y dad is a real man right now 'cause he can support us even though he's unemployed . . . but you know, whenever he had a job, he was doing good. And he supported us, and right now he is showing how he can get us through tough times. . . ." Note that Reynaldo flavors his assessment with a reference to his father's masculinity, by suggesting that he is a "real man" because he is capable of being a family leader with or without a job. For many of the participants, the essence of being a good father is being involved, present and approachable, and being a friend and a measured disciplinarian.

The men's general conception of the "good father" appeared to be closely related to how they assessed their own fathers. Whether they described their fathers as positive or negative role models, the articulated benchmark amounted to a fairly consistent ideal. Typically, their fathers' contributions as disciplinarians and providers were appreciated, but the men wanted these necessary roles balanced with direct involvement and emotional concern. Not surprisingly, the facets in which particular men found their fathers lacking were the ones they seemed most eager to improve on when they themselves become fathers. Similarly, the qualities most appreciated were the ones they hoped to emulate. At one extreme, the men who described physically absent fathers vowed not to be so themselves. The comments of 23-year-old Sean are representative of this small but important group:

> I was just thinking that I didn't want to have children in X number of cities and also have a wife who wasn't the mother of those children 'cause that's pretty much how, what it was with my father. . . . I never felt cheated out of a father, 'cause I think my life turned out a little better, but at the same time I would have liked to [have] known him.

At the other end of the spectrum, some of the men praised their fathers for developing a strong emotional connection with them or knowing how to provide just the right amount of discipline and supervision:

> I'd be a very loving father like my father was. And I would try to model myself as he raised me . . . I'd be firm but I'd never hit the child. I'd be very loving and supportive no matter what. Just be his best friend. (Mitchel, age 22)

> Like my father is good, so I'm gonna pretty much be the same way that he is to me. You know, not strict but having a level head and keeping me down and not letting me get out of control really. Giving me a little bit of line but not too much. (Reynaldo, age 17)

The men whose experiences fell somewhere between the two poles presented a similar dynamic. For instance, 28-year-old David praises his father's achievement of the provider ideal but sees himself as being emotionally closer to his future children:

Well he was a good provider. You know, he worked full-time and he brought home the money, paid the bills, but he wasn't like real affectionate. It didn't seem like he made an effort to like go out of his way to do things with his kids. . . . I think I would be a lot closer to my kids than he was.

Talking about their fathers, then, became an opportunity for these men to refine their visions of themselves as future fathers by reflecting on what they valued or missed in their own experience of being fathered.

Practical Fathering Visions

In chapter 3 we described the concept of child visions as men's mental pictures of their own children. For our sample, this primarily meant visions of children not yet born. A related concept we introduce here, fathering visions, captures the ways in which men fantasized about being involved with or doing things for their children. As noted above, the men sometimes used their fathers as a point of reference to arrive at their own understanding of a "good father."

In some instances, the images the men had of good fathering and their fantasies about fathering their yet-to-be-born children were related to their sense of fatherhood readiness. If they had settled thoughts about what they would do with or for their children, then they were more likely to have criteria to use in judging their current ability to make the images and fantasies come true.

The participants varied considerably in the extent to which they had visualized themselves as active fathers at some point. Not surprisingly, the ones with a pregnant partner appeared to recall spending more time fantasizing about involvement in a prospective child's life. Given the nature of cognitive recall, the men in serious relationships at the time of the interview, especially those with a pregnant partner, were in a better position to recollect and describe their specific fantasies. The men were also more likely to have fathering visions if they had firsthand experience with stepchildren or had socialized with relatives or friends with children. Having watched parents interacting with their children in public is another situation that prompted some of the men to visualize themselves as a father, most commonly as playmate or disciplinarian. Overall, we found that a few have had a very active fantasy life devoted to their impending roles as fathers; some have had occasional thoughts; and others have had no visions.

In chapter 3, we described how Francisco had developed elaborate images of his child Emma prior to her birth. Francisco had also visualized his fathering roles. Compared to the other participants, Francisco had spent more time and energy fantasizing about a prospective child. Some of his images sprang from conversations with his pregnant partner about what they would do with Emma and where they wanted her raised: "Like I want to take her to Disney World and wanna have a nice house. . . . I wanna live in a nice neighborhood. I've been looking at that a lot. I want her to go to a nice school. I'd like [her to] associate with a certain type of people." Francisco talks, too, of wanting to provide Emma with opportunities to travel and of how he planned to be involved with her school activities and friendships. He also saw himself doing things with her, like walking the beach holding hands and playing catch. A unique feature of Francisco's images is that he apparently devoted a fair amount of time and energy thinking about ways to enhance his daughter's social capital.[13]

Applied to fathers' involvement with their children, *social capital* refers to ways men can contribute to family- and community-based relations that can benefit their children's cognitive and social development. *Family-based relations* refers to the kinds of involvement fathers have with their children and their children's mothers that originate in trust, mutual expectations, and a sense of loyalty. *Community-based relations* refers to men's interactions with individuals and organizations in the community—particularly school, neighborhood, and church. By maintaining contact with adults (e.g., coaches, teachers, ministers) who interact with their children, and sometimes providing their children with resources or opportunities, fathers can be aware of what is going on in their children's lives. Fathers can also foster social capital for their children by developing positive relationships with their children's friends or incorporating their children into their own social networks (e.g., work environment).

Generally speaking, the men's visions of fathering focused primarily on more direct forms of interaction with their children by entering into their play activities. For instance, Arthur reports that he had occasionally fantasized about spending time with his prospective children: "Oh yeah, take'em to the ballpark. Teach'em to play ball. Buy a remote-controlled airplane, stuff like that. Fun stuff." He had had some of these thoughts before a former partner's pregnancy; most after he learned that she was expecting.

Unlike Arthur, Jake has had hands-on child care experience, having acted as a stepfather for a few years to the 4-year-old daughter of his cohabiting partner. It sensitized him to the financial and emotional aspects of being a father and provided an everyday context that prompted day-dreaming about what it would be like to have a biological child. Reflecting on the daydreaming, he says that

> every time I do something with her [his stepdaughter] 'cause I'm daddy to her now 'cause her father ain't no around nowhere. Don't pay child support or nothing, so I'm daddy now, so when I'm playing with her and doing things with her and you know pushing her on the swing and all this other stuff. I think about her being my own [biological child] and what I feel like I'm going to have with it being my blood, trying hard not to show favoritism and . . . all the sets of things I'm going to be doing with her and hoping that everything works out for the best [minor medical problems associated with the pregnancy], that way I can be with her.

Manhood and Fatherhood

Much is often said about men's using their sexuality and procreative abilities to express their masculinity,[14] yet little available qualitative research has explored how young men actually think and feel about these matters. Accordingly, young men's reflections on whether they believe being a man and fathering a child are related are useful. Our effort here, then, takes on special significance given the youthful composition of our sample, which includes a number of males who are making the transition from boyhood to manhood.

Numerous participants assert that by itself paternity does not prove manhood insofar as the qualities popularly ascribed to it are understood. Austin imparts his thinking on gender and procreation by first characterizing himself as someone who isn't a "womanizing, beer-guzzling frat boy, stereotyped white guy," but "even though I'm not that kind of guy, I'm still a man" who has "guy tendencies." Even so, he doesn't have this "ultimate definition of a man in my head." Asked about how he would be affected if he were not able to father a biological child, he begins, "I don't feel that manly. I mean, I don't feel powerful or, I mean strong, I have my own will, and my own pride and morals, but I don't feel, I don't feel this ultimate manliness." He continues "[I] wouldn't feel any less of a man . . . I would just feel incompetent . . . as a person, but not as a man." For Austin, the ability to father a biological child has little meaning as a badge of manhood.

Rather, he sees it as a competency fundamental to a human being. He values paternity but apparently not for what it might say about him as a man.

Despite not equating paternity with "being a man," paternity or the thought of it brought emotional responses from some of the men. Frank, a 29-year-old father of twins who had experienced a miscarriage with another partner, entertainingly describes how he felt when he first learned of that pregnancy: "If I was an animal I would feel like a lion and I would be up on a mountain and I would just roar . . . it's an animal instinct or an animal that came out . . . I felt like I needed to be home. Like I needed to protect, I needed to provide." Struggling to find the right words, Frank talks animatedly about his strong feelings and sense of leonine empowerment.

The men typically emphasized mature, responsible masculinity as an ideal. They tended to declarations that manhood should be evaluated on the basis of how men treat their children. For representative statements, listen to Cecil, Paul, Harper, and Arthur relating their thoughts on the relationship between being a man and fatherhood.

> I see that any man can father a child, right, but I see a really good man as being the man who, pretty much, it's everything after fathering the child, that's like really, the actions, the words and actions after that, are what, make a man, but to say "make a man"—I think it's more important to say, like, "make a good man." (Cecil, age 26)

> [H]aving a baby, it will make you prove your manhood. It won't necessarily make you a man, but it will make you prove what kind of man you really are . . . like any 13-year-old kid can make a baby . . . but that doesn't make him a man. (Paul, age 21)

> You take care of your kids, you're responsible, you're there for them. Whatever they need. I think that makes you a man. (Harper, age 29)

> Pretty much anybody can be a father, you know. Go out with a girl on the street and be a father right here. Never see her again, but I think a man's gonna know if he gets a girl pregnant. Marry her, take care of his kid. 'Cause its his. . . . Can't see somebody just abandoning their kid. "Here, I'll pay you twenty-five bucks a week 'til the kid's eighteen, go away." No, that's not, that's just the coward's way out of it. (Arthur, age 21)

Cecil and Harper, as well as other participants, stressed that producing offspring does not distinguish individuals as "men." Biological paternity was not seen as an emblem for masculinity, as shown by Paul's saying that, "any 13-year-old kid can make a baby." The bigger challenge is to assume paternal responsibility for their children and families.

Meeting the challenge is consistent with the more general theme of "responsibility" that many participants identified as essential to manhood. From Antoine's perspective, being a man means "taking responsibility. When you make mistakes, own up to your mistakes, your actions, being able to handle whatever comes with life and responsibility that you make."

Being responsible also means being in control and, for some of the men, achieving an independent status, not beholden to anyone. They saw the assumption of control as signaling a crossing over into the world of adulthood. In many ways, the men tended to equate manhood with responsible adulthood. When Marcus, 19, emphasizes "responsibility" he is speaking of the transition process he is going through: "I still have the part of me that wants to be a kid, but then again it's that part of me that wants to get ready to keep growing up, grow up and jis' keep going to be a man." He stresses the need to accomplish things in order for him to consider himself a man, such as owning a car, having an apartment, and of graduating from school. In a moment of adult-like reflection, Marcus observes that "it's a lotta young boys who have childs [*sic*] that are not being a man about their child." Reynaldo echoes the sentiment that males are men who can handle problems and applies the concept to his own future: "[When] I'm able to do everything and support a family and raise a family. That's that day I'll be a real man."

Although most of the men placed a premium on financial responsibility as an important component of manhood, Jerry interprets it more broadly, declaring that the way a man treats his children in general is paramount. He speaks thusly of responsibility because he sees some men staying at home while their wives work yet acknowledges that he would gladly be one such man if his partner had a good job.

With few exceptions, the young men in our study conveyed strong sentiments about the need for men to assume a range of paternal responsibilities when they become fathers. It is a sentiment clearly at odds with the day-to-day reality that many fathers experience once the romantic relationship with the mother of the children ends. The conviction heard so clearly in our sample of young men's voices before fatherhood is apparently dampened by contextual factors when a romantic relationship dissolves. Other research has demonstrated that many nonresident fathers are quick to talk about the struggles they face in dealing with an uncooperative and bitter former partner and her family, the logistics of overcoming physical distance and separate households, and the unsupportive attitudes toward fathers who are unable to fulfill the breadwinner role adequately.[15] A more cynical view of men's declining commitments is that for many men, the rhetoric of paternal responsibility is much more apparent than its practice.[16] Or, to steal a phrase from popular culture, "It is one thing to talk the talk, quite another to walk the walk."

Making Use of the Ideal Father Image

Of the five properties we discussed in connection with fatherhood readiness, focus of attention, degree of clarity, and temporal orientation are the most relevant to how the participants attempted to bridge the conceptual divide between the father ideal and how they expect to be with their children. As they contemplated their future fathering behavior, the men's focus of attention typically involved a child or children and the dynamic relationship that would prevail. For a few of the men, the focus of attention had to do with some type of child development and/or family-process philosophy. Miller, for instance, forcefully concludes that

> kids are spastic. What are you going to do? . . . I hate that, when you constantly see parents who are like, "Don't do that. No, don't touch that. No don't do that. No don't do this." I mean, for Christ's sake, just buy a leash, put the kid on the leash, and deal with it that way, if you're going to be that neurotic about it.

With this philosophy as a guide, Miller asserts: "My kids are going to experience and go out and do and see the stuff. Because that's how life should be." His comments illustrate that Miller, a father-in-waiting, has some clarity about children's personalities in general and the nature of his future role as a laid-back father.

Sean, a 23-year-old, provides another angle on the degree-of-clarity concept: His vision of what he would be like as a father, in the context of a story featuring the pitfalls of parenting. He recalls that his mother once "beat" him and his sister because his sister did something wrong but would not "fess up." Sean disliked that treatment at the time yet now anticipates that as a father he will not be able to guarantee that it will never arise, any more than his mother could have done. Consequently, he has resigned himself to the idea that fathering will be a "learning experience": "I can have a blueprint set up right now and then when you have children, who's to say that that blueprint is going to work?" Ironically, Sean asserted his clarity about fathering by emphasizing what he perceives to be the uncertainty associated with it. Notice, too, that he did so through a temporal construct. He first looked to the past and then applied it to his hypothetical future.

In most cases, the men's visions of themselves as fathers carried implicit or explicit visions of their children. As we showed in chapter 3, the men emphasized gender, personality, and physical features, in addition to their engaging in specific activities with their children. For the men who had envisioned their children, some tended to focus on their early years; others referenced their children's adolescent development. Justin, an 18-year-old, tries to imagine his and his partner's children, "but at most they're just like infants, really young children." In contrast, Tom thinks about the differences in raising a girl or a boy through adolescence. From his perspective, gender differences do not become relevant to parenting until the children reach puberty, at which point, he anticipates that if he had a daughter he would be uncomfortable with her emerging sexuality:

[L]ike girls would start getting interested in boys and start looking at them. Uhm, I'd don't think I'd be as comfortable taking them to like baseball games and stuff. [Interviewer: why not?] Uhm. I don't know. I've seen a lot of like young girls out there . . . hollering at the guys. I don't know. I wouldn't even want to think that my daughter's got [to] that part where the rearends get her excited.

Justin and Tom differ in the length of their projections but also in focus. Justin's child visions are linked to a specific partner; Tom's are independent of a particular relationship.

There are, then, various ways for men to envision aspects of being fathers before the reality sets in. The three dimensions we have identified (fatherhood readiness, father ideals, and father visions), along with the five theoretical properties associated with fatherhood readiness (degree of collaboration, focus of attention, temporal orientation, experience, and degree of clarity) advance the social psychology of fatherhood by emphasizing aspects of prospective fatherhood. These sensitizing concepts provide a foundation for an expanded conceptualization of fatherhood and father involvement that includes men's subjective experiences prior to conception and birth. Insights related to our work with these concepts can inform other researchers interested in doing either qualitative or survey research with similar or different samples of young men (or women). Further, they furnish useful tools for developing programs designed to enlighten young men about the dangers and joys associated with sex, paternity, and social fathering.

7

Looking Forward

Getting young single men to speak candidly about highly personal issues allowed us to explore aspects of men's inner worlds that have largely been ignored by the research community. Listening to the participants' intimate stories about their sex lives, romantic relationships, procreative experiences, and visions of fathering yielded clues for unveiling some of the conceptual complexities associated with men's procreative identities. That the young men were so willing to share their stories of such deep nature with us may surprise some folks. We had our own doubts when we launched our study, but they quickly disappeared once we heard the men talk openly, often passionately, about their personal lives. As we have chronicled, they were forthright in discussing past and present sexual exploits and relationships, feelings of lust and betrayal, embarrassing moments purchasing condoms and failed attempts to use them, fearful and tearful experiences with pregnancy scares and a partner's pregnancy, contested and consensual negotiations dealing with abortions, the intense anguish over miscarriages, the sense of euphoria in being present when a child is born, ethical and legal dilemmas about establishing paternity, and involvement with real and imaginary children.

Given the exploratory nature of our study and the kinds of issues we wanted to address, we selectively used the symbolic interactionist perspective and several sensitizing concepts to frame the questions we asked our participants. The approach enabled us to deepen and refine the way we think about men's sexual and procreative experiences. It stressed the value of understanding the meanings men assign to their experiences. Unfortunately, as we noted in the opening chapter, this study does not enable us to say much about men's procreative identities from a developmental, race/ethnic, or ecological perspective. We plan to address these issues in subsequent research.

For now, we complete our initial exploration of our participants' sexual and procreative lives by reflecting on and integrating what we have learned from their interviews. We summarize our findings in a manner that enables us to move forward in the way we theorize, conduct research, develop social policy, and design programmatic initiatives that address young men's procreative identities and experiences.

Overall, our participants were instrumental in helping us clarify new research questions and programmatic challenges for getting men to make responsible decisions about sex, contraception, and other fertility-related matters. From our perspective, a logical first step toward accomplishing this goal is to help young single men become more fully aware of their ability to create human life and of the implications of fathering a child. Studying these personal accounts as we did brings us closer to realizing our goal.

Throughout, we emphasized the value of viewing men's experiences through a gender lens. Gender shapes the physiological and social circumstances that provide the foundation for boys' and young men's subjective experiences with their sexuality and procreative potential. Coming to terms with how the experiences are influenced by gender is therefore critical to theoretical as well as programmatic efforts in this area.

Explaining Men's Subjective Experiences

When we began this study, we wanted to explore how young single men learn to see themselves as persons capable of making babies. What are some of the ways they experience this realization that accentuates a connection between their thinking and physical self? How do they manage their awareness as they experiment with romantic involvements, become sexually active, and develop a sexual history replete with different partners, types of relationships, and fertility-related experiences? Our analysis has highlighted the conceptual complexity of the content of men's thoughts and feelings in the procreative realm. We have clarified the processes affecting how men's identities and perspectives change, and we have uncovered some of the contextual factors that influence how these transformations unfold.

Because we employed several sensitizing concepts to guide significant portions of our interviewing, we have not, in a conventional sense, tried to develop a grounded theory of young men's procreative identities. Rather, we have used our sensitizing concepts (procreative consciousness, procreative responsibility, and turning points) and the constant comparative method to deepen and expand our understanding of several theoretical issues. This approach led us to consider how well men's accounts of their experiences fit with the concepts we used to launch the study. The accounts also helped us to identify and sharpen new concepts and their properties that capture aspects of men's subjective experiences. Several of the key concepts that fit this description include fatherhood readiness, father ideals, fathering visions, and child visions. The interviews were particularly useful in generating new properties for the procreative consciousness, turning point, and fatherhood readiness concepts. In each case, we were able to identify a number of theoretical properties that gave greater meaning to our understanding of how men subjectively experience aspects of their lives as persons capable of procreating. These properties also raised new questions.

Because we were interested in young men's inner worlds, our main objective was to explore the facets of our participants' procreative consciousness, including their sense of acting responsibly. The interviews reinforced our original perceptions about young men's procreative consciousness: it is layered, dynamic, and has numerous associated contextual qualities. Similar to how individuals in other life domains express awareness, young men's procreative consciousness often shifts back and forth: inactive one moment, in a state of heightened awareness and activity the next. The inactive and active forms of consciousness can be viewed as loosely connected layers that make up young men's awareness within the procreative realm.

We were especially interested in the types of processes and experiences that activated latent thoughts and feelings. When and why did individual men in the sample become more conscious of their ability to procreate and their potential fertility-related roles? To what extent were others involved in this shift? Can these types of cognitive transitions be cued so they occur more frequently and perhaps become a more permanent feature of young men's self-awareness, a part of their global procreative consciousness? These kinds of questions, of course, assume that young men already have a meaningful relevance structure that they can tap into. In other words, they must have a pre-existing base of knowledge about the reproductive process and about their own ability, at least presumed ability, to procreate. They may even find their sense of being infertile to be relevant knowledge. A basic understanding of key concepts and issues provides young men with the needed foundation to bring latent thoughts and feelings into their wideawake consciousness in a meaningful way. How they acquire an initial base of knowledge is therefore a crucial matter.

The process by which young men acquire knowledge, change identities, and alter their perspectives reflects the dynamic quality of their active consciousness. We discerned that although most in our sample find it unremarkable when they initially learn and come to believe that they can procreate, some see it as a highly significant transition. This first shift in knowledge and perspective, as well as other transitions experienced once they become aware, can occur in various ways.

We were reminded, too, of how important it is to consider the processes, context, and conditions associated with how young men's procreative identity comes into play and how it changes. Generally speaking, our sample of men seem to activate their procreative consciousness when they are engaged in a type of real or imagined problem-solving exercise, envisioning aspects of the procreative realm, or participating in some form of observational learning. Each of these general processes is linked to specific knowledge, tasks, and activities associated with such areas as fecundity, contraception, pregnancy, abortion, children, and fathering.

Not surprisingly, the men in the sample seemed most likely to activate their procreative consciousness when faced with problem-solving scenarios. Creative problem solving, real as well as hypothetical, prompted them to consider their beliefs, preferences, and potential roles and responsibilities. Dealing with the problems at times resulted in the men's feeling as though they had entered a turning point that fundamentally shaped their perspective on their ability to procreate, or their ability to be a good father. As we have emphasized in previous chapters, these scenarios typically dealt in some way with unplanned pregnancies. The men's concerns about how a pregnancy should be resolved and their perceptions about whether they were ready to become fathers were prominent features in the interviews.

Much of the time, the men's sexual partners, and friends and family to a lesser extent, were involved in the problem-solving processes. Unfortunately, we cannot conclude whether turning points are more likely to occur when others intimately participate in young men's experiences. No doubt more attention needs to be given to the impact that others, especially romantic partners, have on the experiences. Much more can be learned about how women help men to coconstruct their procreative consciousness and identity. Future research should consider the possibility that when young single males actively share an event or experience with someone else, compared to "going it alone," they may be more likely to see it as a turning point. The emotional energy, good or bad, associated with the sharing could be a distinctive factor, especially when it involves a highly volatile crisis or a remarkably blissful occasion. The emotional energy may be accentuated when the man is encouraged or forced to discuss specific issues. These exchanges may inspire thinking more deeply about the experience. One possible outcome is that the event becomes a part of the man's relevance structures that shape future decision making related to sex, relationships, and contraception.

An approach that examines young men's romantic relationships over time, as well as their interactions with peers and family, should help discover how past experiences shape their current outlook and behavior. Because the men in our sample often did not consider these problem-solving scenarios in a vacuum, theoretical analyses of the scenarios are likely to be enhanced if they explore how different relationship contexts influence the way men experience their procreative identities. How young men communicate with a partner is often related to the way they define their type of involvement with that partner. Is she a serious girlfriend who could be a future spouse or simply a "fuck buddy" who is pursued only for physical gratification?[1]

Many young men, prior to becoming fathers, entertain visions of what their future children might be like and the type of father they hope to become. The men we talked to were most likely to fantasize about these eventualities when they were in a significant relationship. Some of the men talked about establishing informal, private rituals with a partner in which at times they discussed what potential children might look like and how they might act. At other times, they also discussed with a partner how they would want to resolve an unplanned pregnancy were it to occur. Some of the men were interested as well in finding out what a casual partner would do if she were impregnated then and there. Our general impression is that having a serious relationship provided a context and an interpersonal connection that enabled men to have more extended intimate conversations with a partner.

The nature of our study does not permit us to say much specifically about how reproductive physiology structures young men's views of relationships and their procreative potential. Nonetheless, we suspect that some connection exists. Although policymakers in recent years have accelerated their efforts to hold married and unmarried fathers accountable financially for children they father, men do not have to deal directly with gestation. They are essentially free and clear of the physical consequences of pregnancy even though some may have limited experiences in the form of the couvade. As mentioned elsewhere, men generally are less likely than women to think about contraception and pregnancy issues; presumably in part, because of their immunity from the physical consequences of pregnancy. Unlike postmenarche women, they are also immune from monthly reminders of their procreative potential. Together, these gendered realities result in men's being less likely than women to equate their sexual and romantic relationships with the type or frequency of their thoughts about personal procreative issues. It is a situation that can change significantly for individual men if they encounter a pregnancy scare, a pregnancy, a miscarriage, and an abortion. In a related vein, we did not regularly ask the men in our sample directly if and when they systematically take into account whether they see a woman as a potential mother of their children. However, the way some of them spoke about a partner revealed that they see a partner as suitable or unsuitable to have their children.

The final process that enabled the men to activate their procreative consciousness, observational learning, was significant for a small contingent. It made possible their vicariously becoming more aware as they noticed how others were being affected by procreative events. For some, seeing others undergo hardship or pleasure meant that they began to imagine themselves similarly situated and then assess how they would feel and react. In a few cases, the learning episodes combined observations of and discussions with the person being observed.

Being able to understand from a theoretical perspective the processes that enable men to experience their procreative identities is essential. Likewise, it is crucial to grasp the content of men's procreative consciousness. The task is to identify and examine the properties that define how men think and feel, and to figure out how the properties are interrelated. From reviewing our young men's interviews, we discovered four properties: knowledge, emotional response, temporal orientation, and child visions. Our analysis of the properties shows that procreative consciousness is a multifaceted and complex concept, and that men's knowledge about procreative issues is the core.

When we focused on the young men's core knowledge area, we identified several key dimensions, but our theoretical analysis of these dimensions is somewhat limited because our data can take us only so far. Future attempts to explore these dimensions should at least take into account whether men come to know certain things through experiential or indirect means, the breadth and depth of their knowledge, and whether different pieces of knowledge are technical or emotionally laden. Special attention should be given to fecundity perceptions because they represent the most basic feature of male knowledge in the procreative realm. These perceptions include men's understanding of their own and others' ability to procreate, their degree of potency, and whether they have confirmed their ability to procreate—either through an article of faith that a partner is pregnant with their child or through the more reliable DNA testing procedure.

Similarly, future research should continue to explore issues raised by our analysis of our young men's comments concerning their current readiness to become fathers. Studying men's perceptions of their readiness calls for a broad approach to conceptualizing fatherhood. It shifts attention to men's wide-ranging experiences as procreative beings, not simply their treatment of children who have already been born. Framing fatherhood in such fashion accentuates the value of seeing responsible fatherhood as inclusive of men's conscientious efforts to defer paternity until they are ready to assume roles associated with fathering. Men, some more than others, are capable of imagining what they might be like as fathers. We saw this vividly in 21-year-old Kyle who spoke enthusiastically about his biblical project that had him scouring the Scriptures for ideas that would help him prepare to be a good, Christian family man. Gender-based ideologies were also influential for some of the men who contemplated their willingness to nurture and care for children in ways that have typically been associated with mothering. Understanding more fully when and how young men think about their future procreative selves should lead to promising opportunities to work with them on sex and pregnancy matters.

When we looked at our young men's views about fatherhood readiness, five key properties emerged from the analysis: degree and form of collaboration; focus of attention; temporal orientation; experience; and degree of clarity. These properties should be explored more systematically in future research. In some ways, the participants' views on their fatherhood readiness are a special case of procreative consciousness, and it therefore makes sense to explore more fully how women collaborate in shaping men's sense of readiness. Our study showed that the young men's feelings for a partner can sometimes affect how they assess their degree of readiness, but much more work needs to be undertaken. Little is known about how men's styles of communicating and managing relationships with women affect their experiences as sexual persons capable of fathering children.

Along a similar line, we documented that the men focused their attention on themselves, a partner, their children, or some combination. Even so, we are not in a position to say much about which types of personal characteristics or circumstances influenced the way the men developed their views. Presumably, men with different relationship circumstances, personality traits, employment opportunities, and cultural experiences differ in how they construct their sense of readiness. More needs to be learned about the conditions under which some men have a much stronger feeling than do others about their level of readiness. Why do some but not other men use childhood experiences with a birth family's poor financial circumstances as an incentive to avoid becoming a father before they are financially stable?

Finally, there is widespread interest in how men change identities and perspectives on fertility-related issues. Given the importance of fertility events for many persons, we found it useful during various phases of the study to draw upon Strauss's insights regarding turning points. Studying the unique set of changes that result from the five kinds of turning point experiences we considered provides a useful theoretical approach for understanding men's lives. The eight properties we found relevant to how the men in our sample described their experiences in the procreative realm—degree of control; duration; presence of subjective and behavioral changes, individual or shared, vicarious or personal; type and degree of institutional context; centrality; emotional response and evaluation—highlight the nuances of the men's turning point experiences. Our study enabled our exploration of some of the specific ways men experience turning points in this area and incorporate their reactions into their identity. In the future, more focused interviews are needed to expand and deepen our understanding of why and how these transitional processes take place and affect men's inner worlds.

Although examining change in all its forms intrigued us, we were most interested in how procreative and nonprocreative turning point experiences can affect men's lives in the procreative realm. Because some of these events in the participants' lives were unplanned, the men did not always recognize them as turning points at the time. Notwithstanding the unplanned events, each turning point experience we identified represented a critical juncture, as defined by the men themselves, that led them to transform their procreative identities in a distinctive and timely fashion.

Understanding the nature of how men change their procreative identities has both theoretical and programmatic significance. At every turn in our study, we have stressed the importance of viewing the men's identities as dynamic. We have tried to capture the dynamic features by having the men reflect on their lives so they could convey to us their thoughts and feelings they had about their relationships, sexual histories, and procreative experiences. In addition, they recalled how they behaved with particular partners.[2]

The best way to capture the processes by which young men develop and manage their procreative identities over time would be to enroll them at a relatively early age in a panel design. One viable strategy would be to recruit a sample of men aged 18–22 who are at a similar phase of psychosocial development. This cohort would be useful because psychologists see its members as making a transition into the dynamic period of young adulthood characterized by experimentation with relationships; they are often learning by trial and error how to be involved in sexual, and frequently more serious relationships.[3] The age range would also be relevant from a social policy perspective because of young adult men's role in unplanned teenage pregnancies and childbearing.[4] A panel design with a narrowly defined age group would be appealing because it would allow further exploration of the properties, contexts, phases, and consequences of the critical concepts and processes that have emerged in our study.

One of the methodological issues this type of panel design raises has to do with whether the first interview influences the way men subsequently experience their procreative identity. To what extent, if any, does it encourage men to be more introspective and attentive to their lives as sexual persons who are presumably capable of creating human life? The ideas expressed and language used during that interview could very well lead some participants to see the procreative realm and their association differently. Participants could be asked in the follow-up interview to reflect on the initial interview's effect. This sequential procedure may produce some clues for developing programs aimed at encouraging young men to become more cognizant of their procreative abilities. Introducing a set of concepts and easy-to-remember terms might help them become more self-aware about this area of their lives.

Our research did show that men do not necessarily partition their subjective experiences with specific procreative events. Rather, they develop and modify their identities as they weave together thoughts and feelings about experiences and relationships. Future research based on the panel design suggested or a single interview strategy similar to ours should explore more systematically the interconnections between men's subjective experiences as they relate to various procreative events.

For this study, we primarily looked into how men's procreative identities evolve, emphasizing the role of turning point experiences in the process. Uncovering the properties associated with how men define and interpret their changing self was a significant feature. Though important, understanding the processes related to the changes is only part of a bigger picture. Future research also needs to consider how personal characteristics, social circumstances, and processes reinforce existing behavioral patterns and perspectives. Just as key events can represent turning points in men's lives, other events may reaffirm for men that the path being followed or the perspective currently held, is meaningful to them.[5] Recognizing something as meaningful requires that men have a certain level of procreative consciousness. Establishing a line of inquiry attentive to such a reinforcement or support process will deepen understanding of young men's procreative identities.

In some instances, turning point experiences at one moment in time may later serve to reinforce the transformed identity. For example, men who have turning point experiences that hinge on exposure to particular ideologies (say, Christianity, feminism) may begin to see their procreative identities in a new light because they see the world in a new way. If these men continue to hold the values associated with the ideologies, they will probably recognize at times how the ideologies reinforce aspects of their procreative identities. At other times, men may encounter significant events unrelated to any ideological belief system that profoundly remind them of their beliefs and may reaffirm that fathering a biological child is important to them; how critical it is that they be precoitally clear about a partner's preferences for resolving a pregnancy; or that much effort goes into caring for a child. Turning point experiences are noteworthy because they may prevent men from reverting to an earlier way of behaving or thinking about sexual and procreative issues.

Because we interviewed only men for this study, we can do no more than speculate as to gender comparisons.[6] We suspect that women are probably more likely than men to spend time in social settings and conversations that prominently feature issues associated with pregnancy and children. Hence, men may be less likely, on average, to encounter situations that would prompt a turning point in procreative identity. Even though some kinds of turning points and their properties may be similar for men and women, we can anticipate that significant differences persist because of gendered lives.

Another meaningful set of issues that should be addressed involves how the concepts we generated and expanded are relevant to categories of men with various developmental, racial, cultural, religious, and socioeconomic backgrounds. Different models of masculinity and gender relations are likely to intersect with the previously mentioned characteristics and influence approaches to sex, relationships, contraception, and fatherhood. Men are likely to experience their procreative identities in sundry ways that depend on their definitions of masculinity. For example, defining masculinity in terms of the ability to be a spiritual leader of a family is at odds with defining it as the ability to "score" with women.

Unfortunately, the kinds of substantive issues we could pursue were in some ways constrained by our sample. The sample included young men from diverse educational, economic, and racial/ethnic backgrounds but was relatively small, and the number representative of any one category was even smaller. If this sort of sample were to be expanded in future research, it would allow easier examination of within- and between-group data. Researchers could ascertain the similarities and dissimilarities in, for example, the father visions of specific groups such as young inner-city African American and Hispanic males, rural males, males with varying degrees of experience with sex and pregnancy, males of different religious persuasions, and so on. Also whether men living in different ecological settings tend to experience features of their procreative consciousness in unlike ways. Are there unique ecological factors conducive to procreative responsibility's being expressed, or expressed in certain ways? For instance, it may be that the skewed gender ratio among African Americans results in black men's being less trusting of black women during sexual episodes and relationships because of high competition for eligible young black men. This condition might encourage black men to experience their procreative identities in particular ways. Some, especially those with economic means, may be more apt than white counterparts to feel susceptible to a woman's intentionally becoming pregnant. In addition, because black men are more likely to date and marry women outside their race than are white men,[7] they may tend to be more conscious of their procreative abilities if the prospects of having mixed-race offspring are salient to them and/or a partner.

Although these ideas are purely speculative at this point, they typify the kinds of issues that need to be addressed next. If researchers were to consider how procreative consciousness and other concepts are expressed in a range of ways by young men in a range of social categories, they could enhance our theoretical understanding of the men's experiences in the procreative realm. The researchers' theoretical explanations can be enriched immensely by constantly comparing incidents between and among the categories. This process will not only enhance the fit and utility between the theoretical accounts and the experiences of a wide variety of young men but should lead the way to group-specific program development.

It would be useful as well to augment our type of theoretical sampling by obtaining more data that would permit closer study of issues. Such issues would include the connection between the nature of men's heterosexual relationships and their procreative consciousness and how their experiences with multiple sexual partnering influences their procreative consciousness. In addition to enhancing our theoretical understanding of men's lives, the new data would provide a basis for developing more client-specific pregnancy prevention and fatherhood programs.

This kind of qualitative research, though valuable in its own right, can also serve to suggest concepts or categories for quantitative analysis. Survey instruments can be designed based on our concepts/categories. Survey methodologies and representative sampling strategies should help to expand our understanding of how selected variables (e.g., race, age, socioeconomic status) influence men's procreative identities. These survey data can then be used to expand and further generate theory while controlling for such factors as developmental stage, race, class, and socioeconomic status. The studies would complement the NSAM studies on young men that have been fielded in recent years.

Social Policy

That policymakers have become increasingly interested in men's roles in sex, contraception, pregnancy, childbearing, and fatherhood is well known. Prompted in part by academic researchers, policymakers are eager, at least in principle, to find ways to incorporate men into creative efforts to reduce rates of STD and HIV/AIDS transmission, unplanned pregnancies, out-of-wedlock births, and children born without a legal father. For various reasons, the most diligent policy efforts have focused on increasing paternity establishment and child-support collection. The two issues provide clear-cut opportunities for legislative interventions that, when implemented, will lessen state expenditures. A key approach for reducing the numbers of children who will become wards of the state includes aggressive efforts to hold men financially accountable for their biological children. This strategy also reaffirms a husband's responsibility for children not genetically related to him, but who were conceived extramaritally by his wife.[8]

In contrast, social policy that targets young men who have not yet impregnated a partner has lagged, partly because the issue appears less pressing and the financial payoffs are less obvious. Even so, social policy initiatives can and should be devised to heighten young men's procreative consciousness before they impregnate a partner. Looking to Sweden for guidance, we find that the government there has taken an active role in advocating that men, in principle, should be as responsible as women are for childcare.[9] Broadly defined, Swedish social policies and specific legislative initiatives reinforce the idea that men should develop strong, nurturing bonds with their children. In the United States, public policy that supports the growing number of pregnancy prevention and fathering programs is needed. These programs provide men with learning opportunities to become more aware of their procreative abilities and responsibilities, as well as to understand how their lives are influenced by their desire to achieve a masculine self.

Policies directed at men must encourage them to develop strong ties with their children that transcend their romantic involvements with women; an approach that must be reconciled with pro-choice laws. Obviously, it will remain a challenge to inspire some men to feel invested in their children from the start if they are simultaneously excluded from the emotionally laden pregnancy resolution process.[10] Although we agree that women's voices should be privileged in decisions about abortion, policymakers can still promote efforts to sensitize men to children's needs. The efforts should involve men during the pre- and postnatal periods. As much as possible, policies should acknowledge that fathers have the right to solidify a commitment to their children that is in some ways independent of their relationship to the children's mother, even though efforts to foster coparental cooperation would be the ideal.[11]

Irrespective of policies that might be implemented, it would be wise not to overestimate the government's ability to foster significant and immediate changes in how men (and women) actually express gender within romantic relationships and families. The Swedish experience has documented that governmental policies can have a part in bringing about modest changes in men's willingness to take paternity leave, but it is far more difficult for government to bring about truly substantive changes in how people think about and organize their work and family roles. A male-dominated corporate culture, a gender-segregated labor force, and an imbalanced gender-wage ratio, will continue to have a strong bearing on individuals' perceptions of the provider and caretaker roles. These entrenched phenomena portend that any fundamental change in men's orientation toward children will involve a protracted process requiring widespread support from various institutions.[12]

One indirect way that policymakers have participated in elevating interest in men's family roles is by funding national surveys of adolescent and young adult men's (and women's) sexual, contraceptive, fertility, and paternal attitudes and behavior. To the extent that social policy on those issues is informed by social science research, it is most often guided by national surveys that document the social demography of sex, contraception, and fertility. The surveys identify, for example, the demographic profiles of persons most likely to have sexual intercourse at a young age; have multiple sex partners; engage in risky contraceptive behavior; and get involved in an unplanned pregnancy. Smaller-scale and more substantively oriented regional studies can also be useful. Take for instance, the 1995 survey of 4,159 students in grades 9-12 in randomly selected Massachusetts high schools that enabled the correct classification of 89.9 percent of males involved in a pregnancy based on their self-reports of forced sexual contact, frequency of weapon carrying on school property, number of cigarettes smoked daily, number of sexual partners in the previous three months, and condom nonuse at last intercourse.[13]

To date, minimal attention has been accorded the findings of qualitative studies such as ours. That qualitative studies tend to carry far less weight than national surveys for policymakers, the general public, and the larger research community should not diminish our study's contribution to the theoretical, policy, and programmatic efforts targeting young men's procreative lives. Though not based on a nationally representative sample, our findings address issues central to the national debate. The strength of our approach is that it begins to lay bare the depth and complex web of men's subjective experiences that influence their thoughts, feelings, and decisions related to sex, relationships, contraception, pregnancy, abortion, and fathering. Without a thorough understanding of the dynamic social psychological processes underlying men's experiences in these areas, policymakers and program developers will be handicapped in their ability to incorporate men into initiatives designed to promote reproductive health and positive outcomes for sexual partners and, in some cases, their children. In consequence, efforts to delineate policy, programmatic, and research agendas should strive to coordinate large-scale surveys and more focused qualitative inquiries.

Program Interventions

In recent years, there has been a sizeable increase in the number of pregnancy prevention and male involvement programs that reach out to young men, those who have become fathers and those who have not. Many of the programs are community based and funded by a combination of public and private sources. Our findings complement the insights gleaned from a survey of social service providers who have developed these types of programs throughout the United States.[14] After reviewing a variety of such programs in the mid-1990s, Freya Sonenstein and her colleagues summarized their findings:

> Most of these programs are set up in response to high teen pregnancy rates in low-income, economically and politically alienated inner-city communities. . . . [T]hese programs try to change males' attitudes toward themselves, their relationships with women, and their futures. Most focus on comprehensive life issues—improving self-esteem, relationship skills, and employment skills—to give young men the tools they will need to take control in multiple areas of their lives, to exercise responsibility, and to give them hope for positive futures . . . they focus heavily on nurturance, role-modeling, and consistency/dependability to rebuild a young man's vision of himself and his future as positive. . . . Accepting males as they are and then working with them to bring about positive changes is central to the programs' approaches. Theoretically, greater self-respect translates into more responsible behavior and "smarter" decision-making.[15]

Most of the ideas about why programs are effective have emerged from interventions in low-income, inner-city areas, but some of these proposals can and should be adapted to teenage and young adult men living in more advantaged neighborhoods, as well as to other groups (e.g., military and prison populations).

Our own research reinforces the premise that much can be done at a programmatic level to improve young men's awareness of their procreative abilities and to encourage them to act more responsibly when it comes to sex, contraception, paternity, and social fathering. We suspect that just as some of the men in our study had unplanned turning point experiences that led to positive outcomes for their procreative identity, it is possible to foster similar types of outcomes for men based on what we learned from our qualitative interviews.

Although our interviews enabled us to explore the social psychology of young men's procreative identity in general terms, we have already acknowledged that we are not able to consider thoroughly how their subjective experiences are shaped by the complex interplay among race, ethnicity, class, and neighborhood culture. These issues, important as they are, are beyond the reach of this study. The factors' influence is best studied through intensive work by ethnographers, who become intimately familiar with participants within a particular ecological environment. Thus, at this time, we limit our recommendations to general observations and make only passing reference to how certain intervention strategies might take into account the local sociocultural context.

From a programmatic perspective, our research has clear practical implications. Recall that much of our discussion focused on how the young men in our sample experience their procreative consciousness, in particular, on how the men become aware of their ability to impregnate a sex partner; draw upon their procreative awareness to make decisions about sex, relationships, contraception, and pregnancy resolution; and envision aspects of becoming a father. As noted earlier, the four properties that emerged from our analysis were knowledge, emotional response, temporal orientation, and child visions. The men's perceptions of fatherhood evolve around three key interrelated substantive concepts: fatherhood readiness, father ideals, and fathering visions. Each concept is relevant to the expanding number of male involvement and pregnancy prevention programs in the United States. Taken together, they provide a substantive foundation for such interventions. Likewise, the five theoretical properties associated with fatherhood readiness that emerged from our interviews (degree and form of collaboration; focus of attention; temporal orientation; experience; and degree of clarity) are instructive because they provide insights for strengthening these kinds of programs. We can use the properties to supplement the practical advice Sonenstein and her colleagues offer in their review of model programs.[16] The properties are also relevant to programs suitable for high schools, colleges, the military, and prisons.

Our purpose here, then, is to show briefly how the key concepts we highlight, especially the five interrelated theoretical properties that relate to fatherhood readiness, can inform initiatives to heighten young men's procreative responsibility and encourage them to consider their long-term visions for fathering prior to impregnating a partner. We specifically recommend that programs develop opportunities for men to address at least the following six areas: (1) self knowledge, appraisals, and aspirations; (2) relationship issues with partners; (3) past experiences with fathers (painful and valued); (4) paternal role models; (5) philosophies of fathering; and (6) child visions.[17]

We base these and subsequent suggestions on two main assumptions. First, it is worthwhile to recruit and incorporate young men into programs that are designed to promote their awareness about procreative issues and to teach them about various aspects of father involvement. Second, it is possible and essential to reach males prior to their involvement in an unplanned pregnancy, but concerted efforts should nonetheless be made to incorporate males who have already been responsible for a pregnancy.

Consistent with Sonenstein and her colleagues' stated goal of encouraging men to respect themselves, we add that it is critical for young men to "know" themselves. Efforts to enhance men's self-awareness should not only encourage men to become more aware of how they perceive their key personal attributes (negative and positive character portrayals) and long-term aspirations but also encourage them to identify the sources that have affected their perceptions. Program facilitators can ask men what they value and how they came to feel that way. What are their long-term aspirations in terms of education, employment, finances, and family? Do they want to father children? If so, in what kind of situation? How important do they feel it is to travel, be independent, spend time with friends, and nurture others? How do they define *manhood* and how does it relate to their sexuality and paternity? For some, it is possible that this self-knowledge may have little, if anything, to do directly with their views on fathering, children, and family. However, men's values and perceptions about human capital issues are likely to be related indirectly to their future approach to family-related matters, and opportunities should be created for men to discover these connections.

Part of men's self-knowledge involves understanding how their identities as men are affected by their perceptions of a romantic partner(s) and/or women in general.[18] Most of the men in our study were able to define and differentiate the types of relationships they had with partners but were less likely to comment on how the relationships influenced their sense of self as men. Similarly, men need to consider systematically how their relationships with women affect their perceptions of procreative issues. Are men's views about contraception, paternity, and potential fatherhood responsibilities influenced by particular kinds of situations and the women with whom they are involved? When and why are women able to get some men to think in specific ways about their ability to procreate? And, when men are influenced by a partner's orientation toward procreative issues, to what extent, under what conditions, and how do they incorporate the new perspective into their romantic episodes and relationships with new partners?

Programs can provide an invaluable service by getting men to think and talk about their concrete experiences with relationships and procreative issues. Men should be asked to reflect on questions such as What are the qualities you would like in a partner? How does your involvement with a particular type of woman make you feel, especially as a man and a person capable of creating human life? What are the qualities you would want in the mother of your child? What does a "good" relationship look like? Encouraging men to think about these and related issues should, in many instances, lead them to become introspective and to evaluate themselves, partners, family, and friends.

These questions may also assist men in considering alternative definitions of masculinity. Ideally, programs should help men expand their self-knowledge by enlightening them about masculinity's competing images and how the images implicate different ways to relate to a partner. Depending on the nature of the program, a range of ideological perspectives on gender relations from profeminism to religious conservatism could be presented and debated. We recognize that there are alternative means to achieve at least some of the same objectives with young men, that is, providing them with the will and interpersonal skills needed to avoid unplanned pregnancies and to show a partner respect. How men define and express "respect" depends on the ideological perspective they embrace. For example, those who adopt a profeminist or religiously conservative perspective are likely to have distinctive views. Men relying on any ideology should at least be concerned about how an unplanned pregnancy and birth would affect a partner's life chances and emotional well-being, as well as their own.

We found that men's interactions with a female partner contribute to the diverse criteria they use to evaluate their sense of being ready for fatherhood. Efforts to raise young men's level of procreative consciousness should, therefore, encourage men to recognize how their sense of readiness may be related to a partner's perceptions and experiences. By alerting young men explicitly to the three primary foci of attention we have discussed (self, partner, and child), programs could help them recognize that their procreative abilities can have diverse consequences, not only for themselves but others.

Developing men's gender/partner sensitivity and child sensitivity is crucial. For example, assisting men to forecast the short- and long-term outcomes of a birth for a partner and for the unintended child may promote a re-visioning of that scenario. Such discussions could also sensitize men to a range of possible situations they or others might encounter. Facilitators might remind them that some males who perceive themselves to be in love with a partner may be more likely than those in casual dating relationships to recognize the possible negative consequences an unplanned pregnancy and birth may have for her. Or men could be told that affection for a partner may in some instances obscure their ability to see beyond the idealized image of creating a child (and family) with her. The lesson: romanticized visions should be tempered with a hard dose of reality. Messages such as these can sharpen men's understanding of the tacit and explicit collaboration that can take place among partners as men develop a sense of readiness for fatherhood. At the very least, young men should be encouraged to have explicit discussions with a partner about the sense of readiness of each in the relationship to deal with pregnancy, childbearing, and parenting issues.

Programs that focus on men's relationships will need to be sensitive to the participants' stage of socioemotional development. Men in their teens are likely to have a different sense of themselves and relationships than young men in their early twenties. By then, many have begun to make the transition to a more independent lifestyle and have more relationship experience. Many have developed strong ties to the labor market; formulated career goals; lived away from parents; witnessed friends, family, and peers getting married and/or having children; have had serious relationships wherein they entertained at least passing thoughts about marriage and paternity; and have dealt with the coupling and uncoupling process with different women. Such men are likely to have a better grasp of seeing beyond themselves than their adolescent counterparts. Extra effort will need to be devoted to help teenage males move beyond an ego-centered life perspective and physiological urges while reinforcing their awareness of how they can affect others' lives.

One way to have young men think about how much people can be influenced by others is to ask them to think about their relationships with their fathers (and mothers), as well as the relationships between their fathers (stepfathers) and mothers (stepmothers). Our research, consistent with other studies,[19] showed that men felt that their relationships with their fathers played a significant role in shaping their views about the ideal father and about the visions they had of fathering their own children. When given a chance, the men in our study often linked their visions about their future experiences as fathers with their positive and negative experiences with their fathers. This pattern suggests that programs should provide young men opportunities to think seriously about how they connect their childhood experiences with their fathering visions. Some men are likely to have already thought about such connections; others may become more aware of their views when they participate in a program. Men participating in a program may have their feelings awakened as they work through these issues with a facilitator and listen to peers' views. For some, this may be the first time they have thought or talked about their feelings for their fathers and about their own prospective fathering.

Young men, especially those whose fathers have not been positive role models, should be encouraged to identify other men in their lives who are role-model fathers. They should be asked to talk about why they think a relative, friend's father, or clergyman is a positive role model. Some may have to look to media personalities to find a suitable model, but most should be able to look to someone to fill the bill. By getting young men to identify with a father figure, social service providers can help enable their becoming more aware of and possibly developing their own fathering philosophies. How should fathers relate to and interact with their sons and daughters of various ages? How should fathers support, nurture, teach, and discipline their children? What specific rights and responsibilities should fathers have when it comes to their children?

As young men reflect on these matters and clarify their fathering philosophies, they should be reminded that fathering occurs within a larger social, cultural, legal, and political context. For example, they should receive specific information about public policies regarding paternity rights, paternity establishment, child support, and visitation. They should then be asked to think about and comment on how these public policies could enhance or impede their efforts to realize their fathering visions. For instance, young men might consider what their chances would be of fulfilling their fathering visions if they do not establish legal paternity or live with their children? Though these hypothetical applications are inherently limited, those that are most realistic could deepen some young men's procreative consciousness and understanding of their fatherhood readiness. The challenge, then, is to convert this heightened awareness into behavior that reduces the risk of unplanned pregnancies and promotes healthy romantic and parenting relationships.

In addition to having men identify their personal visions of fathering, programs can encourage them to consider how they perceive children in general and whether they have given thought to what their own children might be like. A number of the men in our study remarked that they "loved" or "really liked" children and enjoyed "playing" with them. Although a few mentioned that firsthand experiences with everyday care made them question whether they were ready for fatherhood, many of the men had a limited understanding of the demands of full-time parenting. Thus, whenever possible, programs should provide young men supervised opportunities to shoulder the responsibilities of actual child care. A number of innovative programs have already been developed to encourage male involvement in children's lives.[20] What is needed now is to introduce such programs to a wider range of young men and thereby encourage greater self-awareness concerning how they can affect children's lives.

It may be challenging to design programs sensitive to the various developmental stages experienced by teenage and young adult males, but we found that males of varying ages are eager to talk about fatherhood and related issues. Our data, along with the results from the previously mentioned survey of U.S. pregnancy prevention programs, suggest that getting young men to take an active interest in sexual and procreative issues is possible. Some of the suitable programs can be stand-alone projects; others can be folded into ongoing projects that address larger issues.

Getting men not only to understand the full significance of paternity and social fatherhood but also to make sexual and contraceptive decisions that reflect their understanding should be a primary objective for those who work with young men in schools, social service agencies, the military, prisons, the health care arena, and other settings. Our research leads us to support programs that promote introspection, self-evaluation, and a temporal orientation that assists men in establishing a clear sense of where they have been, where they are, and where they would like to be in the future. Having men examine their past and present in order to project their future is an invaluable exercise in accentuating men's procreative identities. Men can be encouraged to use this self-reflexive, life-course perspective to think about how a variety of fertility-related experiences relate to other areas of their lives.

Men should benefit from programs that provide an organizational setting, a structured format, and an appropriate set of concepts (e.g., procreative consciousness, procreative responsibility, fatherhood readiness, father ideals, fathering visions, child visions, turning points) to help them frame their thoughts. With this type of arrangement, men can construct and share narratives about their procreative selves and relationships in the presence of peers or in one-on-one sessions with trusted program staffers trained in health care and family planning matters. By being exposed to a few key terms, they can begin to enrich and organize their thinking about their procreative potential and individual responsibility in the sexual and procreative realms.

As men share stories and dreams, facilitators can help them recognize the types of narratives they use and the motives that infuse the narratives. One way to think about how individuals organize their stories is to distinguish between what have been referred to as "stability," "progressive," and "regressive" narratives.[21] Stability narratives emphasize how particular features of a person's life have remained the same over time; progressive and regressive narratives suggest a more dynamic trend, an experience is depicted as having improved or declined in some fashion. The description could focus on the type, quantity, and/or quality of a phenomenon (e.g., desire for children, trust in women, contraceptive diligence, or father involvement). Some men will use a progressive or a regressive narrative to describe a feature of their lives; others will use both. They can employ these styles sequentially to talk about the highs and lows of an experience as it has unfolded over time. Or they may use both together to refer to aspects of the same phenomenon. One way to think of the latter is to imagine a man reflecting on his childhood and talking about how his father became a better economic provider over time but concurrently grew more emotionally distant.

In addition to the three types of narratives, it may be useful to keep in mind two motives ("agency" and "communion") commonly found among life stories.[22] These may be relevant to how men talk about their involvement in areas related to the procreative realm. *Agency* refers to men's desire to master the environment in a manner that enables them to achieve a goal; it conveys a need to maintain a sense of power, achievement, and control in pursuit of a goal. These experiences are deeply rooted in typical expressions of masculinity. *Communion*, emphasizes the tendency for men to integrate themselves with an entity other than themselves (e.g., child, girlfriend, family, peers, community) and to seek intimacy, and it signifies a "readiness for experiences of feeling close to and in communion with others, engaging in warm, friendly, and mutual interaction."[23] Such experiences are often associated with females' interpersonal activities and hence are viewed as more feminine, though variations on the integration theme may be assigned masculine value, especially in the context of sports or all-male group activities. Young men may weave one or both motives into their narratives before or after they have fathered a child.

Narrative strategies also can give meaning to the potential interactions between how men emphasize aspects of self, a relationship with a particular child, and involvement with a romantic partner and/or the mother of the child. We have no illusions of facilitators as being trained to do elaborate narrative analysis "on the fly" as they listen to young men talk about their lives. Still, we suspect that being sensitive to narrative strategies provides facilitators the opportunity to help the men understand and talk about their relationships and procreative identities. Facilitators may enhance their effectiveness if they become more sensitive to how men holding different views on gender relations and their own manhood conceptualize and narrate their sexual and procreative experiences.

Whereas the concepts mentioned above might prove initially useful in thinking about types of narratives (stability, progressive, regressive) and motives (agency, communion), future research should aim to develop other ways of thinking about men's procreative narratives. Qualitative research always involves a struggle to understand and explain others' experiences. In our future work, we plan to clarify the diverse narratives young men use and identify a language that enables them to express the varied and complex nature of those experiences. Ideally, with newly generated concepts grounded in data, we will be able to help young men think and talk about their experiences in ways that ring true to them, and thereby assist them in learning about themselves and others. This knowledge, it is hoped, will allow them then to make choices that are beneficial to a partner, their children, and themselves. Facilitators can also use this knowledge to help young men understand themselves and their options.

One key programmatic matter that eventually needs to be addressed is whether programs targeting young men should be gender segregated.

Would boys and young men feel more comfortable and stand to gain more in an all-male group or in a mixed group by being directly exposed to young women's voices about the relevant issues?

Because young men appear to be more comfortable talking about sex, relationships, and procreative issues in male-only groups, it seems reasonable to suggest that some programs, particularly those that reach boys at a young age, target males separately. This approach appeals to scholars of boyhood[24] and is consistent with the basic philosophy of outreach service programs: to work with males where they are, both in terms of their physical location and state of mind. The stance makes sense, but it would be an oversight to ignore the influence of the politics of gender on the way young men communicate with others. Programs that bring young men and women together should offer them unique opportunities to discover and discuss how persons of the opposite gender think about sex and various procreative issues. Mixed-gender discussions about issues dealing with trust and intimacy in romantic relationships are definitely desirable. Many young men have serious concerns about trusting a partner. Opportunities to address these issues exist in numerous school-based, gender-integrated sex education programs, but similar programs are needed for older teens and young adults not in school. A gender-integrated program is meaningless, though, unless the teacher or facilitator provides individuals the direction and freedom to discuss relevant issues openly and meaningfully. A nonthreatening setting where males and females can honestly share their gendered perspectives on sex, relationships, contraception, fertility, and parenting issues is invaluable.

One way to stimulate unfettered discussion would be to share qualitative interview data similar to those we have generated in this study. Asking for comments on the materials could be a powerful tool for launching sensitive discussion among adolescents and young adults. Jumping into such a discussion about anonymous persons might seem less threatening. Gender-integrated programs, though important, do not need to stand alone; they can build on complementary previous and concurrent same-gender programs.

Gender-integrated programs could be supplemented by institutionalizing arrangements whereby a counselor or facilitator is made available to young couples as part of the standard services offered by a school or a social service organization. This service might be incorporated into school and community-based health clinics. Given males' negative orientation toward family planning clinics,[25] finding creative ways to legitimize couple sessions and to solicit males' involvement would be challenging.

A key program feature for many interventions oriented toward young men should be to teach them how to be observant, reflective, and evaluative of friends and family, and of others. For example, young men could be encouraged to consider procreative themes as they reflect on movie characters, song lyrics, and literature they find appealing. Applying procreative identity concepts to others as well as to themselves should strengthen the message that they can and should think more systematically and responsibly about procreative issues. The focus should encourage young men to see how they, as men, have a role in educating themselves and others about the implications of their sexual, contraceptive, and fertility-related decisions. Sharing ideas in this way will provide the impetus for lively interaction that will allow them to learn from one another as well as from a facilitator.

Another programming issue speaks to the potential need to tailor some programs in a manner sensitive to different cultural groups, particularly along racial lines. Some have advocated this service specialization for programs that involve young fathers.[26] The quality of pregnancy prevention programs that target young men who are not fathers might also be improved if the programs were to take into account cultural traditions and stereotypes, historical experiences, and prevailing economic and community conditions. Program facilitators and teachers who are sensitive to the social ecology of a target population of males are better equipped to secure and sustain males' interest. Although our observations about young men's procreative identities are general, the concepts we introduce can still provide considerable direction to persons working with young men from varying racial and ethnic backgrounds. The concepts we have generated can also be useful in evaluating existing programs and, with further refinement, serve as outcome measures for intervention studies in various types of social ecologies.

The Big Picture

Both our qualitative study of young men's procreative identities, and the expanding number of programs targeting men of this age, are in keeping with the public's, social policymakers', and scholars' keen interest in paternity issues and men's family roles. During the past two decades, we have witnessed a steady flow of cultural messages reminding us of men's role in perpetuating the high rates of teenage pregnancy and out-of-wedlock childbearing. Much has also been made of the competing trends that show that although fathers are increasingly being depicted as hands-on, nurturing caretakers of their children, growing numbers of financially and emotionally irresponsible "dead-beat" dads are saturating the social landscape.[27] As we noted in chapter 1, interest in young men is part of this larger fascination with the economic, psychological, sociological, and legal faces of fatherhood during a period of rapid family change and dynamic gender relations.

These messages are set against a sociocultural backdrop that reaffirms the idea that making babies and raising them is serious business for individuals and society. Over the years, it has become more fashionable to see the transition to parenthood as distinctly an individual's or couple's choice. Some Americans, though, have grown increasingly leery of the pronatalist messages that have historically led some people to want children at an early age simply to keep in step with a time-honored life-course trajectory. This relatively recent middle-class shift has been buttressed by the rise in the proportion of women attending college and working outside the home. Although it is not precisely clear how these phenomena have affected men's procreative consciousness, it is readily apparent that understanding that consciousness is as timely as ever because childbearing is now part of an increasingly negotiated terrain.

In the first author's earlier work, he examined the significant cultural forces and technological factors that have altered or could alter the larger context within which men experience their procreative roles.[28] The present study has taken a new direction: exploring how individual men experience their lives and change within the procreative realm. By revealing some of the broad aspects of a social psychology of men's procreative identity, including its evolution and expression, our study has produced fresh theoretical insights and practical suggestions for program development. In addition, and in the language of grounded theorists, we anticipate that future researchers will tease out dimensions, phases, contexts, degrees, contingencies, types, and other theoretical codes that permit further expansion, integration, and grounding of the concepts we have explored. These efforts will move us closer to theory generation, theoretical work that can promote effective program development by attending to young men's voices about sex, relationships, and fertility-related matters in a range of cultural and economic settings.

Future researchers can build upon our findings by highlighting three overlapping fathering trajectories that guide men's lives in the procreative and paternal realms: self-as-father, father-child, and coparent.[29] Consistent with other social scientists' use of the trajectory concept,[30] we use it to refer to a course or path of experience as represented by the individuals. Trajectories imply a temporal element. Our employment of the "trajectory" metaphor should not be interpreted to mean that men move through a prescribed set of stages. Instead, it suggests that men's lives unfold in various ways along three distinct yet often connected substantive paths; paths that represent a kind of life domain with related experiences. On occasion, the domain may be accentuated by identifiable and significant events that alter or reinforce men's real or imagined identities as fathers and their perspective on fathering.[31]

These broad paths, marked by men's subjective realities and behaviors, represent the micro or personal parameters that give men the chance to construct their identities as "possible" fathers and then as fathers. Though particular trajectories may be irrelevant at times for individuals, some become salient intermittently in response to men's changing life circumstances. The nexus represents an important site for research. In chapter 1 we described how men can experience their procreative consciousness in a manner that is separate from their relationships with particular women. Similarly, men can experience an individual, or self-as-father, trajectory that encompasses their fertility intentions and views about fathering, independent of any specific relationships they may have with a romantic partner or children. The nature and direction of this trajectory can be influenced by processes associated with men's personal development and gendered experiences. As we have shown, whatever types of thoughts and feelings men develop about having children typically originate from their initial awareness that they are capable of impregnating a sex partner. In some cases, boys may have a vague sense, prior to learning about their fecundity, that they will have their own children someday. The awareness may be keen for some, but largely absent for others.[32]

Generally speaking, the self-as-father trajectory captures how men sometimes embrace fathering as an amorphous role or abstract image, not an actual, interpersonal connection to a specific child.[33] When men think about prospective fatherhood, they do so in a general way, sometimes relying on their thoughts and feelings about their own father's previous and current involvement in their lives. Once men become fathers themselves, however, their personal images of fathering and conversations they have about paternity and fatherhood concerns are likely to be deepened through their changed status. Their more general views will be interwoven with their experientially based sentiments for their own children. We saw this with Francisco, for example, whom we interviewed while his partner was pregnant and then shortly thereafter when his daughter was born. Although he said that he sometimes "forgot" that he was a father, he also remarked that he had a strong emotional connection to his daughter and saw the relationship as instrumental in his life. Men's self-as-father trajectories are related as well to their experiences with romantic partners. In the latter instance, the trajectory is likely to become intertwined with their evolving relationship with their partner prior to their child's birth. That relationship typically evolves into a coparental trajectory once the child is born.

One key feature of the self-as-father trajectory is that men associate images of their future fathering roles with images of their "possible selves," as discussed in chapter 1.[34] Their perceptions of how they would like to think, feel, and act as fathers come into play. The trajectory does not necessarily end with the birth of a first child but can evolve beyond it. Once men attain fatherhood, their reflections on the father they would like to be are probably more connected with their actual children—a pattern that should prevail for at least as long as they sustain the identity of father to them. Because many nonresident fathers' commitments to their children wane over time,[35] those fathers (or "stepfathers") may find themselves once again thinking more abstractly about the fathering terrain. The idea of becoming a father again, perhaps in the hope of doing a better job, may influence some men's thinking. For other men, feelings of grief, remorse, or discomfort about an earlier fathering experience may be dissuasive of imagining what it could be like to have another turn at it.

These experiences, then, are likely to shape how men think about, act upon, and articulate their orientation toward becoming and being a father. Some of the emotional, cognitive, and practical energy that they expend as part of this "self-as-father" trajectory can be looked upon as being part of the responsibility domain of father involvement.[36] Images of "possible selves" may motivate men to undertake self-improvement projects that are intended to enhance their prospects of being a responsible father and family man. We saw this with Kyle as he studied biblical passages in search of meaningful advice about men's family roles.[37] Less directly, others among the men sought to improve their human capital by completing their education and establishing themselves financially before having children.

The father-child and coparent trajectories are closely tied to men's parenting identity and men's perceptions of "self-as-solo-parent" and "self-as-coparent".[38] Even though our study did not deal extensively with men's involvement with their children, our findings and the sensitizing concepts we worked with are relevant to this broader domain of men's lives as fathers. The second trajectory involves men's relationships with individual children they father. Fathers who have multiple children have separate father-child trajectories for each. The "father-child" trajectory can include both biological and nonbiological children. In most cases, men develop and sustain some kind of evolving relationship with individual children, although they may produce offspring with whom they never develop a father identity. In the latter instances, father-child relationships may deteriorate to the point that men no longer play an active role in their children's lives. With time, some fathers may rekindle their connection to and involvement with these children, and they may also develop relationships with other children.

It may be useful in some instances to extend our understanding of the father-child trajectory. As some of our participants described, men sometimes have opportunities to develop relationships with particular children that simulate a father-child trajectory outside a conventional father or stepfather arrangement. The children may be those of a romantic partner, platonic friend, or family member. In a functional sense, such relationships may expose them to a form of anticipatory socialization whereby they learn how it feels to be attached to and responsible for a child. The experiences can also affect men's more general sense of "self-as-father" and competence in caring for children.

When men are involved in multiple father-child relationships in which they see themselves as a father or stepfather they are likely to individualize the relationships to varying degrees. Nonetheless, in their minds and narratives, men can represent their fathering experiences in a way that consolidates or summarizes this life domain. In other words, men's awareness of their fathering identity and activities may at times reflect their mutual tendency to aggregate impressions and experiences, especially with regard to children who have the same mother. Although these empirical issues have yet to be explored systematically, it is reasonable to assume that men with children who have different mothers may use the mothers as reference points to compartmentalize the way they consider and represent their fathering experiences. Likewise, men may use the biological or step status of their children to group their subjective understandings of themselves as fathers. Notwithstanding these possibilities, fathers can still develop and be aware of personalized bonds they have with individual children, a reality that may be both cause and consequence of the different ways they involve themselves in their children's lives. The ebb and flow of complex, dyadic father-child interactions are clearly at the crux of distinguishing the father-child trajectory. Relatedly, having multiple father-child relationships provides men with unique opportunities to perceive, compare, and evaluate their involvement with their children. It makes sense, then, to study how fathers subjectively manage and verbally construct their sense of fathering based on their multiple "father-child" trajectories.

The third trajectory refers to men's involvements with the mother (or mothers) of their children. It captures the dyadic, coparental processes involving biological and/or nonbiological children. Fathers' interactions with mothers who serve as gatekeepers to their children is a key element of the coparental trajectory,[39] a defining feature of which has to do with the extent to which fathers see themselves as a coparent rather than solo parent. The dyadic parenting processes that often emerge in fathers' lives—discussions about discipline, values, and monitoring—are intertwined with fathers' efforts to "do fathering" and involve themselves in their children's lives.[40] The trajectory typically refers to men's lives in relation to living children but can be extended to include *copartner* experiences prior to a pregnancy or conception that involve talks and joint fantasizing about having and raising children. As discussed earlier, the fathering and child visions men have prior to their children's being born are in some instances jointly constructed.

Being sensitive to how the three trajectories overlap and influence one another at different times illuminates men's lives as persons who can procreate, act in a fatherly way to biological and stepchildren, or both. An approach that pays attention to the trajectories highlights the value of incorporating men's thoughts, beliefs, feelings, and motives into a larger discussion of father involvement.[41] Thus, understanding how fathers (and prospective fathers) weave together their self-as-father, father-child, and coparental trajectories through narratives is a fruitful line of inquiry for father-involvement research.

The three-pronged approach to men's trajectories as fathers punctuates the value of looking at men's lives through a social psychological lens. This lens draws attention to both the life-span and social dimensions of men's identities that engage either their procreative consciousness or fatherly expressions. From an identity perspective, the fatherhood experience begins before children enter men's lives or are even conceived, and the visions of children and fathering that occur then are relevant to men's identities. The notion of men's "possible selves" reminds us that who people become is often shaped by who they want to be and the life events they experience. It can be assumed, too, that men's self-perceptions as fathers generally become more complex when they start to interact with their children and their children's mother(s). Children and their mother(s) are two of the more important social sources for men's self-assessments about fathering. Thus, men's self-reflections as progenitors and social fathers are shaped in part by their perceptions of how they think others see them in these arenas.

Throughout, we have sought to sharpen our understanding of how young men subjectively experience different events, relationships, and life transitions that relate to sex, procreation, and fathering. Our emphasis on the dynamic aspects of men's lives as persons with sexual and procreative interests lays the foundation for understanding men's eventual involvement with their children in a broader context. The expanded view places a premium on being attentive to how men move through adolescence and then into and out of young adulthood. They make the journey in gendered bodies; bodies in a culture in which gender remains a fundamental organizing principle of social life. To grasp the truly big picture, then, we must continue to explore the connections between men's sexual, procreative, and fathering experiences as they play themselves out across the gendered landscape. This integrative work is necessary to improve our theoretical understanding of men's procreative lives. It can also guide initiatives to encourage men to be mindful about having sex, making decisions that involve contraception and pregnancy, and being involved in their children's lives in healthy ways.

With these activities in mind, we can turn to the future and ask: Are men likely in the years ahead to become more aware of their procreative abilities and take them seriously? If they do, how will it affect our society? To the first question, we offer a qualified yes. We suspect that an increasing proportion of men can and will develop a heightened awareness of their ability to procreate at various points during their life course and perhaps even more frequently in their daily lives. Slowly, but surely, men have the potential to become more enlightened about their sexual and reproductive well-being and the responsibilities associated with their ability to create human life. Lessons learned from research and program initiatives, in combination with structural changes in the larger culture and gender relations, should provide the impetus. However, without resources and a commitment from local communities, the pattern is likely to occur unevenly from place to place.

Turning to the second question, there is little doubt that our society would be decidedly different if more men were mindful of their ability to procreate and genuinely concerned, prior to conception, about how a new baby, and the child's mother might fare in the society. Although it is guesswork to estimate the scope and impact of such a development, it seems safe to assume that it would lead to fewer unplanned and unwanted pregnancies, fewer abortions, fewer turbulent couple relationships, fewer fragile families living in poverty, and lower rates of child abuse. In short, more people would be healthy and happy. Lest we leave the impression that positive outcomes for men, women, and children are assured if ways are found to heighten men's procreative consciousness, this is not a certain outcome. Men could, theoretically, become more aware of their ability to procreate, yet become more invested in procreating purely out of self-interest. The trick is to foster men's awareness of their own "gift" to create human life while having them recognize that the ability can influence others' lives either positively or negatively depending upon circumstances.

The ultimate challenge is twofold. First, help young men at an early age, ideally before they become sexually active, to achieve and sustain a deeper self-awareness of their power to create human life. Second, encourage men to be attentive to the best interests of others, as well as their own, as they contemplate their readiness to become biological and social fathers. Meeting this twofold challenge should bring about an improved quality of life for many; ignoring the challenge will reinforce the prevailing pattern of troubled lives and unrealized dreams. If our participants' enthusiasm for talking to us is an accurate gauge, young men from around the country would be highly receptive to national and local initiatives that confront this weighty challenge.

Appendix
Participant Profiles

Key

REC (RECRUITING)

  ABL: Able Body Labor
      (employment center)
   AC: Abortion clinic
  CBC: Childbirth class
 DMV: Department of
      Motor Vehicles
   DK: Don't know
  FUI: Follow-up interview
  LOF: Lofton High school
  PNC: Prenatal Clinic
      (Jacksonville)
  SFH: St. Francis House
      (homeless shelter)
  UHE: University Hospital
      Employee (Jacksonville)
WOM: Word of mouth

RACE

    B: Black (African American)
 Bi-R: Biracial
    H: Hispanic
  NAI: Native American Indian
  NO: Native of . . .
    W: White

FINANCIAL STATUS

    FS: Receiving food stamps
  LWP: Living with parent(s)
   NP: Not poor
  SLL: Student living on loans
   UN: Unemployed
   NA: Not Applicable

FERTILITY EXPERIENCE

    A: Abortion experience
    F: Father
  FIW: Father-in-waiting
  MC: Miscarriage experience
  NF: New father, second
      interview with previous
      father-in-waiting
  PN: Procreative Novice

*Participants interviewed twice
(once during pregnancy;
once after child was born)

APPENDIX: PARTICULAR PROFILES

Part #	Pseudonym	Rec	Age	Race	Educ.	Financial Status	Relationship/ Marital Status	Fertility Experience					
								PN	F	MC	A	FTW	NF
1	Miller	WOM	28	W	HS grad	DK	Single/liv w partner					X	
2	Allen	WOM	27	W	Less than 12 years	NP	Single		X		X		
3	Tom	DMV	22	NAI	Less than 12 years	Poor	Divorced			X			
4	Mitchel	DMV	22	W	Some college	NP	Single	X					
5	Jake	DMV	27	W	HS grad	NP	Divorced/liv w partner					X	
6	Cecil	DMV	26	W	Some college	Poor	Sep, nearly div	X					
7	Phillip	DMV	23	W	Some college	NP	Divorced		X	X			
8	Harper	DMV	29	B	Some college	UN, LWP	Single	X					
9	Cal	DMV	16	W	Less than 12 years	NP	Single	X					
10	Desmond	DMV	30	B	College grad	UN, NP	Single	X					
11	Kyle	DMV	21	W	Some college	NP	Single	X					
12	Derrick	WOM	19	B	Some college	NP	Single		X				
13	Antoine	WOM	19	B	Some college	Poor	Single		X				
14	Jody	DMV	21	W	Some college	NP	Single	X					
15	Jeffrey	DMV	21	W	Some college	NP	Single	X					
16	Marcus	WOM	19	Bi-R	Some college	NP, LWP	Single	X					
17	Reynaldo	WOM	17	H	Less than 12 years	NP	Single	X					
18	Joseph	DMV	19	W	Some college	NP	Single	X					
19	Justin	DMV	18	W	HS grad	NP	Single	X					
20	Raymond	WOM	19	B	Some college	NP	Single	X					
21	Paul	DMV	21	W	Some college	NP	Single	X					
22	Sean	DMV	23	B	Some college	NP, LWP	Single	X					
23	Alex	DMV	18	W	Some college	NP	Single	X					
24	Garrett	DMV	17	W	Less than 12 years	LWP	Single	X					
25	Martin	LOF	18	B	HS grad	DK	Single				X		
26	Arthur	Fly	21	W	HS grad	DK	Single				X		
27	Austin	AC	21	W	Some college	NP	Single				X		
28	Jerry	AC	19	W	Some college	NP	Single				X		
29	David	ABL	28	W	HS grad	Poor	Single				X		
30	Stephen	AC	18	W	Some college	Poor	Single/liv w partner				X		
31	Francisco*	DK	20	H	Some college	NP,FS	Single/liv w partner						X

#	Name	Code	Age	Race	Education	Economic	Relationship						
32	Kendal	PNC	24	B	Some college	NP	Single						X
33	Reginald*	PNC	20	B	Some college	Poor	Single					X	X
34	Todd	SFH	27	W	Less than 12 years	Poor	Single		X				
35	Gilbert	SFH	20	NAI	HS grad or GED	Poor	Divorced		X		X	X	
36	Frank	SFH	29	B	Some college	"Kinda poor"	Single		X	X			
	Francisco	DK	20	H	Some college	NP, FS	Single/ liv w partner						X
	Reginald	PNC	20	B	Some college	Poor	Single						X
37	Albert	CBC	28	W	Some college	Well off	Divorced/ liv w partner						X
38	Harvey	WOM	25	W	College grad	DK	Single, engaged	X					
39	Bakka	DMV	30	N.O. Ghana	Some college	DK	Single	X					
40	Miles	DMV	29	N.O. Ghana / Ghana	College grad	NP	Single	X					
41	Simone	DMV	23	N.O. Cuba	Some college	Student	Single	X					
42	Ricky	DMV	25	N.O. Cuba	Some college	Poor (SLL)	Single	X					
43	Andy	WOM Jax	30	W	Post-college	Good	Single/liv w partner	X	X				
44	Rudy	WOM Jax	25	W	Some college	NP	Single	X					
45	Terry	WOM Jax	21	W	Some college	NP	Single	X					
46	Ed	UHE Jax	22	B	HS grad	NP	Single		X				
47	Sid	PNC Jax	25	B	HS grad	NP	Single			X		X	
48	Sam	WOM Jax	26	W	HS grad	NP	Liv w partner & 6-yr-old stepchild	X					
49	Oscar	UHE Jax	25	B	HS grad	NP	Single, Liv w partner		X				
50	Ricky	UHE Jax	18	B	HS grad	NP	Single				X		
51	Tim	WOM	24	W	College grad	NP	Single		X				
52	Marcel	WOM	30	W	College grad	Poor	Single	X					

SUPPLEMENTAL SAMPLE

# Part	Pseudonym	Age	Race	Educ.	Financial Status	Relationship/Marital Status	Fertility Experience				
							PN	F	MC	A	FIW
1	Ebeneezer	23	H	Some college	Av	Single				X	
2	Josh	22	W	Some college	Av	Single	X				
3	Butch	21	Am/Asian	Some college	NP	Single			X		X
4	Jared	21	W	Some college	Good	Single	X				
5	Andrew	21	W	Some college	Good	Single	X				
6	Barney	20	W	Some college	Av	Single	X				
7	Fred	23	W	College grad	Av	Single				X	
8	Tripp	23	W	Some college	Av	Single	X				
9	John	20	W	Some college	Poor	Single	X				
10	Tarence	25	B	College grad	Poor	Single	X				
11	Gavin	18	B	HS Grad	Good	Single				X	
12	Mario	20	H	Some college	Good	Single	X				
13	JP	21	Bi-R	College grad	Good	Married					
14	Eric	22	W	HS grad	Poor	Single	X				
15	Sal	20	W	Some college	Av	Single	X				
16	Anonymous	21	H	Some college	Av	Single	X				
17	Stewart	21	W	Some college	Good	Single	X				
18	James	22	H	Some college	n/a	Single					

Notes

Notes to Chapter 1

1. Sonenstein, Stewart, Lindberg, Pernas, and Williams, 1997.

2. Alan Guttmacher Institute, 2002.

3. Abma and Sonenstein, 2001; Alan Guttmacher Institute, 2002; Bachu, 1996; Sonenstein, Stewart, Lindberg, Pernas, and Williams, 1997.

4. Child Trends, 1999; Singh and Darroch, 2000; Ventura, Mathews, and Curtin, 1999; Ventura, Mathews, and Hamilton, 2001; Ventura, Mosher, Curtin, Abma, and Henshaw, 2000, 2001.

5. Alan Guttmacher Institute, 2002; Sonenstein, Stewart, Lindberg, Pernas, and Williams,1997.

6. Furstenberg, 1991, 1992; Geronimus, 1991, 1992.

7. Marsiglio, 1998.

8. Moore, Driscoll, and Ooms, 1997.

9. Lamb, Pleck, Charnov, and Levine, 1987.

10. A number of scholars have commented on how social capital issues are relevant to understanding father involvement (Amato, 1998; Furstenberg, 1998; Furstenberg and Hughes, 1995; Marsiglio and Cohan, 2000; Seltzer, 1998).

11. During the past decade, scholarship on fatherhood was advanced when several journals, including *Families in Societies* (1993), *Journal of Family Issues* (1993 and 1994, 1999), *Demography* (1998), *Journal of Men's Studies* (1998), and *Marriage and Family Review* (2000), devoted special issues to this topic. A number of edited volumes (Booth and Crouter, 1998; Bozett and Hanson, 1991; Daniels, 1998; Garfinkel, McLanahan, Meyer, and Seltzer, 1998; Hawkins and Dollahite, 1997; Hood, 1993; Lamb, 1997; Marsiglio, 1995; Shapiro, Diamond, and Greenberg, 1995) provided additional outlets for the growing body of research on fatherhood. See also Day and Lamb (in press).

12. Several of the primary centers include the National Center for Fathers and Families; Center on Fathers, Families, and Public Policy; National Center for Fathering; National Fatherhood Initiative; and the Fatherhood Project.

13. The main surveys include the Panel Study of Income Dynamics, National Survey of Labor Market Experience—Youth, National Survey of Adolescent Males, National Survey of Families and Households, and National Survey of Family Growth (see Federal Interagency Forum on Child and Family Statistics, 1998).

14. Gerson, 1993.

15. Blankenhorn, 1995; Popenoe, 1996.

16. Daniels, 1998; Griswold, 1993.

17. Marsiglio and Cohan, 2000; Messner, 1997; Stacey, 1998.

18. Federal Interagency Forum on Child and Family Statistics, 1998; Levine and Pitt, 1995; Marsiglio, 1998.

19. During the past few decades, and especially in the 1990s, a number of international organizations and national governments have taken steps to encourage men's involvement in sexual and reproductive health issues in numerous countries. For example, both the 1994 International Conference on Population and Development in Cairo and the 1995 Fourth World Conference on Women in Beijing highlighted men's important role in reproductive responsibilities. More recently, the 1998 Symposium on Male Participation in Sexual and Reproductive Health: New Paradigms, held in Oaxaca, Mexico, highlighted ongoing efforts in Latin America to understand and promote men's involvement in this area (AVSC, 1999a, 1999b).

20. Mead, 1934.

21. Blumer, 1969; Stryker, 1980; see also Holstein and Gubrium, 2000.

22. Strauss and Goldberg, 1999, p. 245; see also Markus and Nurius, 1986; Oyserman and Markus, 1990.

23. Mead, 1934.

24. Armato and Marsiglio, 2002.

25. Marsiglio, 1998; O'Brien, 1981.

26. Schutz, 1970a, 1970b.

27. Although men have always been able to use their hands to detect the fetus's movement within a partner's womb during the latter months of pregnancy, the experience is probably not quite as powerful as the prospective mother's feeling the movement internally.

28. Marsiglio, 1998.

29. Sonenstein, Stewart, Lindberg, Pernas, and Williams, 1997.

30. Townsend, 1998.

31. Furstenberg and Cherlin, 1991.

32. Schwalbe and Wolkomir, 2002.

33. Strauss, 1969.

34. van den Hoonaard, 1997.

35. Blumer, 1969.

36. van den Hoonaard, 1997; Blumer, 1954.

37. van den Hoonaard, 1997, p. 2.

38. van den Hoonaard, 1997.
39. Miller, 1992a.
40. Strauss, 1969, p. 272.
41. Strauss, 1969, p. 269.
42. Cowan, 1991.
43. Glaser 1978, 1992; Glaser and Strauss, 1967.
44. Durkheim, 1895/1982.
45. Glaser and Strauss, 1967, p. 242.
46. Strauss, 1969.

Notes to Chapter 2

1. Allen and Doherty, 1996; Gilmore, DeLamater, and Wagstaff, 1996; Fursten-berg, 1995; Landry and Camelo, 1994; Sugland, Wilder, and Chandra, 1997; Sulli-van, 1989, 1995.

2. We stress that our observations are most relevant to conducting interviews with men, but many of our comments may be equally relevant to interviewing women.

3. Drawing on our qualitative research with single men ages 16–30, we extend the multidisciplinary dialogue about how qualitative methods can be used with different populations (Deatrick and Faux, 1991; Faux, Walsh, and Deatrick, 1988; Fine and Sandstrom, 1988; West, Bondy, and Hutchinson, 1991).

4. Alan Guttmacher Institute, 2002; Grady, Tanfer, Billy, and Lincoln-Hanson, 1996; Kaiser Family Foundation, 1997; Ku, Sonenstein, and Pleck, 1994; Marsiglio, 1993; Marsiglio and Shehan, 1993; Pleck, Sonenstein, and Ku, 1991, 1993, 1996; Shostak, McLouth, and Seng, 1984; Sonenstein, Stewart, Lindberg, Pernas, and Williams, 1997; see also Gohel, Diamond, and Chambers, 1997; Nesmith, Kler-man, Oh, and Feinstein, 1997.

5. Allen and Doherty, 1996; Barker, 1998; Gilmore, DeLamater and Wagstaff, 1996; Furstenberg, 1995; Holmberg and Wahlberg, 2000; Landry and Camelo, 1994; Sugland, Wilder, and Chandra, 1997; Sullivan 1989, 1995; see also Edwards, 1994.

6. Ku, Sonenstein, and Pleck, 1994; Tanfer, Grady, Klepinger, and Billy, 1993.

7. Sugland, Wilder, and Chandra, 1997.

8. This figure is based on a personal communication with Freya Sonenstein, P. I. of the NSAM who conducted an "in-house" analysis of the 1995 NSAM.

9. Alan Guttmacher Institute, 2002. As reported in this AGI report, data from a national study of high school seniors in 1992 found that males were less likely than females (37 percent to 49 percent) to report that having children was "very important in life."

10. Alan Guttmacher Institute, 2002.

11. Sullivan, 1995.

12. Marsiglio, 1993.

13. See Barker, 1998 for a comparative analysis of separate samples of African American and Hispanic young males in Chicago and males in Rio de Janeiro, Brazil.

14. Barker, 1998; Gilmore, DeLamater, and Wagstaff, 1996; Sugland, Wilder, and Chandra, 1997.

15. Holmberg and Wahlberg, 2000; Shostak, McLouth, and Seng, 1984.

16. Schneider and McLean, 2000.

17. Pleck, Sonenstein, and Ku, 1996.

18. Marsiglio, 1993.

19. Allen and Doherty, 1996; see Kiselica, 1995.

20. Kaiser Family Foundation, 1997.

21. Marsiglio and Shehan, 1993.

22. Nelson, Coleman, and Swager, 1997; Rosenwasser, Wright, and Barber, 1987.

23. Boggess and Bradner, 2000.

24. Sandelowski, 1995, p. 179.

25. In recent years, some researchers have questioned and studied the completeness of men's fertility reporting (Lindberg, Sonenstein, Martinez, and Marcotte, 1998; Mott and Gryn, 2001; Rendall, Clarke, Peters, Ranjit, and Verropoulou, 1999). Although Lindberg and her colleagues concluded that it is possible to obtain accurate reporting from young fathers using survey instruments, we recognized that some males might have been reluctant to report abortions, miscarriages, and births to us. The candor with which men spoke about sex, relationships, contraception, and procreative experiences lead us to feel confident that participants provided us with honest reports.

26. Schwalbe and Wolkomir, 2002.

27. Glaser, 1978, 1992; Glaser and Strauss, 1967.

28. Glaser and Strauss, 1967; Glaser, 1978, 1992.

29. In Glaser's (1978) iteration of the grounded theory method, these "families of theoretical codes" would be used during data analysis to tease out theoretical codes.

30. Lincoln and Guba, 1985.

31. Faux, Walsh, and Deatrick, 1988.

32. McKee and O'Brien, 1983.

33. Reissman, 1991.

34. See Schwalbe and Wolkomir (2002) for their discussion about masculine styles of impression management.

35. Landry and Camelo, 1994.

36. Munhall and Boyd, 1993.

37. Schwalbe and Wolkomir, 2002.
38. Schwalbe and Wolkomir, 2002.
39. Krueger, 1994.
40. Deatrick and Faux, 1991, p. 215.
41. Schatzman and Strauss, 1973.
42. Mallory (2001) advocates an "analysis of difference" whereby the interviewer thoughtfully analyzes the possible effects that race/ethnicity, gender, and social status may have on interviews when differences exist between interviewer and participant. At one point she suggests that the interviewer ask the participant what barriers he/she perceives between himself/herself and the researcher, and what preconceptions the participant might have of the researcher. The aim is to improve the accuracy and legitimacy of the research. Mallory also cautions us to be aware that by focusing on such differences, researchers may overlook the similarities they have to a participant and therefore be inattentive to relevant substantive issues.

43. Of particular interest in our study was the stark contrast in participant and interviewer characteristics in the thirteen interviews conducted by Hutchinson, six of which involved African American men. To gain perspective on these interviews, we turn to Arendell's (1997) reflexive article on interviewing divorced men. Arendell emphasizes how men enacted gender in her interviews, specifically their assertion of gender identity and gender hierarchy. She found herself in a paradoxical position during the interviews because although most of the men were highly critical of women, they shared their feelings and experiences with her because she was a woman. Other men, they believed, would likely be critical of them and their vulnerabilities. In contrast to Hutchinson's experiences interviewing men in our study, Arendell found the divorced men in her research to be challenging, controlling, asserting superiority, denigrating toward women in general, aggressive, seductive, and in a few cases protective. The different topics in the two studies (divorce, procreative identities), the age difference between the interviewer and participants (Arendell was close to the participants' ages; Hutchinson could have been the men's mother, and in some cases even their grandmother) surely influenced gender enactment. Whereas Ardendell was perceived at different times as a former wife, an honorary male, and a nurturing woman, Hutchinson always appeared to be in the role of a nurturing, caretaking woman who was interested in whatever story they had to tell, or whatever feeling they wanted to express.

44. Faux, Walsh, and Deatrick, 1988; Ginsberg and Opper, 1979. With the younger men, and sometimes others, it is probably advisable to state that there are no right or wrong answers a few times during the interview. Reiterating the statement on the informed consent that their answers will not be shared with their parents may also be helpful. We also wondered about our recruiting strategy: we invited participants to discuss how they think about "dating, pregnancy, birth

control, and fatherhood issues" without warning them about the personal, intimate nature of the questions. We were curious, too, about the influence of cultural and age-related proscriptions against discussing sensitive topics with strangers; participants' embarrassment or concern about the accuracy of their sexual/procreative knowledge; and the propriety of being sexually active at their age.

45. Strauss, 1969.

46. We emphasize the need to seek clarity not only of language but also of any affective nuances or tone. In the following example, the interviewer checked out her understanding. When asked when he first thought about getting a girl pregnant, a 29-year-old male said, "Oh Jeez, she was 14. I was 15 in her parents' house. We dated on and off almost five years. And, I guess she wasn't on the pill at the first, at least the first year or so, and her parents wouldn't even hardly let her see me. Kinda weird . . . I just pulled out." I: "Oh, withdrawal?" R: "Yeah." Earlier in the interview when talking about his partner's pregnancy, he said, after laughing loudly, "Somebody shoot me." I: "You really feeling that way?" In the latter instance, the interviewer tries to understand where the participant is coming from, to see if his verbal comments square with his nonverbal behavior. Throughout the interview this participant used a lot of sarcasm, laughed loudly at serious moments, made contradictory statements, and used very strong language to express angst over his situation, which had numerous complicating factors. The interviewer was uncertain at times of what he was really feeling and how to get at the meaning of such strong emotional language, for example, calling his partner's son "a bastard" and his own fetus "the devil seed" and "the spawn of Satan." She pressed him at one point, asking him if that is really how he felt. Pointing out contradictions and asking for clarification was helpful in this unusual situation. Ultimately, she felt like she was witnessing his confusion and powerful contradictory feelings.

47. We plan to explore men's use of language for their partners more carefully in future studies.

48. Crabtree and Miller, 1992.

49. Mason, 1996, p. 6.

NOTES TO CHAPTER 3

1. Morris, 1997.

2. Sonenstein, Pleck, and Ku, 1989; Sonenstein, Stewart, Lindberg, Pernas, and Williams, 1997.

3. DeLamater, 1987; In a study of 1,114 primary female caregivers (mothers and daycare workers) in Minnesota and California researchers found relatively small gender differences in the observed masturbation behavior of children aged 2–12. (Friedrich, Fisher, Broughton, Houston, and Shafran, 1998).

4. Marsiglio, 1988.

5. Marsiglio, 1998.

6. This scenario is most likely to involve males who are thinking about their own potential contribution to a pregnancy, but some men will quickly learn from a new sexual partner, perhaps even prior to having sex for the first time, that she is currently late with her period. Although the male will realize he is not the potential father in this case, discussions of the topic can still activate his procreative consciousness.

7. Other research in this area is quite sparse, but the ethnographic study we mentioned in chapter 2, using a sample of teenage and young adult men living in Brooklyn, New York, briefly deals with the "consciousness" and "awareness" theme of interest to us (Sullivan, 1995).

8. Marsiglio, 1998.

9. Rogow and Horowitz, 1995, p. 146; see also Clark, 1981; Ilaria, Jacobs, Polsky, Knoll, Baron, MacLow, and Armstrong, 1992; Pudney, Oneta, Mayer, and Seage, 1992.

10. LaRossa and LaRossa, 1989; Walzer, 1998.

11. Johnson and Puddifoot, 1996; Puddifoot and Johnson, 1997.

12. Shostak, McLouth, and Seng, 1984.

13. Furstenberg and Cherlin, 1991; Furstenberg and Harris, 1993.

NOTES TO CHAPTER 4

1. Hart (1992) provides a general discussion of the psychological processes associated with young men's transition from adolescence to adulthood. He focuses on issues associated with the development of an ideal self, moral development, and the acquisition and use of adaptation styles. For a discussion of the issues African American males face in making the transition to adulthood, see Billson, 1996.

2. Glaser, 1978; Strauss, 1969.

3. Gaylin, 1992; Marsiglio, 1998.

4. This research is relevant to various theoretical, research, and social policy agendas, some of which address men's involvement in preventing or dealing with unplanned pregnancies, as well as their commitments to their children (Federal Interagency Forum on Child and Family Statistics,1998; Marsiglio, 1998; Sonenstein, Stewart, Lindberg, Pernas, and Williams, 1997).

5. Blumstein, 1991.

6. Strauss, 1969.

7. Glaser and Strauss, 1967.

8. Belsky and Miller, 1986; Berman and Pedersen, 1987; Cowan, 1988, 1991; Jordan, 1996; Herzog, 1982; LaRossa and LaRossa, 1989; Puddifoot and Johnson,

1997; Shostak, McLouth, and Seng, 1984; Snarey, 1993; Strauss and Goldberg, 1999; Walzer, 1998; Zayas, 1988.

9. Daniels and Weingarten, 1982.

10. Molinaro, Woolfolk, and Palkovitz, 1997.

11. Daniels and Weingarten, 1982, p. 161.

12. Belsky and Miller, 1986; Marsiglio and Cohan, 1997.

13. Walzer, 1998, p. 16.

14. LaRossa and LaRossa, 1989.

15. Bansen and Stevens, 1992; Brier, 1999.

16. Miller, 1992b; Miller, Pasta, and Dean, 1998.

17. Decisions about whether males should be involved in making abortion decisions, and if so, to what extent, are highly controversial (Coleman and Nelson, 1999).

18. Ryan and Plutzer, 1989; Zelles, 1984.

19. In data collection for a new study of stepfathers, for example, the first author has recently heard men talk about how their repeated incarceration and the witnessing of a stepchild's nearly drowning were turning point experiences that affected their procreative and paternal consciousness.

20. Schutz, 1970a, 1970b.

21. LaRossa and LaRossa, 1989; McMahon, 1995; Trebilcot, 1983; Walzer, 1998.

Notes to Chapter 5

1. For many young men, learning how to manage their sexuality often begins within a romantic relationship (Graber, Britto, and Brooks-Gunn, 1999).

2. As shown in Furman, Brown, and Feiring's edited volume (1999), various theoretical perspectives can inform the study of adolescent relationships. These include social exchange theory, developmental theory, attachment theory, theories of emotions, and sociobiological and contextual theories of family functioning. Future research might consider ways to link concepts central to these theories with our ideas about the development of procreative identity.

3. Sonenstein, Stewart, Lindberg, Pernas, and Williams, 1997.

4. Billy, Tanfer, Grady, and Klepinger, 1993; see also Sabogal, Faigeles, and Catania, 1993.

5. One study used the grounded theory method to generate a model that illuminated how the African American adolescents in the study viewed sex as a set of interrelated games including a courtship game, duplicity game, disclosure game, and prestige game. Sexual pleasure was only part of the picture. The social action consequences were highly important and competed with or overrode the pregnancy and disease issues (Eyre, Hoffman, and Millstein, 1998).

6. Reiss, 1986.

7. Buzwell and Rosenthal (1996), who noted the connection between sex and romance in Australian adolescents, generated a typology of adolescents' sexual styles, including the sexually naive, sexually unassured, sexually competent, sexually adventurous, and sexually driven. The model was predictive of how the adolescents thought and behaved in regard to sex and relationships. Precursors to these sexual styles, however, are not yet known.

8. Other researchers support our finding that the nature of a relationship affects procreative consciousness and behavior in men; some note that this holds true for women as well. Reisen and Poppen (1995) found that college women described regular (almost every time) and consistent (every time) condom use more often in shorter relationships. Regular condom use was present in high-trust relationships; consistent condom use was common for women in a first sexual relationship. As did men, women used condoms less frequently as relationships evolved and trust increased. The nature of the relationship also influences other types of contraceptive use.

Landry and Camelo's (1994) focus group study with men and women aged 16–29 living in Denver revealed that condom use was more common in short-term, casual sexual relationships; more effective methods of contraception were chosen for long-term relationships. The Denver participants, as did ours, admitted that they occasionally did not use any contraception/protection with casual partners. Critelli and Suire (1998), in their study of 237 college students, found that in short-term monogamous relationships the use of other forms of birth control was associated with decreased condom use, putting individuals at risk for STDs and HIV/AIDS. Rather than mitigating risk, the trend toward short-term serial monogamous relationships negates STD prevention. Less than 50 percent of the participants knew if their partners were infected with HIV, and 19 percent admitted having sexual contact with another while in their "monogamous" relationship. We learned from our research, a bit late, that asking questions about multiple sexual contacts during a supposed monogamous relationship is important. Each of these smaller-scale studies is consistent with contraceptive patterns based on national survey data of young men (Ku, Sonenstein, and Pleck, 1994).

Understanding how young men think about monogamy and how they behave in monogamous relationships is essential for risk reduction and the development of relevant reproductive health programs. As Reisen and Poppen (1995) note, the issue of trust, a critical emotional and psychological feature of a relationship, influences risk perception and risk taking. Consequently, qualitative researchers who study both men and women can help gain more insight about this concept by asking What is it? How and when do partners decide to trust? Based on what? How does it change over time? To what extent and how do concerns about trust relate to individuals' pregnancy resolution perceptions?

9. Ku, Sonenstein, and Pleck, 1994.

10. Although little research has focused on young men's emotional reactions

and interpersonal relations with partners who are considering and/or undergoing abortions, an earlier study found that most teenage males want to be included in the decision-making process. They also are interested in receiving emotional and social support (Redmond, 1985). A grounded-theory study of eighteen Swedish young men aged 15 to 26 also suggested that the nature and quality of the men's relationship with a partner influenced the decision-making process (Holmberg and Wahlberg, 2000). The young men valued confidentiality when they sought abortion information, professional secrecy about their decision, and organized support to help them with their decision.

11. Bogren, 1983; Clinton, 1987; May and Perrin, 1985; Munroe, Munroe, and Nerlove 1973; Strikland, 1987.

12. Some researchers of the couvade, taking their cues from animal behavior, advocate shifting the focus from the anthropological, psychological, and sociological to a biological perspective. The new research agenda would include efforts to develop measurements of the physiological change in "pregnant" men and a search for the factors producing this change. Researchers interested in this line of research believe that it could have implications for understanding paternal and abusive-fathering behaviors (Mason and Elwood, 1995).

13. Mason and Elwood, 1995, p. 137.

14. One critical time for men to relate to a pregnant partner is during labor and delivery. A few of our participants commented on their positive experiences during this time, but research has shown that some men experience fear, anxiety, and disappointment. A qualitative study based on in-depth interviews with first-time white fathers who wanted to be present during the labor and delivery process found that some experienced fear and anxiety in response to the pain their wives encountered and the outcome of the birth process (Chandler and Field, 1997). They also were disappointed and frustrated at times when they felt "tolerated" rather than included as part of a "laboring couple." The authors of this study urge midwives to view the men as partners and not relegate them to supportive roles. In another small, intensive qualitative study, researchers studied six men who participated in four two-to-three hour meetings prior to the birth and in one meeting after the birth, followed by individual interviews that served as a validity check (Donovan, 1995; see also Barclay, Donovan, and Genovese, 1996). Observations at public and private hospitals and midwife classes also provided data. Men described their relationship with a partner as being in a state of disequilibrium. They felt ambivalent, separate from her and the pregnancy, that the relationship with the baby was "unreal," and that they had lost their previous lifestyle and role. They noted that the partner had become more emotional and their sexual relationship was diminishing, both of which contributed to their feeling isolated from the partner. The latter study also highlights men's anxiety and frustration during a partner's pregnancy along with their lack of understanding of what was occurring. Although prepared-childbirth classes have become more popular in recent decades and the public typically wants men to be

supportive of a pregnant partner, much more needs to be done to facilitate men's support and increase their comfort levels.

15. For a discussion of betrayal ("overlapping relationships") in adolescent relationships, see Graber, Britto, and Brooks-Gunn (1999, pp. 374–377).

16. Barker (1998) identifies the nature of mistrust in male-female relationships in his sample of low-income men in Chicago and Rio de Janeiro, Brazil: The men thought that a partner would betray them by going out with another man; that a partner would talk about the men's thoughts and behavior to their friends; and that a partner's interest lay in money.

17. Lamanna (1999) presents four discourse schemas (accidental, pair-bond, developmental, protective) relative to sex, reproduction, and relationships that she heard in interviews and focus groups with adolescent females. In our data, we heard young males use accidental and pair-bond schemas but not the latter two. Research that specifically examines male discourse more closely would enhance our understanding of the similarities and differences in gendered discourse.

18. Coleman and Ingham, 1999.

19. Interestingly, Barker (1998) notes that it was generally in committed relationships where talking about sex and contraception occurred. With the exception of Kyle, we found this to be true also.

20. Various issues are relevant to understanding the dynamics of young men's and women's communication patterns that involve sex and contraception. Building on Levinson's prior work that used self-efficacy as a theoretical framework with adolescent girls, Van den Bossche and Rubinson (1997) conducted a comparative study of male and female college students aged 18–20. Their survey focused on barriers to contraceptive use and contraceptive self-efficacy practices. This study underscores the need for men and women to learn how to communicate more effectively about contraceptive issues. The gender differences that surfaced suggest that women need to assume more responsibility in acquiring contraceptives and that men need to learn to refuse sexual intercourse without contraception.

21. In their focus-group study with men and women ages 16–29 living in Denver, Landry and Camelo (1994) found as we did that talking about contraception was less likely to occur in casual relationships and early in a relationship than in long-term committed relationships.

NOTES TO CHAPTER 6

1. Allen and Doherty, 1996; Furstenberg, 1995.

2. Marsiglio, 1998.

3. Herzog, 1982; May, 1980; Sherwen, 1987; Soule, Stanley, and Copans, 1979; Zayas, 1988.

4. Gohel, Diamond, and Chambers, 1997.

5. Federal Interagency Forum on Child and Family Statistics, 1998; Levine and Pitt, 1995; Marsiglio, 1998; Moore, Driscoll, and Ooms, 1997; Sonenstein, Stewart, Lindberg, Pernas, and Williams,1997.

6. Achatz and MacAllum, 1994; Anderson, 1993; Doherty, Kouneski, and Erickson, 1998; Wattenberg, 1993.

7. Furstenberg and Cherlin, 1991.

8. These findings supplement survey research conducted in the 1980s with high school students from a metropolitan area (Marsiglio, 1989; Marsiglio and Menaghan, 1990). This study examined students' perceptions about how likely it would be for them to experience different types of consequences by resolving an unplanned pregnancy with a hypothetical partner in a particular way. They were asked to assume that they had been dating the partner for a year and that they would be living with the partner and child. African American teenage males felt this type of decision would limit their ability to make plans for their life without worrying about others, limit their chances to spend time with friends, and enable them to assume financial responsibility for the situation. In addition to the last two consequences, white teenage males anticipated that living with a partner and child would lessen their chances of obtaining their desired level of education, give them a chance to care for the daily physical needs of their child, and require them to get a steady job. When compared to the young women, men were less likely to feel as though this arrangement would limit their education and more likely to require them to have a steady job, assume financial responsibility for the situation, and limit their chances to spend time with their friends.

9. Lamb, 1997; Parke, 1996.

10. Denzin, 1987.

11. Hawkins and Dollahite, 1997.

12. Allen and Doherty, 1996; Daly, 1993.

13. Amato, 1998; Furstenberg, 1998; Furstenberg and Hughes, 1995; Marsiglio and Cohan, 2000.

14. Gaylin, 1992; Marsiglio, 1988; 1998.

15. Braver and O'Connell, 1998, Furstenberg, 1995.

16. Bertoia and Drakich, 1995; Coltrane and Hickman, 1992.

NOTES TO CHAPTER 7

1. We echo other researchers who ask about the relationship between sex and romance under varied conditions, and the characteristics of healthy and unhealthy relationships (Furman, Brown, and Feiring, 1999).

2. Recall that we conducted follow-up interviews with only two men. The initial interview took place during their partners' pregnancies and the follow-up interview a few months after the births.

3. Erikson, 1950, 1964; Gould, 1978.

4. Landry and Forrest, 1995.

5. McAdams, 1990.

6. The first author has supervised twenty brief pilot in-depth interviews with young women that explore their understanding of how they became aware of their reproductive potential, the turning point experiences they have had, and their sense of readiness for motherhood. Although it is premature to draw any conclusions from these data, analyses that compare men's and women's inner worlds related to reproductive issues are likely to produce some intriguing findings.

7. Crowder and Tolnay, 2000.

8. Marsiglio, 1998; Schneider and McLean, 2000; Uniform Parentage Act, 1973.

9. Haas, 1992.

10. Marsiglio, 1998.

11. Dowd, 2000. In some ways this sentiment differs from Dowd's legal interpretation because she is more willing to stress the necessity for men to support the children's mother in a manner that assumes that all mothers, seemingly regardless of their behavior, deserve this type of support.

12. Haas and Hawng, 1995.

13. Pierre, Shrier, Emans, and DuRant, 1998. In a related study using the 1993 Massachusetts Youth Risk Behavior Survey conducted on a random sample of 3,054 ninth to twelfth graders (Springarn and DuRant, 1996), researchers compared the use of tobacco, alcohol, and other drugs; early and multiple sexual experiences; fighting resulting in injury; and demographic variables between sexually active young men involved in a pregnancy ($n=82$) and their counterparts ($n=537$) who reported that they had never caused a pregnancy. These researchers described a "risk behavior syndrome" based on their findings that a history of being involved with a pregnancy clustered with other health-risk and problem behaviors.

14. Kiselica, 1995; Levine and Pitt, 1995; Sonenstein, Stewart, Lindberg, Pernas, and Williams, 1997.

15. Sonenstein, Stewart, Lindberg, Pernas, and Williams, 1997, p. 143.

16. Sonenstein, Stewart, Lindberg, Pernas, and Williams, 1997.

17. See Barker (1998) for a brief discussion of suggestions for how youth-servicing organizations can encourage young males to adopt more "progressive versions of masculinity" that would enhance their opportunities for engaging in responsible sexual, contraceptive, and paternal behavior.

18. Downey, Bonica, and Rincon (1999) emphasize the importance of understanding normative developmental changes in adolescent dating prior to identifying maladaptive patterns. We believe that the search for both types of relationship patterns—normative and maladaptive—is critical to our ability to understand the evolutionary process of procreative identity development.

19. Daly, 1993; Lewis, 1986.

20. Levine and Pitt, 1995; Levine, Murphy, and Wilson, 1993.

21. Gergen and Gergen, 1997.

22. Bakan, 1966; McAdams, 1990.

23. McAdams, 1990, p. 158.

24. Pollack, 1998.

25. Danielson, McNally, Swanson, Plunkett, and Klausmeier, 1988; Schulte and Sonenstein, 1995. For a description of the successful Young Men's Clinic in New York City, see Armstrong, Cohall, Vaughan, Scott, Tiezzi, and McCarthy (1999) and Sonenstein, Stewart, Lindberg, Pernas, and Williams, 1997.

26. Kiselica, 1995. See also Majors (1994) and Billson (1996) for discussions about various educational and mentoring strategies for working with African American young males. Some of these strategies promote an Afrocentric ideology.

27. Furstenberg, 1988; Pleck, 1997.

28. Marsiglio, 1998.

29. Marsiglio, in press.

30. Glaser, 1978; Glaser and Strauss, 1968.

31. McAdams, 1990; Strauss, 1969.

32. Theorists of adult life interested in generativity issues also add their voice to this train of thought by discussing the developmental and motivational forces propelling adult men to seek opportunities to nurture children (Hawkins and Dollahite, 1997; McAdams, 1990; Snarey, 1993).

33. See related discussion of "imago" as a "personified and idealized image of the self . . . [that structures] a person's life story" (McAdams, 1990, p. 191).

34. Markus and Nurius, 1986; Oyserman and Markus, 1990; Strauss and Goldberg, 1999.

35. Furstenberg and Cherlin, 1991.

36. Lamb, Pleck, Charnov, and Levine, 1985, 1987; Pleck and Stueve, in press.

37. Researchers who do discourse analysis may look at the interpretive resources young men use in their accounts as they talk about their future romantic and domestic lives—including paternity experiences (see Edley and Wetherell, 1999).

38. Pleck and Stueve, in press; Stueve and Pleck, 2001.

39. Allen and Hawkins, 1999.

40. One concrete and innovative measure of men's orientation in this regard is revealed in their narratives that are organized around the "parenting voice" ("I only" or "we joint" pronouns) that men use in describing meaningful parenting experiences to interviewers, and presumably others outside a research context (Stueve and Pleck, 2001).

41. Although motivation can be discussed as a separate factor related to fathers' involvement, men's concerns about and efforts to achieve certain fathering ideals can be seen as a dimension of a broader view of father involvement that is independent of specific children (Marsiglio, Day, and Lamb, 2000; Pleck and Stueve, 2001).

References

Abma, J. C. and Sonenstein, F. L. (2001). Sexual activity and contraceptive practices among teenagers in the United States, 1988 and 1995. Vital Health Stat, 23 (21). Hyattsville, MD: National Center for Health Statistics.

Achatz, M. and MacAllum, C. A. (1994). *The young unwed fathers demonstration project: A status report.* Philadelphia: Public/Private Ventures.

Alan Guttmacher Institute. (2002). *In their own right: addressing the sexual and reproductive health of American men.* New York.

Alexander, C. N., Jr. and Wiley, M. (1981). Situated identity and identity formation. In M. Rosenberg and R. H. Turner (Eds.), *Social psychology: Sociological perspectives* (pp. 269–289). New York: Basic Books.

Allen, D. A. and Doherty, W. J. (1996). The responsibilities of fatherhood as perceived by African American teenage fathers. *Families in Society: The Journal of Contemporary Human Services*, March, 142–155.

Allen, S. M. and Hawkins, A. J. (1999). Maternal gatekeeping: Mother's beliefs and behaviors that inhibit greater father involvement in family work. *Journal of Marriage and the Family*, 61, 199–212.

Amato, P. (1998). More than money? Men's contributions to their children's lives. In A. Booth and N. Crouter (Eds.), *Men in families: When do they get involved? What difference does it make?* (pp. 241–278). Mahwah, NJ: Lawrence Erlbaum Associates.

Anderson, E.(1993). Sex codes and family life among poor inner–city youths. In R. I. Lerman and T. J. Ooms (Eds.), *Young unwed fathers: Changing roles and emerging policies* (pp. 74–98). Philadelphia: Temple University Press.

Arendell, T. (1997). Reflections on the researcher–researched relationship: A woman interviewing men. *Qualitative Sociology*, 20, 341–368.

Armato, M. and Marsiglio, W. (2002). Self structure, identity, and commitment: Promise Keepers' Godly man project. *Symbolic Interation*, 25, 41–65.

Armstrong, B., Cohall, A. T., Vaughan, R. D., Scott, M., Tiezzi, L., and McCarthy, J. F. (1999). Involving men in reproductive health: The young men's clinic. *American Journal of Public Health*, 89, 902–905.

AVSC. (1999a). Literature review for the Symposium on Male Participation in Sexual and Reproductive Health: New Paradigms. New York: AVSC International Planned Parenthood Federation, Western Hemisphere Region.

AVSC (1999b). Five case studies for the Symposium on Male Participation in Sexual and Reproductive Health: New Paradigms. New York: AVSC International Planned Parenthood Federation, Western Hemisphere Region.

Bachu, A. (1996). *Fertility of American men*. Population Division Working Paper No. 14. Fertility Statistics Branch. Washington, DC: U.S. Bureau of the Census.

Bakan, D. (1966). *The duality of human experience: Isolation and communion in Western men*. Boston: Beacon Press.

Bansen, S. S. and Stevens, H. A. (1992). Women's experiences of miscarriage in early pregnancy. *Journal of Nurse Midwifery*, 37, 84–90.

Barclay, L., Donovan, J., and Genovese, A. (1996). Men's experiences during their partner's first pregnancy: A grounded theory analysis. *Australian Journal of Advanced Nursing*, 13, 12–24.

Barker, G. (1998). Boys in the hood, boys in the bairro: Exploratory research on masculinity, fatherhood and attitudes toward women among low income young men in Chicago, USA, and Rio de Janeiro, Brazil. Paper presented at IUSSP/CENEP Seminar on Men, Family Formation and Reproduction. Buenos Aires, May.

Belsky, J. and Miller, B. C. (1986). Adolescent fatherhood in the context of the transition to parenthood. In A. B. Elster and M. E. Lamb (Eds.), *Adolescent fatherhood*. Hillsdale, NJ: Lawrence Erlbaum Associates.

Berman, P. W. and Pedersen, F. A. (1987). Research on men's transitions to parenthood: An integrative discussion. In P. W. Berman and F. A. Pedersen (Eds.), *Men's transitions to parenthood: Longitudinal studies of early family experience* (pp. 217–242). Hillsdale, NJ: Lawrence Erlbaum Associates.

Bertoia, C. E. and Drakich, J. (1995). The fathers' rights movement: Contradictions in rhetoric and practice. In W. Marsiglio (Ed.), *Fatherhood: Contemporary theory, research, and social policy* (pp. 230–254). Thousand Oaks, CA: Sage.

Billson, J. M. (1996). *Pathways to manhood: Young black males struggle for identity*. New Brunswick, NJ: Transaction Pubishers.

Billy, J. O. G., Tanfer, K., Grady, W. R., and Klepinger, D. H. (1993). The sexual behavior of men in the United States. *Family Planning Perspectives*, 25, 52–60.

Blankenhorn, D. (1995). *Fatherless America: Confronting out most urgent social problem*. New York: HaperCollins.

Blumer, H. (1954). What is wrong with social theory? *American Sociological Review*, 19, 3–10.

Blumer, H. (1969). *Symbolic interactionism*. Englewood Cliffs, NJ: Prentice-Hall.

Blumstein, P. (1991). The production of selves in personal relationships. In J. Howard and P. Callero (Eds.), *The self-society dynamic* (pp. 305–322). New York: Cambridge University Press.

Boggess, S. and Bradner, C. (2000). Trends in adolescent males' abortion attitudes, 1988–1995: Differences by race and ethnicity. *Family Planning Perspectives*, 32, 118–123.

Bogren, L. Y. (1983). Couvade. *Acta Psych Scand*, 68, 55–65.

Booth, A. and Crouter, N. (1998). *Men in families: When do they get involved? What difference does it make?* Mahwah, NJ: Lawrence Erlbaum Associates.

Bozett, F. W. and Hanson, S. M. H. (1991). *Fatherhood and families in cultural context.* New York: Springer.

Braver , S. L. and O'Connell, D. (1998). *Divorced dads: Shattering the myths.* New York: Tarcher/Putnam.

Brier, N. (1999). Understanding and managing the emotional reactions to a miscarriage. *Obstetrics Gynecology*, 93, 151–155.

Buzwell, S., and Rosenthal, D. (1996). Constructing a sexual self: Adolescents' sexual self–perceptions and sexual risk–taking. *Journal of Research on Adolescence*, 6, 489–513.

Chandler, S. and Field, P. (1997). Becoming a father: First–time fathers' experience of labor and delivery. *Journal of Nurse Midwifery*, 42, 17–24.

Child Trends. (1999). Facts at a glance. www.childtrends.org

Clark, S. D. (1981). An examination of the sperm count of human pre–ejaculatory fluid. Master's thesis, Johns Hopkins University, Baltimore.

Clinton, J. (1987). Physical and emotional responses of expectant fathers throughout pregnancy and the early postpartum period. *International Journal of Nursing Studies*, 24, 59–68.

Coleman, L. M. and Ingham, R. (1999). Exploring young people's difficulties in talking about contraception: How can we encourage more discussion between partners? *Health Education Research*, 14, 741–750.

Coleman, P. K. and Nelson, E. S. (1999). Abortion attitudes as determinants of perceptions regarding male involvement in abortion decisions. *Journal of American College Health*, 47, 164–171.

Coltrane, S. and Hickman, N. (1992). The rhetoric of rights and needs: Moral discourse in the reform of child custody and child support laws. *Social Problems*, 39, 401–420.

Cowan, P. A. (1988). Becoming a father: A time of change, an opportunity for development. In P. Bronstein and C. P. Cowan (Eds.), *Fatherhood today: Men's changing role in the family* (pp. 13–35). New York: John Wiley and Sons.

Cowan, P. A. (1991). Individual and family life transitions: A proposal for a new definition. In P. A. Cowan and E. M. Hetherington (Eds.), *Family transitions* (pp. 3–30). Hillsdale, NJ: Lawrence Erlbaum Associates.

Crabtree, B. and Miller, W. (1992). *Doing qualitative research.* Newbury Park, CA: Sage.

Critelli, J. and Suire, D. (1998). Obstacles to condom use: The combination of other forms of birth control and short–term monogamy. *Journal of American College Health*, 46, 215–219.

Crowder, K. and Tolnay, S. E. (2000). A new marriage squeeze for black women: The role of racial intermarriage by black men. *Journal of Marriage and the Family*, 62, 792–807.

Daly, K. (1993). Reshaping fatherhood: Finding the models. *Journal of Family Issues*, 14, 510–530.

Daniels, C. R. (1998). *Lost fathers: The politics of fatherlessness in America*. New York: St. Martin's Press.

Daniels, P. and Weingarten, C. (1982). *Sooner or later*. New York: W. W. Norton and Co.

Danielson, R., McNally, K., Swanson, J., Plunkett, A., and Klausmeier, W. (1988). Title X and family planning services for men. *Family Planning Perspectives*, 20, 234–237.

Day, R. D. and Lamb, M. E. (in press). *Conceptualizing and measuring paternal involvement*. Mahwah, NJ: Lawrence Erlbaum Associates.

Deatrick, J. and Faux, S. (1991). Conducting qualitative studies with children and adolescents. In J. Morse (Ed.), *Qualitative nursing research: A contemporary dialogue* (pp. 203–223). Newbury Park, CA: Sage.

DeLamater, J. (1987). Gender differences in sexual scenarios. In K. Kelly (Ed.), *Females, males and sexuality: Theories and research* (pp. 178–191). Philadelphia: Temple University Press.

Denzin, N. K. (1987). *The recovering alcoholic*. Thousand Oaks, CA: Sage.

Doherty, W. J., Kouneski, E. F., and Erikson, M. F. (1998). Responsible fathering: An overview and conceptual framework. *Journal of Marriage and the Family*, 60, 277–292.

Donovan, J. (1995). The process of analysis during a grounded theory study of men during their partners' pregnancies. *Journal of Advanced Nursing*, 21, 708–715.

Dowd, N. E. (2000). *Redefining fatherhood*. New York: New York University Press.

Downey, G., Bonica, C., and Rincon, C. (1999). Rejection sensitivity and adolescent romantic relationships. In W. Furman, B. Brown, and C. Feiring (Eds.), *The development of romantic relationships in adolescence* (pp. 148–174). Cambridge, UK: Cambridge University Press.

Durkheim, E. (1895/1982). *The rules of the sociological method*. New York: Free Press.

Edley, N. and Wetherell, M. (1999). Imagined futures: Young men's talk about fatherhood and domestic life. *British Journal of Social Psychology*, 38, 181–194.

Edwards, S. R. (1994). The role of men in contraceptive decision–making: Current knowledge and future implications. *Family Planning Perspectives*, 26 (2), 77–82.

Erikson, E. (1950). *Childhood and society*. New York; Norton.

Erikson, E. (1964). *Insight and responsibility*. New York: Norton.

Eyre, S., Hoffman, V., and Millstein, S. (1998). The gamesmanship of sex: A model based on African American adolescent accounts. *Medical Anthropology Quarterly*, 12, 467–489.

Faux, S., Walsh, M., and Deatrick, J. (1988). Intensive interviewing with children and adolescents. *Western Journal of Nursing Research*, 10, 180–194.

Federal Interagency Forum on Child and Family Statistics (1998). *Nurturing fatherhood: Improving data and research on male fertility, family formation, and fatherhood*. Washington, DC.

Fine, G. and Sandstrom, K. (1988). *Knowing children: Participation observation with minors*. Newbury Park, CA: Sage.

Friedrich, W. N., Fisher, J., Broughton, D., Houston, M. and Shafran, C. R. (1998). Normative sexual behavior in children: A contemporary sample. *Pediatrics*, 101, 1–8.

Furman, W., Brown, B., and Feiring, C. (1999). *The development of romantic relationships in adolescence*. Cambridge, UK: Cambridge University Press.

Furstenberg, F. F., Jr. (1988). Good dads—bad dads: Two faces of fatherhood. In A. J. Cherlin (Ed.), *The changing American family and public policy* (pp. 193–218). Washington, DC: Urban Institute.

Furstenberg, F. F., Jr. (1991). As the pendulum swings: Teenage childbearing and social concern. *Family Relations*, 40, 127–138.

Furstenberg, F. F., Jr. (1992). Teenage childbearing and cultural rationality: A thesis in search of evidence. *Family Relations*, 41, 239–243.

Furstenberg, F. F., Jr. (1995). Fathering in the inner city: Paternal participation and public policy. In W. Marsiglio (Ed.), *Fatherhood: Contemporary theory, research, and social policy* (pp. 119–147). Thousand Oaks, CA: Sage.

Furstenberg, F. F., Jr. (1998). Social capital and the role of fathers in the family. In A. Booth and N. Crouter (Eds.), *Men in families: When do they get involved? What difference does it make?* (pp. 295–301). Mahwah, NJ: Lawrence Erlbaum Associates.

Furstenberg, F. F., Jr. and Cherlin, A. J. (1991). *Divided families: What happens to children when parents part*. Cambridge: Harvard University Press.

Furstenberg, F. F., Jr. and Harris, K. (1993). When and why fathers matter: Impacts of father involvement on the children of adolescent mothers. In R. Lerman and T. Ooms (Eds.), *Young unwed fathers: Changing roles and emerging policies* (pp. 117–138). Philadelphia: Temple University Press.

Furstenberg, F. F., Jr. and Hughes, M. E. (1995). Social capital and successful development among at–risk youth. *Journal of Marriage and the Family*, 57, 580–592.

Garfinkel, I., McLanahan, S., Meyer, D., and Seltzer, J. (1998). *Fathers under fire: The revolution of child support enforcement*. New York: Russell Sage Foundation.

Gaylin, W. (1992). *The male ego*. New York: Penguin Books.

Gergen, K. J. and Gergen, M. M. (1997). Narratives of the self. In L. P. Hinchman and S. K. Hinchman (Eds.), *Memory, identity, community* (pp. 161–184). Albany: State University of New York Press.

Geronimus, A. T. (1991). Teenage childbearing and social and reproductive disadvantage: The evolution of complex questions and the demise of simple answers. *Family Relations*, 40, 463–471.

Geronimus, A. T. (1992). Teenage childbearing and social disadvantage: Unprotected discourse. *Family Relations*, 41, 244–248.

Gerson, K. (1993). *No man's land: Men's changing commitments to family and work.* New York: Basic Books.

Gilmore, S., DeLamater, J., and Wagstaff, D. (1996). Sexual decision–making by inner–city black adolescent males: A focus group study. *Journal of Sex Research*, 33, 363–371.

Ginsberg, H. and Opper, S. (1979). *Piaget's theory of intellectual development* (2nd ed.). Englewood Cliffs, NJ: Prentice–Hall.

Glaser, B. (1978). *Theoretical sensitivity*. Mill Valley, CA: Sociology Press.

Glaser, B. (1992). *Basics of grounded theory analysis*. Mill Valley, CA: Sociology Press.

Glaser, B. and Strauss, A. (1967). *The discovery of grounded theory: Strategies for qualitative research.* Chicago: Aldine de Gruyter.

Glaser, B. and Strauss, A. (1968). *Time for dying.* Chicago: Aldine Publishing.

Gohel M., Diamond, J. J., and Chambers, C. V. (1997). Attitudes toward sexual responsibility and parenting: An exploratory study of young urban males. *Family Planning Perspectives*, 29, 280–283.

Gould, R. (1978). *Transformation, growth and change in adult life.* New York: Simon & Schuster.

Graber, J., Britto, P., and Brooks–Gunn, J. (1999). What's love got to do with it? Adolescents' and young adults' beliefs about sexual and romantic relationships. In Wyndol Furman, B. Bradford Brown, et al.(Eds). *The development of romantic relationships in adolescence* (pp. 364–395). Cambridge studies in social and emotional development. New York: Cambridge University Press.

Grady, W. R., Tanfer, K., Billy, J. O. G., and Lincoln–Hanson, J. (1996). Men's perceptions of their roles and responsibililities regarding sex, contraception and childbearing. *Family Planning Perspectives*, 28, 221–226.

Griswold, R. L. (1993). *Fatherhood in America: A history.* New York: Basic Books.

Haas, L. (1992). *Equal parenthood and social policy.* Albany: State University of New York Press.

Haas, L. and Hawng, P. (1995). Company culture and men's usage of family leave benefits in Sweden. *Family Relations*, 44, 28–36.

Hart, D. A. (1992). *Becoming a man: The development of aspirations, values, and adaptation styles.* New York: Plenum Press.

Hawkins, A. J. and Dollahite, D. (1997). *Generative fathering: Beyond deficit perspectives.* Thousand Oaks, CA: Sage.

Herzog, J. M. (1982). Patterns of expectant fatherhood: A study of fathers of premature infants. In S. H. Cath, A. R. Gurwitt, and J. M. Ross (Eds.), *Father and child: Development and clinical perspectives* (pp. 301–314). Boston: Little, Brown.

Holmberg, L. I. and Wahlberg, V. (2000). The process of decision–making on abortion: A grounded theory study of young men in Sweden. *Journal of Adolescent Health*, 26, 230–234.

Holstein, J. A. and Gubrium, J. F. (2000). *The self we live by: Narrative identity in a postmodern world*. New York: Oxford University Press.

Hood, J. (1993). *Men, work, and family*. Newbury Park, CA: Sage.

Hutchinson, S., Wilson, M., and Wilson, H. (1994). Benefits of participating in research interviews. *Image, Journal of Nursing Research*, 26(2), 161–164.

Ilaria, G., Jacobs, J. L., Polsky, B., Knoll, B., Baron, P., MacLow, C., and Armstrong, D. (1992) Detection of HIV–I DNA sequences in pre–ejaculatory fluid, *Lancet*, 340, I, 469.

Jacobs, M. (1995). The wish to become a father: How do men decide in favour of parenthood? In M. C. P. van Dongen, G. A. B. Frinking, and M. J. G. Jacobs (Eds.), *Changing fatherhood: An interdisciplinary perspective* (pp. 67–83). Amsterdam, The Netherlands: Thesis Publishers.

Johnson, M. P. and Puddifoot, J. E. (1996). The grief response in the partners of females who miscarry. *British Journal of Medical Psychology*, 69, 313–328.

Jordan, W. J. (1996). *Role transitions: A review of the literature*. Philadelphia: National Center on Fathers and Families.

Kaiser Family Foundation. (1997). The 1997 Kaiser Family Foundation Survey on Men's Role in Preventing Pregnancy: Questionnaire and Toplines. Menlo Park, CA.

Kiselica, M. S. (1995). *Multicultural counseling with teenage fathers: A practical guide*. Thousand Oaks, CA: Sage.

Krueger, R. (1994). *Focus groups: A practical guide for applied research* (2nd ed.), Thousand Oaks, CA: Sage.

Ku, L., Sonenstein, F. L., and Pleck, J. H. (1994). The dynamics of young men's condom use during and across relationships. *Family Planning Perspectives*, 26, 246–251.

Lamanna, M. A. (1999). Living the postmodern dream: Adolescent women's discourse on relationships, sexuality, and reproduction. *Journal of Family Issues*, 20, 181–217.

Lamb, M. E. (1997). *The role of the father in child development* (3rd ed.). New York: John Wiley and Sons.

Lamb, M. E., Pleck, J. H., Charnov, E. L., and Levine, J. A. (1985). Paternal behavior in humans. *American Zoologist*, 25, 883–894.

Lamb, M. E., Pleck, J. H., Charnov, E. L. and Levine, J. A. (1987). A biosocial perspective on paternal behavior and involvement. In Lancaster, J. B., Altmann, J.,

Rossi, A. S., and Sherrod, L. R. (Eds.), *Parenting across the lifespan: Biosocial dimensions* (pp. 111–142). Hawthorne, NY: Aldine de Gruyter.

Landry, D. J. and Camelo, T. M.. (1994). Young unmarried men and women discuss men's role in contraceptive practice. *Family Planning Perspectives*, 26 (5), 222–227.

Landry, D. J. and Forrest, J. D. (1995). How old are U.S. fathers? *Family Planning Perspectives*, 27, 159–163, 165.

LaRossa, R. and LaRossa, M. M. (1989). Baby care: Fathers vs. mothers. In B. J. Risman and P. Schwartz (Eds.), *Gender in intimate relationships: A microstructural approach*. Belmont, CA: Wadsworth.

Levine, J. A., Murphy, D. T., and Wilson, S. (1993). *Getting men involved: Strategies for early childhood programs*. New York: Families and Work Institute.

Levine, J. A. and Pitt, E. W. (1995). *New expectations: Community strategies for responsible fatherhood*. New York: Families and Work Institute.

Lewis, C. (1986). *Becoming a father*. Milton Keynes, UK: Open University Press.

Lincoln, Y. and Guba, E. (1985). *Naturalistic inquiry*. Beverly Hills, CA: Sage.

Lindberg, D. L., Sonenstein, F. L., Martinez, G., and Marcotte, J. (1998). Completeness of young fathers' reports of fertility. *Journal of Economic and Social Measurement*, 24, 15–23.

Majors, R. (1994). Conclusion and recommendations: A reason for hope—an overview of the new black male movement in the United States. In R. G. Majors and J. U. Gordon (Eds.), *The American black male: His present status and his future*. Chicago: Nelson–Hall.

Mallory, C. (2001). Examining the differences between researcher and participant: An intrinsic element of grounded theory. In R. Schreiber and P. Stern (Eds.) *Using grounded theory in nursing*. (pp 85–95). New York: Springer.

Markus, H. and Nurius, P. (1986). Possible selves. *American Psychologist*, 41, 954–969.

Marsiglio, W. (1988). Adolescent male sexuality and heterosexual masculinity: A conceptual model and review. *Journal of Adolescent Research*, 3, 285–303.

Marsiglio, W. (1989). Adolescent males' pregnancy resolution preferences and family formation intentions: Does family background make a difference for blacks and whites? *Journal of Adolescent Research*, 4, 214–237.

Marsiglio, W. (1993). Adolescent males' orientation toward paternity and contraception. *Family Planning Perspectives*, 25, 22–31.

Marsiglio, W. (1995). *Fatherhood: Contemporary theory, research, and social policy*. Thousand Oaks, CA: Sage.

Marsiglio, W. (1998). Procreative man. New York: New York University Press.

Marsiglio, W. (in press). Studying fathering trajectories: In–depth interviewing and sensitizing concepts. In R. Day and M. E. Lamb (Eds.); *Conceptualizing and measuring paternal involvement*. Mahwah, NJ: Lawrence Erlbaum Associates.

Marsiglio, W. and Cohan, M. (1997). Young fathers and child development. In M. E. Lamb (Ed.), *The role of the father in child development* (3rd ed.) (pp. 227–244). New York: John Wiley and Sons.

Marsiglio, W. and Cohan, M. (2000). Contextualizing father involvement and paternal influence: Sociological and qualitative themes. *Marriage and Family Review,* 29, 75–95.

Marsiglio, W., Day. R. D., and Lamb, M. E. (2000). Exploring fatherhood diversity: Implications for conceptualizing father involvement. *Marriage and Family Review,* 29, 269–293.

Marsiglio, W., Hutchinson, S., and Cohan, M. (2000). Envisioning fatherhood: A social psychological perspective on young men without kids. *Family Relations,* 49, 133–142 .

Marsiglio, W., Hutchinson, S., and Cohan, M. (2001). Young men's procreative identity: Become aware, being aware, and being responsible. *Journal of Marriage and the Family,* 62, 123–135.

Marsiglio, W. and Menaghan, E. G. (1990). Pregnancy resolution and family formation: Understanding gender differences in adolescents' preferences and beliefs. *Journal of Family Issues,* 11, 313–333.

Marsiglio W. and Shehan, C. (1993). Adolescent males' abortion attitudes: Data from a national survey. *Family Planning Perspectives,* 25, 162–169.

Mason, C. and Elwood, R. (1995). Is there a physiological basis for the couvade and onset of paternal care? *International Journal of Nursing Studies,* 32, 137–148.

Mason, J. (1996). *Qualitative researching.* Thousand Oaks, CA: Sage.

May, K. A. (1980). A typology of detachment/involvement styles adopted during pregnancy by first–time fathers. *Western Journal of Nursing Research,* 2, 445–453.

May, K. A. and Perrin, S. P. (1985). Prelude: Pregnancy and birth. In S. M. Hanson and F. W. Bozett (Eds.), *Dimensions of fatherhood* (pp. 64–91). Beverly Hills, CA: Sage.

McAdams, D. (1990). Unity and purpose in human lives: The emergence of identity as a life story. In A. I. Rabin, R. A. Zucker, R. A. Emmons, and S. Frank (Eds.), *Studying persons and lives* (pp. 148–200). New York: Springer.

McKee, L. and O'Brien, M. (1983). Interviewing men: Taking gender seriously. In Eva Gamarnikow, David Morgan, June Purvis, and Daphne Taylorson (Eds.), *The public and the private* (pp. 147–161). London: Heinemann.

McMahon, M. (1995). *Engendering motherhood: Identity and self–transformation in women's lives.* New York: Guilford Press.

Mead, G. H. (1934). *Mind, self, and society: From the standpoint of a social behaviorist.* Chicago: University of Chicago Press.

Messner, A. M. (1997). *Politics of masculinities: Men in movements.* Thousand Oaks, CA: Sage.

Miller, W. B. (1992a). Personality traits and developmental experiences as antecedents of childbearing motivations. *Demography*, 29, 265–285.

Miller, W. B. (1992b). An empirical study of the psychological antecedents and consequences of induced abortion. *Journal of Social Issues*, 48, 67–93.

Miller, W. B., Pasta, D. J., and Dean, C. L. (1998). Testing a model of the psychological consequences of abortion. In L. J. Beckman and S. M. Harvey (Eds.), *The new civil war: The psychology, culture and politics of abortion* (pp. 235–267). Washington, DC: American Psychological Association.

Molinaro, J., Woolfolk, T., and Palkovitz, R. (1997). Developing the fatherhood identity: Processes, themes and influences. Paper presented at the Theory Construction and Research Methodology Workshop, Crystal City, VA, November.

Moore, K. A., Driscoll, A. K., and Ooms, T. (1997). *Not just for girls: The roles of boys and men in teen pregnancy prevention*. Washington, DC: National Campaign to Prevent Teen Pregnancy.

Morris, L. A. (1997). *The male heterosexual*. Thousand Oaks, CA: Sage.

Mott, F. L. and Gryn, T. A. (2001). Evaluating male fertility data: Who reports consistently and what are the analytical implications. Paper presented at the Meetings of the Population Association of America, Washington, DC, March.

Munhall, P. and Boyd, C. (1993). *Nursing research: A qualitative perspective*. New York: National League for Nursing Press.

Munroe, R. L., Munroe, R. H., and Nerlove, S. B. (1973). Male pregnancy symptoms and cross–sex identity: Two replications. *Journal of Social Psychology*, 89, 147–148.

Nelson, E. S., Coleman, P. K, and Swager, M. J. (1997). Attitudes toward the level of male involvement in abortion decisions. *Journal of Humanistic Education and Development*, 25, 217–224.

Nesmith, J. D., Klerman, L. V., Oh, M. K., and Feinstein, R. A. (1997). Procreative experiences and orientations toward paternity held by incarcerated adolescent males. *Journal of Adolescent Health*, 20, 198–203.

O'Brien, M. (1981). *The politics of reproduction*. Boston: Routledge and Kegan Paul.

Oyserman, D. and Markus, H. R. (1990). Possible selves and delinquency. *Journal of Personality and Social Psychology*, 59, 112–125.

Parke, R. (1996). *Fatherhood*. Cambridge: Harvard University Press.

Pierre, N., Shrier, L., Emans, J., and DuRant, R. (1998). Adolescent males involved in pregnancy: Associations of forced sexual contact and risk behaviors. *Journal of Adolescent Health*, 23, 364–369.

Pleck, J. H. (1997). Paternal involvement: Levels, courses, and consequences. In M. E. Lamb (Ed.), *The role of the father in child development* (pp. 66–103, 325–332). New York: John Wiley and Sons.

Pleck, J. H., Sonenstein, F., and Ku, L. (1991). Adolescent males' condom use: Relationships between perceived costs–benefits and consistency. *Journal of Marriage and the Family*, 53, 733–745.

Pleck, J. H., Sonenstein, F., and Ku, L. (1993). Changes in adolescent males' use of and attitudes toward condoms, 1988–1991. *Family Planning Perspectives*, 25, 106–109, 117.

Pleck, J. H., Sonenstein, F., and Ku, L. (1996). Effects of pregnancy experience on young males' subsequent fertility behavior. Unpublished manuscript.

Pleck, J. H. and Stueve, J. L. (2001). Time and parental involvement In K. Daly (Ed.), *Minding the time in family experience: Emerging perspectives and issues*. (pp. 205–226). Oxford, UK: Elsevier Science.

Pleck, J. H. and Stueve, J. L. (in press). Assessing paternal identity through narratives: The importance of parental identity "conjointness." In R. D. Day and M. E. Lamb (Eds.), *Conceptualizing and measuring paternal involvement*. Mahwah, NJ: Lawrence Erlbaum Associates.

Pollack, W. (1998). *Real boys: Rescuing our sons from the myths of boyhood*. New York: Henry Holt and Company.

Popenoe, D. (1996). *Life without father*. New York: Free Press.

Puddifoot, J. E. and Johnson, M. P. (1997). The legitimacy of grieving: The partner's experience at miscarriage. *Social Science and Medicine*, 45, 837–845.

Pudney, J., Oneta, M., Mayer, K., Seage, G., III, and Anderson, D. (1992). Pre–ejaculatory fluid as a potential vector for sexual transmission of HIV–I. *Lancet*, 340, I, 470.

Redmond, M. A., (1985). Attitudes of adolescent males toward adolescent pregnancy and fatherhood. *Family Relations*, 34, 337–342.

Reisen, C., and Poppen, P. (1995). College women and condom use: Importance of partner relationship. *Journal of Applied Social Psychology*, 25, 1485–1498.

Reiss, I. L. (1996). *Journey into sexuality: An exploratory voyage*. Englewood Cliffs, CA: Prentice-Hall.

Reissman, C. (1991). When gender is not enough: Women interviewing women. In J. Lorber and S. Farrell (Eds.), *The social construction of gender* (pp. 217–236). London: Sage.

Rendall, M. S., Clarke, L., Peters, H. E., Ranjit, N., and Verropoulou, G. (1999). Incomplete reporting of men's fertility in the United States and Britain: A research note. *Demography*, 36, 135–144.

Rogow, D. and Horowitz, S. (1995). Withdrawal: A review of the literature and an agenda for research. *Studies in Family Planning*, 26, 140–153.

Rosenwasser, S. M., Wright, L. S., and Barber, R. B. (1987). The rights and responsibilities of men in abortion situations. *Journal of Sex Research*, 23, 97–105.

Ryan, B. and Plutzer, E. (1989). When married women have abortions: Spousal notification and marital interaction. *Journal of Marriage and the Family*, 51, 41–50.

Sabogal, F., Faigeles, B., and Catania, J. A. (1993). Multiple sexual partners among Hispanics in high–risk cities. *Family Planning Perspectives*, 25, 257–262.

Sandelowski, M. (1995). Sample size in qualitative research. *Research in Nursing and Health*, 18, 179–183.

Schatzman, L. and Strauss, A. (1973). *Field research: Strategies for a natural sociology*. Englewood Cliffs, NJ: Prentice–Hall.

Schneider, W. H. and McLean, C. (2000). 'Pregnant on the sly.' *Report Newsmagazine*, April 24, 52–53.

Schulte, M. M. and Sonenstein, F. L. (1995). Men at family planning clinics: The new patients? *Family Planning Perspectives*, 27, 212–225.

Schutz, A. (1970a). *On phenomenology and social relations*. Chicago: University of Chicago Press.

Schutz, A. (1970b). *Reflections on the problem of relevance*. New Haven: Yale University Press.

Schwalbe, M. L. and Wolkomir, M. (2002). Interviewing men. In J. F. Gubruim and J. A. Holstein (Eds.), *Handbook of interview research: Context and method* (pp. 203–219). Thousand Oaks, CA: Sage.

Seltzer, J. A. (1998). Men's contributions to children and social policy. In A. Booth and N. Crouter (Eds.), *Men in families: When do they get involved? What difference does it make?* (pp. 303–314). Mahwah, NJ: Lawrence Erlbaum Associates.

Shapiro, J. L., Diamond, M. J., and Greenberg, M. (1995). *Becoming a father*. New York: Springer.

Sherwen. L. N. (1987). The pregnant man. In L. N. Sherman (Ed.), *Psychosocial dimensions of the pregnant family* (pp. 157–176). New York: Springer.

Shostak, A. B., McLouth, G., and Seng, L. (1984). *Men and abortion: Lessons, losses, and love*. New York: Praeger.

Singh, S. and Darroch, J. E. (2000). Adolescent pregnancy and childbearing levels and trends in developed countries. *Family Planning Perspectives*, 32, 14–23.

Snarey, J. (1993). *How fathers care for the next generation: A four-decade study*. Cambridge: Harvard University Press.

Sonenstein, F. L., Pleck, J. H., and Ku, L. (1989). Sexual activity, condom use and AIDS awareness in a national sample of adolescent males. *Family Planning Perspectives*, 21, 152–158.

Sonenstein, F. L., Stewart, K., Lindberg, D. L., Pernas, M., and Williams, S. (1997). *Involving males in preventing teen pregnancy: A guide for program planners*. The California Wellness Foundation: The Urban Institute.

Soule, B., Stanley, K, and Copans, S. (1979). Father identity. *Psychiatry*, 42, 255–263.

Springarn, R. and DuRant, R. (1996). Male adolescents involved in pregnancy: Associated health risk and problem behaviors. *Pediatrics*, 98, 262–268.

Stacey, J. (1998). Dada–ism in the 1990s: Getting past baby talk about fatherlessness. In C. R. Daniels (Ed.), *Lost fathers: The politics of fatherlessness in America* (pp. 51–83). New York: St. Martin's Press.

Strauss, A. (1969). Turning points in identity. In *Mirrors and masks: Transformations of identity* (pp. 92–100). New York: Macmillan.

Strauss, A. and Corbin, J. (1990). *Basics of qualitative research: Grounded theory procedures and techniques.* Newbury Park, CA: Sage.

Strauss, R. and Goldberg, W. A. (1999). Self and possible selves during the transition to fatherhood. *Journal of Family Psychology*, 13, 244–259.

Strikland, O. L. (1987). The occurrence of symptoms in expectant fathers. *Nursing Research*, 36, 184–189.

Stryker, S. (1980). *Symbolic interactionism: A social structural version.* Menlo Park, CA: Benjamin/Cummings.

Stryker, S. and Serpe, R. T. (1982). Commitment, identity salience, and role behavior. In I. W. Ickes and E. Knowles (Eds.), *Personality, roles and social behavior* (pp. 199–218). New York: Springer–Verlag.

Stueve, J. L. and Pleck, J. H. (2001). "Parenting voice": Solo parent identity and co–parent identities in married parents' narratives of meaningful parenting experiences. *Journal of Social and Personal Relationships*, 18, 691–708.

Sugland, B. W., Wilder, K. J., and Chandra, A. (1997). Sex, pregnancy and contraception: A report of focus group discussions with adolescents. Unpublished paper. Washington, DC: Child Trends.

Sullivan, M. (1989). Absent fathers in the inner city. *Annals of the American Academy of Political and Social Science*, 501, 48–58.

Sullivan, M. (1995). Teenage males' beliefs and practices about contraception: Findings from comparative ethnographic research in high–risk neighborhoods. Paper presented at the Annual Meetings of the Population Association of America, San Francisco, April.

Tanfer, K., Grady, W. R., Klepinger, D. H., and Billy, J. O. G. (1993). Condom use among U.S. men, 1991. *Family Planning Perspectives*, 25, 61–66.

Townsend, J. (1998). *What women want—what men want: Why the sexes still see love and commitment so differently.* New York: Oxford University Press.

Trebilcot, J. (1983). *Mothering: Essays in feminist theory.* Totowa, NJ: Rowman & Allanheld.

Uniform Parentage Act, 9B U.L.A. (1973).

Van den Bossche, F. and Rubinson, L. (1997). Contraceptive self–efficacy in adolescents: A comparative study in male and female contraceptive practices. *Journal of Sex Education and Therapy*, 22, 23–29.

van den Hoonaard, W. C. (1997). Working with sensitizing concepts: Analytical field research. *Qualitative Research Methods*, 41.

Ventura, S. J., Mathews, T. J., and Curtin, S. C. (1999). Declines in teenage births rates, 1991–1998: Update of national and state trends. Vital Health Stat, 47 (26). Hyattsville, MD: National Center for Health Statistics.

Ventura, S. J., Mathews, T. J., and Hamilton, B. E. (2001). Births to teenagers in the United States, 1940–2000. National Vital Statistics Reports, 49 (10). Hyattsville, MD: National Center for Health Statistics.

Ventura, S. J., Mosher, W. D., Curtin, S. C., Abma, J. C., and Henshaw, S. (2000). Trends in pregnancies and pregnancy rates by outcome: Estimates for the United States, 1976–96. Vital Health Stat, 21 (56). Hyattsville, MD: National Center for Health Statistics.

Ventura, S. J., Mosher, W. D., Curtin, S. C., Abma, J. C., and Henshaw, S. (2001). Trends in pregnancy rates for the United States, 1976–97: An update. National Vital Statistics Reports, 49 (4). Hyattsville, MD: National Center for Health Statistics.

Walzer, S. (1998). *Thinking about the baby: Gender and transitions into parenthood.* Philadelphia: Temple University Press.

Wattenberg, E. (1993). Paternity actions and young fathers. In R. I. Lerman and T. J. Ooms (Eds.), *Young unwed fathers: Changing roles and emerging policies* (pp. 213–234). Philadelphia: Temple University Press.

West, M., Bondy, E., and Hutchinson, S. (1991). Interviewing institutionalized elders: Threats to validity. *Image, Journal of Nursing Research*, 23, 171–176.

Zayas, L. H. (1988). Thematic features in the manifest dreams of expectant fathers. *Clinical Social Work Journal*, 16, 282–296.

Zelles, P. (1984). Feedback from 521 waiting room males. In A. B. Shostak, G. McLouth, and L. Seng (Eds.), *Men and abortion: Lessons, losses, and love* (pp. 299–304). New York: Praeger.

Index

About the Authors

William Marsiglio, Professor of Sociology at the University of Florida, has written extensively on the social psychology of men's sexuality, fertility, and fatherhood. His most recent books include *Procreative Man* (1998) and *Fatherhood: Contemporary Theory, Research, and Social Policy* (1995; Ed.). He is currently writing a book on stepfathering.

Sally Hutchinson, Professor of Nursing at the University of Florida, teaches qualitative methods to doctoral students and has published more than sixty articles on the method or product of qualitative health research. As an international speaker and consultant in qualitative research, she has worked in Brazil, Australia, Egypt, Canada, Scandinavia, and East Africa.

www.ingramcontent.com/pod-product-compliance
Lightning Source LLC
Chambersburg PA
CBHW032120020426
42334CB00016B/1019